British-Jewish writers are increasingly addressing challenging questions about what it means to be both British and Jewish in the twenty-first century. *Writing Jewish* provides a lively and accessible introduction to the key issues in contemporary British-Jewish fiction, memoirs and journalism, and explores how Jewishness exists alongside a range of other different identities in Britain today.

By interrogating myths and stereotypes and looking at themes of remembering and forgetting, belonging and alienation, location and dislocation, Ruth Gilbert examines how these writers identify the particularity of their difference – while acknowledging that this difference is neither fixed nor final, but always open to re-interpretation.

RUTH GILBERT is Senior Lecturer in English at the University of Winchester, UK and Honorary Fellow of the Parkes Institute Research Centre at the University of Southampton, UK. She has published a number of articles on Jewish literature and is the author of *Early Modern Hermaphrodites: Sex and Other Stories*.

Writing Jewish

Contemporary British-Jewish Literature

RUTH GILBERT

palgrave
macmillan

Arts & Humanities
Research Council

First published 2013 by
PALGRAVE MACMILLAN

Palgrave Macmillan in the UK is an imprint of Macmillan Publishers Limited, registered in England, company number 785998, of Houndmills, Basingstoke, Hampshire RG21 6XS.

Palgrave Macmillan in the US is a division of St Martin's Press LLC, 175 Fifth Avenue, New York, NY 10010.

Palgrave Macmillan is the global academic imprint of the above companies and has companies and representatives throughout the world.

Palgrave® and Macmillan® are registered trademarks in the United States, the United Kingdom, Europe and other countries

ISBN: 978–0–230–27555–3   (hardback)
ISBN: 978–0–230–27556–0   (paperback)

This book is printed on paper suitable for recycling and made from fully managed and sustained forest sources. Logging, pulping and manufacturing processes are expected to conform to the environmental regulations of the country of origin.

A catalogue record for this book is available from the British Library.

A catalog record for this book is available from the Library of Congress.

Printed in China

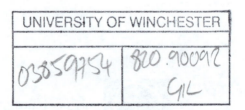

For Isaac and Sam

Contents

Acknowledgements

I am grateful to the AHRC for funding the research leave that allowed me to complete this book. I would also like to thank the University of Winchester for the sustained support they have shown during the time that I have been working on this project. Inga Bryden has provided invaluable advice on funding and research development over a number of years. I am especially indebted to my departmental colleagues, Mick Jardine and Nick Rowe, for their exceptional good grace in covering my teaching when I have been on research leave.

I am grateful to Jenna Steventon, Lucinda Knight and Felicity Noble at Palgrave, and Vidhya Jayaprakash at Newgen, for their help in bringing this book to publication. I am also grateful to the anonymous readers of both the AHRC funding application and the draft of the book for their thoughtful and perceptive comments. I would also like to thank Tony Kushner and the Parkes Institute, University of Southampton, for encouragement from the early stages of this project.

Earlier versions of parts of Chapters 1, 2, 3, 4 and 8 have been published in articles in *Jewish Culture and History* and *Holocaust Studies*. I am grateful to Vallentine Mitchell for permission to reproduce this material. I am also grateful to Bernard Kops for granting permission to quote from his poem 'Diaspora'; to Rockingham Press for permission to quote from Lotte Kramer's poem, also titled, 'Diaspora' (first published in *New and Collected Poems,* Rockingham Press, 2011); to Menard Press and Sheila Gilbert for permission to quote from A.C. Jacobs', 'Alien Poem' (all of which are discussed in Chapter 4). Ruth Fainlight's 'The English Country Cottage' (discussed in Chapter 4) and Joanne Limburg's 'Mother Chicken Soup' and 'The Nose on My Face' (which I look at in Chapter 7) are printed by permission of Bloodaxe Books Ltd. The extract from *Two Thousand Years* by Mike Leigh (© Mike Leigh 2006) is printed by permission of United Agents (www.unitedagents.co.uk<http://www.unitedagents.co.uk>) on behalf of Mike Leigh. The photograph of *Klezmer Fest* (figure 1) is reproduced by permission of Judah Passow.

I am aware that the lives and thoughts of real people are often embedded in my discussions and I am grateful to the writers from whose work I draw. Their sometimes highly personal accounts provide the material for some of my analysis. I hope that *Writing Jewish* treats these with sensitivity.

Many people have provided support in many ways throughout the writing of this book. Amanda Boulter helped shape the project and I appreciate the intelligence and care that she brought to its early development. I am, as ever, indebted to Peter Betts who has been a consistently loyal and thoughtful friend. I am immeasurably grateful to Julia Waterfield. Her insight, wisdom and generosity have helped me in many ways. I would also like to thank Caroline Fawcett. In the final stages of the project she has provided a new perspective.

A book such as this perhaps inevitably connects the academic to the personal. My own family aptly demonstrates the variety of contemporary British-Jewish identities that are possible in contemporary Britain. In many respect, their stories are the story of this book. My father, Ivan Gilbert, knows from experience the many differences that can be generated within just one Jewish family. He is a Tevye for our times. Finally, I would like to thank my sister, Zara McQueen, soup-maker and Jewess extraordinaire, for her unstinting support throughout and beyond the period of writing this book.

Preface: 'No Place Like Home'

In March 2012 I visited *No Place Like Home*, an exhibition of photographs at the Jewish Museum in London. The exhibition marked the culmination of a year-long project in which the photojournalist, Judah Passow, had surveyed a range of personal and public moments in order to explore 'what it means to be British and Jewish in the 21st Century'.[1] As Passow's photographs documented the diversity and variations of contemporary British-Jewish life, the exhibition demonstrated, above all, that being British and being Jewish can mean many things.

Passow's images depicted orthodox and liberal Jews, yeshiva students, brides, barmitzvah boys, footballers, doctors, butchers, bagpipers, prisoners, police officers, fundraisers and street performers. They captured key moments of celebration and demonstration, ritual and reflection, study and recreation. As I made my way round the exhibition, I was struck, in particular, by the extent to which it was saturated with textual images and signs: most obviously in books and newspapers, but also on cars, on bodies, in shops, synagogues and on the street. My focus in *Writing Jewish* is on reading more conventional texts, in the form of literature of various kinds, but these photographs resonated with some of my own reflections on contemporary British-Jewish life, and the ways in which this is being written, in a range of ways.

The Jewish Museum as a setting also provided an impetus for contemplation. It is a crisp and contemporary space which, in itself, presents a self-assured statement about Jewish life in Britain today. The exhibition reflected this confidence. Many images were celebratory and vibrant. But Passow's photographs also captured some more hesitant and indefinable moments. A number of them showed interactions between different types of British Jews, different generations, different ethnicities and different races. In this respect, the exhibition was a record of and a testament to the power of connection; but it did not gloss over moments of disagreement, or of isolation. So, for example, whilst some photographs showed British Jews celebrating Israel, others recorded protests against current Zionist ideology. And, as well as the many photographs of Jews in the company of others, there were also some haunting images of disconnection and loss.

Historically, Jews have been seen as eternal outsiders, a people who have been cast adrift in the uncertainties of the diaspora and are perhaps never truly at home. In this context, the title of the exhibition, *No Place Like Home*, is evocative. Passow's photographs show that Jews are very much at home in today's Britain, but the title can be read in a variety of ways. It suggests simultaneously, familiarity and estrangement, belonging and alienation, the particular and the universal. These too are the ambiguities that *Writing Jewish* sets out to explore.

Some of the photographs in the exhibition were specifically and unmistakably Jewish in content, others less obviously so. Several images featured powerful emblems of identity, such as the Star of David, and several included the Union Jack flag. In observing the ways in which these signifiers of Jewishness and Britishness are juxtaposed, the viewer was encouraged to reflect on issues of different, dual and maybe multiple identifications. Perhaps unsurprisingly, some of the more explicitly patriotic statements of belonging were seen in relation to the older generation of British Jews. So we saw iconic images of Britishness within particularly Jewish contexts: a portrait of Churchill on the wall of a care home in Brighton; the annual parade of the Association of Jewish Ex-Servicemen at Whitehall; the Prayer for the royal family displayed at a London synagogue; and 'Rule Britannia' being sung in an East End day centre.

These images assert Jewish affiliation to Britain, but there were also more ambiguous signifiers of both connection and disconnection threaded through the exhibition. So, for example, there was an image of a Maccabi Lions footballer in the foreground of one photograph. He has the word 'Israel' tattooed in Hebrew on his upper back. In the background, one of his teammates is wrapped in a Union Jack towel. How we interpret such potentially overdetermined signifiers of identity is uncertain. Or, we might reflect on the figure that stands with their back to a Star of David outside, what the caption informs us, is an orthodox synagogue in Southend, Essex. The Star of David is stark, angular and eerie. It dominates the picture but appears to be strangely detached, as if it floats, unanchored, against the dense black wall behind. The figure in the foreground seems to be turning away from this symbol of Jewishness. In a complex gesture, they are lifting their outer top to cover their face. We do not know if they are male or female, Jewish or gentile, or why they are hiding their face. Images such as these are subtle and disconcerting and they complicate any straightforward ideas about belonging for British Jews.

Passow has spoken about what he sees as the peculiar ability of British Jews to adapt to changing conditions, arguing that it is this 'capacity to question and reinvent themselves' that is key to Jewish survival.[2] And the thrust of the exhibition is about resilience. It suggests, overall, a developing confidence in British Jewish life. As Jonathan Freedland writes in his essay accompanying the exhibition, 'while once Jews whispered their identity – their voices literally falling in volume when saying the J- word in a public place – today's Jews are much more out and proud'.[3]

Certainly, a recent wave of popular media depicting Jews in Britain seems, on the surface, to attest to this sense of increasing visibility. Indeed, for some cultural commentators, British Jewishness has now become 'a hip cultural talking point'.[4] However, as Josh Appignanesi, the director of the Jewish-Muslim comedy film *The Infidel* has noted: 'the complications of Anglo-Jewish relations over the past 700 years are not reducible to some flippantly amusing stereotypes on some passing TV shows'.[5] Such responses indicate the tenor of current conversations that British Jews are having, in public, about what it means to be a Jew in Britain today and how this could or should be represented in the mainstream media. These are often lively, heated and noisy exchanges. *Writing Jewish* looks at some of these communal discussions and at popular depictions of contemporary British-Jewish life; but it also focuses on quieter, more internal, matters of subjectivity and identification.

Returning to *No Place Like Home*, we are presented with the numerous modalities of such debates. In a defining photograph of the exhibition we see two men in conversation at the 2009 Klezmer Fest in Regent's Park (see Figure 1). The occasion and the image seem to sum up the 'out and proud' mood that Freedland suggests; but the photograph also points to the more irreducible ambiguities that are perhaps innate within contemporary British Jewishness. A middle-aged man holds his hands open and upwards in an archetypal Jewish gesture. His shrug is directed towards a younger man who looks back at him with apparent attention. This younger man has a Mohican and a pin pierced through his upper ear. He is wearing a Union Jack t-shirt and reveals a forearm that is tattooed with delicate interlocking shapes. The sleeve of his t-shirt is ripped to show another, Celtic-style, tattooed band on his upper arm. He thus displays, on his body, complex layers of tribal inscription. As he clasps his hand to his neck, the gesture contrasts to the older man's open-handed and expressive pose. Of course, we do not know what is being said, but the body language encapsulates

Figure 1: © Judah Passow, Klezmer Fest, Regent's Park (2009)

what seems to be a moment of connection between the generations. It suggests different, but not necessarily incompatible, ways to be both Jewish and British.

It is a powerful image that was reproduced extensively in the publicity material for the exhibition. It captures a moment that is contemporary, energetic and vibrant. But, it is also an image that is hard to read. It hints at the possibility of tension as well as connection, defiance as well as conviviality, ambiguity as well as assertion. It raises questions about Jewish identity in today's Britain which are not easy to answer. In this way, it presents an apt opening to this book. *Writing Jewish* will draw from a range of contemporary British-Jewish literature to explore other equally such complex moments of signification. It will suggest some of the ways in which, through reading, we also write Jewishness within the culture of contemporary Britain.

Notes

1. Jewish Museum, *No Place Like Home: Photographs by Judah Passow*, p.2. I am grateful to Judah Passow for permission to reproduce his photograph and for his generous engagement with my ideas about his work in an email dialogue about the exhibition.

2. Judah Passow in conversation with Robin Lustig, Jewish Museum, 11 March 2012.
3. Jonathan Freedland, 'Minority Report', *No Place Like Home: Photographs by Judah Passow*, p.5.
4. Stephanie Theobald, 'We're All Kosher Now', *Sunday Times*, 4 November 2012. I am grateful to the anonymous reader for Palgrave who alerted me to this article.
5. 'We're All Kosher Now'.

1

British-Jewish Writing Today

The Jewish writer is *not* particularly different...from any other writer except in that the fate of the Jews has been exceptionally contradictory and has led to a fiction which seeks, in the profoundest sense, to reconcile the irreconcilable. The Jewish writer in Britain is thus called upon to draw from a rich vein of paradox and ambiguity out of which a field of meaning can be constructed.

Michael Woolf (1995)[1]

I was an English Jew – that was my dysfunction.

Howard Jacobson (2007)[2]

In May 2012 *New Statesman* published a special issue on British-Jewish identity.[3] Its editorial opens by recalling Tony Blair's 2006 address to the Anglo-Jewish population on the 350th anniversary of the Jewish readmission to Britain. In a speech given at Bevis Marks, the oldest synagogue in London, Blair commended British Jews for retaining a distinct faith-based identity whilst also showing their loyalty and commitment to Britain.[4] Blair's words had obvious implications for other immigrant communities in Britain at the time, especially in view of the tensions that followed the London terrorist attacks of 2005.[5] So are British Jews, as Blair suggested, an exemplar of assimilation? As the *New Statesman* leader rightly points out, the British-Jewish experience is far from that straightforward: 'the history of Jewish cultural, religious and intellectual life in Britain', it argues, 'shows just how complex are such questions of identity and belonging'.[6] *Writing Jewish* explores some of this complexity.

1

This introductory chapter sets out a framework for reading a
range of contemporary British-Jewish literature. It looks at some
of the contexts that inform this writing and introduces ideas about
Jewishness, Britishness, belonging and identification that will be
developed throughout the book. The two quotations cited above
present the parameters of the discussion. Michael Woolf's proposition, that British-Jewish writers must somehow 'reconcile the irreconcilable' in order to construct 'a field of meaning', requires some
interrogation. Paradox and ambiguity might inform the experience of
British Jews, but these uncertainties surface in different ways, take
a variety of forms and suggest a plurality of meanings. If, as Max,
Jacobson's caustically self-aware character in *Kalooki Nights*, puts
it, being an English Jew is a form of dysfunction, then perhaps the
work of the contemporary British-Jewish writer (and indeed critic),
is to face that dysfunction: to examine its roots, to explore the ways
in which it becomes manifest, and to consider the impact it has on the
expression of both individual and collective identities. In order to do
this, it is necessary to look at the gaps and inconsistencies that exist in
the representation of these issues and to be open to the possibilities as
well as the pains of dysfunction. As the discussions throughout *Writing
Jewish* will suggest, reading contemporary British-Jewish literature
need not be a lachrymose task. Self-awareness, wit and subtle forms
of subversion exist alongside more intense and agonized explorations
of British-Jewish identities and the reader of such writing needs to be
attuned to these different modes of expression.

I shall argue during the course of this book that the British-Jewish
experience, although nuanced and diverse, is also specific. *Writing
Jewish* focuses on the contemporary but, in order to reflect on these
recent representations of British-Jewish identities, it is necessary to
be aware of the particular histories that impact on such writing. In
the words of one historian, Anglo-Jewish history is 'little more than
a bland and lukewarm chronicle'.[7] It has been dismissed by others as
'petty', 'unimportant', and singularly lacking in drama.[8] In comparison
to the histories of Jews elsewhere in the world this might well seem to
be the case. However, whilst in many respects the fate of Anglo-Jewry
can be viewed as a success story, and British Jews have been compara-
tively fortunate, this is by no means an unambiguous or uncompli-
cated tale. Jews were expelled from England in 1290 and readmitted
in 1656. Since then various waves of immigration have brought Jews
to Britain. From the seventeenth-century Sephardic resettlements,
the Ashkenazi dispersals from Central and Eastern Europe in the

nineteenth and early twentieth-centuries, and the migrations of refugees from Nazi Europe, Jews have made their homes in Britain for many reasons and in many ways. The story of Britain's Jewish past is a story that features moments of remarkable cruelty and acts of profound generosity. It is a story of persecution and assimilation; lingering prejudice and progressive liberalism; quiet derision and singular opportunity. British-Jewish writers today inherit this history in direct and indirect ways.[9] Literature, perhaps more than any other form of cultural production, is able to articulate the powerful effects of such a past whilst also drawing on the complexities of the present.

British-Jewish: 'A Category Error'

In 2003 Bryan Cheyette posed a question that underpins much subsequent work in British-Jewish studies. 'What is it about Britishness', asked Cheyette, 'that is so deforming?'[10] Again, British-Jewishness is seen as a kind of 'dysfunction' and this question has in recent years become an increasingly significant focus of enquiry for historians, as well as literary critics, fiction writers, memoirists and journalists.[11] In 1994, David Cesarani argued that British-Jewish culture has been characterized by 'a tradition of self-deprecation and a lack of collective self-esteem'.[12] Cesarani, and other key British-Jewish historians, such as Tony Kushner, have provided vital insights into the ways in which ideas about Jewishness have been constructed in British culture.[13] In fact, many recent developments in British-Jewish studies could not have progressed without such careful historical contextualization. As a result, literary critics, cultural commentators and writers are now far more prepared to explore the complexities of what it means to be a British Jew, including the difficulties of the past, than they might have been 20 years ago.

Cultural histories reveal that, whilst generally Jews have been tolerated in Britain, a deep well of antisemitic prejudice has also rippled beneath the surface of Anglo-Jewish life. Written and anecdotal accounts suggest that Jews in Britain, even during the twentieth century, routinely encountered antipathy and discrimination that was subtle, pervasive and undermining.[14] In the inter-war years and beyond this was the kind of antisemitism that resulted in exclusion from golf clubs and Masonic lodges, quotas for admission into public schools and universities, difficulties in obtaining employment and so on. Many middle-aged and older Jews in Britain today recall childhood experiences of what the American critic, Leslie Fiedler, has termed Britain's 'mild-as-milk, matter-of-fact; antisemitism'.[15] In the post-war period British Jews continued to experience the effects of such antisemitism. They understood, for example, that a job application from somebody with an obviously Jewish name might be quietly rejected. They learned to ignore casual jokes and mildly antisemitic comments. Instead they set up their own golf clubs and they anglicized their Jewish-sounding names. So, Kahanskys became Kanes, Levis became Lewises, and Goldbergs became Gilberts.

Many accounts of growing up in the 1940s, 50s and even 60s describe an atmosphere of quiet repression that permeated Anglo-Jewish consciousness. As one British Jew recalls it, post-war Jews mitigated their feelings of underlying anxiety by 'being quiet, keeping a low profile, not wanting to be ruffled by anything, not ruffling anything'; adding, 'I suppose we were colluding with each other to disappear into England and lose our identity'.[16] This culture of apology and self-effacement is transmitted in subtle ways. As Anne Karpf notes, 'British antiSemitism is particularly pernicious because for much of the time it's covert and based on the suppression of difference'.[17] She cites a Jewish acquaintance who, leaving Britain for the US, bemoaned the way that British Jews 'retreat, as though living in a constant state of repressed anxiety about it. In that sense, they are being very English – trapped in passivity, unwilling to react, rock the boat, make a fuss' (216).

This sense, that British Jews are, and are not, 'English' surfaces repeatedly as a point of tension throughout British-Jewish writing.[18] As Jacobson put it in *Roots Schmoots*, recalling his own childhood sense of split identity whilst growing up in 1950s Manchester, 'we faced in opposite directions, we were our own antithesis'.[19] This ironic but nonetheless seemingly impossible contradiction in British-Jewish identity is a recurring theme in many recent memoirs and novels and a prevailing tone of irresolution runs through this writing. Karpf has described eloquently her own sense of division as the British child of immigrant Holocaust survivors. She recalls that:

> As a child and young adult I'd always found it maddening when my mother asked if someone was 'English' – her euphemism for non-Jewish...it implied you couldn't be simultaneously English and Jewish – you weren't *really* English. But she was right all along...I've always automatically said 'they' about the English. (51)

This question, about whether one could be both Jewish and 'English', runs deep in the Anglo-Jewish consciousness. These complex issues of identification will be discussed throughout *Writing Jewish*. Ideas about memory underpin many of these discussions and I shall spend some time laying the foundations for an exploration of these themes in Chapters 2 and 3. Chapter 2 considers theories of memory in order to look at the role that memory plays in constructing a sense of identity for British Jews. Chapter 3 develops these themes in relation to the lasting effects of the Holocaust on British-Jewish consciousness. Here the delicate interplay between remembering and forgetting is a key focus of the discussion.

The ways that the past plays into a sense of present-day identity is a structuring theme throughout the book. In *Jacob's Gift: A Journey into the Heart of Belonging* (2006), a family memoir and thoughtful exploration of what it means to be both British and Jewish, Jonathan Freedland recounts a story that exemplifies a typical experience for many British Jews who descend from immigrants. 'Once', he writes of his early schooldays, 'there was a family tree project':

> Each of us had to trace our ancestors back as far as we could. Boys with names like Lowe, Sutherland and Blyth returned with hefty, parchment-style scrolls – unfurling forebears whose lives were etched on church records stored since medieval times in villages in Suffolk or Cornwall. One boy had gone all the way back to 1066; his scroll touched the floor. I held a single sheet of A4 paper bearing the names of my great-grandparents and the – estimated – date of 1880. That was as far back as I could go.[20]

The memory sums up a recognition of what it means to be a child, grandchild or even great-grandchild of immigrants in a country that has traditionally valued continuity and longevity in lineage.

This lack of rootedness, the flimsy connection to the British past, symbolized by Freeland's undersized family tree, is a recurring theme in other second and third generation Jewish writing. In some ways this typifies the immigrant experience in general. But for many British Jews of Eastern European heritage, this is further complicated by the fact that places of Jewish history were brutally annihilated in the Holocaust. The rupture from the past is, in this respect, unnaturally abrupt and deeply traumatic and many diasporic Jews have to rely on memory rather than place in order to make and renew identities. These themes will be developed in Chapters 4 and 5 which, building on the previous two chapters' discussion of memory, focus on issues of identity and location. Here, ideas about how British-Jewish writers present their connections to Britain, in terms of place, and how a notion of home is conceived in relation to Eastern Europe and Israel will be discussed.

The sense of marginalization that Freedland describes, of not being quite 'English', can of course evoke a desire for the other that is pleasurably charged as well as potentially alienating. Freedland outlines this effect when he recalls his schoolboy awareness of the fundamental difference between 'the bright, bespectacled Jewish young women, their talk full of ideas, their hair full of dark curls' and 'the others, the Kates, Katherines and Sophies who were unmistakably *other*'. He goes on to explain that 'their very ordinariness, the straightness of their hair, the button brevity of their noses, made them irresistibly exotic. They were so *English*' (15). The erotic charge of this frisson has been exploited to comic effect by Jacobson among others. His fiction is populated by a series of hapless Jewish men who suffer repeated romantic and sexual humiliations at the hands of the heartless Aryan women whom they find unbearably cruel and magnetically irresistible. Chapter 6's discussion of Jewish masculinity will explore some of these complex aspects of male desire by focusing on the ways that contemporary British-Jewish writing presents issues relating to identity, gender and sexuality.

A sense of confused identification, ranging from the erotic to the emotive, underlies many of these explorations of British-Jewish masculinity. Unsurprisingly, some of these issues, especially in relation to ontological uncertainty, also inform contemporary writing by British-Jewish women. For Linda Grant, the child of Jewish immigrants who grew up in post-war Britain, a sense of internal contradiction was formative. 'While slavishly trying to imitate *them*, – the English', she recalls, 'I also became self-divided'.[21] Reflecting on memories of her loud, generous and, to her teenage eyes, painfully embarrassing father, Grant observes that she took for granted the 'vulgar luxuries' that he could provide yet she also longed for 'a dry, mild, laconic father with a name like James or Charles or Timothy and a distinguished war record' (71–2). Similarly, Anne Karpf recalls her fantasized adolescent identity as 'Toni', a Barbie doll projection of perfect femininity, who would contain 'no cell of Jewishness' (41). These teenage recollections, whilst typical of adolescent angst in more general terms, suggest the particularly complex aspects of identification that British Jews of this generation have had to negotiate. Chapter 7's discussion of the representation of Jewish women builds on such moments of discomfort. It looks at the ways that stereotypes of Jewish femininity have impacted on contemporary representations of Jewish women and the ways in which such stereotypes are both reiterated and subverted in recent writing.

The sense of split identification that contemporary British-Jewish literature so often explores is evidently a potentially troubling issue. One cannot read this material without becoming aware of this discomfort. However, it is also apparent that difference is not always a cause for concern. In the increasingly fluid and decentred conditions of the contemporary world, discontinuous narratives of identity, in some contexts, bestow a certain cultural cachet. In 2006 Grant described herself as 'a category error', explaining that 'everyone knows that the British are tactful, decorous, well-mannered, prudent, prone to meaningful silences, and Jews are – well, the opposite'.[22] Elsewhere Grant has coined the phrase 'shouty Jews'.[23] This characterization, which is humorous, confident and self-aware, demonstrates a shrewd understanding of identity in contemporary Britain. It suggests the absurdity as well as the difficulty of identification and sets a tone for thinking about the current field of British-Jewish writing. Sometimes, as we shall see throughout *Writing Jewish*, a sense of disconnection is expressed as a yearning for wholeness and these are meaningful reflections on the difficulties engendered by difference; but the uncertainties associated with being a 'category error' are also potentially playful and productive. In her contribution to the *New Statesman* special issue, Grant wrote that 'the British Jew is an oddity; we're so out of kilter with universal experience that we are a minority taste'.[24] Recent developments in contemporary literature suggest that, rather than apologizing for itself, this 'oddity' is becoming increasingly more vocal, perhaps even 'shouty', in articulating its peculiarity.

British-Jewish literature: coming from behind?

Jewish writing has contributed significantly to British cultural life over many decades. It has, however, arguably gained a new visibility and momentum in recent years. In fiction, memoirs and journalism, writers are addressing increasingly challenging questions about what it means to be both British and Jewish in the twenty-first century. In his 2001 study, *Post-War Jewish Fiction*, David Brauner detected a shift in attitude, from when he was researching the subject as a doctoral student in the 1990s, to the publication of his book at the turn of the millennium. Like Bryan Cheyette, who noted in 2003 that 'there exists a commonplace perception, despite a good deal of evidence to the contrary, that Jewish writers in Britain do not exist', Brauner recounts that he had been met repeatedly with a sense of disbelief that there was such a thing as British-Jewish fiction.[25] 'Over the last few years', he notes, 'whenever I have mentioned the subject of my work in progress to friends and colleagues, their first response has been to ask, with various degrees of flippancy, whether there is any British-Jewish fiction' (x).

Until quite recently there has been a pervading sense that American writing has somewhat dominated the literary and cultural agenda. As a result, current studies are increasingly recognizing the need to untangle the British experience from the American and the wider European perspectives and focus on the *particularity* of the Anglo-Jewish context. In a lecture given in 2006 to commemorate the readmission of the Jews to England in 1656, Howard Jacobson, on particularly bullish form, confronted some of these issues. He argued that English Jews have historically been mired by self-consciousness and, in order to avoid accusations of 'introversion' and parochialism, have deliberately avoided writing explicitly about their own experiences.[26] Jacobson claimed that the aggressive confidence of American Jewish writers such as Saul Bellow and Philip Roth has not been repeated in the English context because Jews have only been 'welcomed' to this country with a degree of caution. Furthermore, English Jews have not reshaped 'what is meant by Englishness' because it is only recently that Britain has acknowledged that it is very much a culture under construction.[27] Unlike Americans, Jacobson argues, British Jews have been absorbed into the existing fabric of British life rather than redefining the weave itself. Grant's 2012 *New Statesman* piece makes a similar point. 'The US dazzles and obliterates', she says, 'whereas the British Jewish experience is one of uncertainty' (51). So we have, for example, in the title of Anthony Blond's memoir, *Jew Made in England* (2004), a rather astute recognition of the thoroughly integrated yet fundamentally distinct relationship between Jew and country.[28]

For Jacobson, Jews have been inhibited by the 'tranquillity', the lack of crisis, of British life. Ultimately, he suggests that we need to find ways to be Jewish that are not based on denial, apology, weak imitation of the American model, or 'the anguished spirit of the Eastern European shtetl' (46). He concludes (in a pleasingly 'shouty' way) that:

> We have been in this country a while now. The story of our finely tuned accommodations to English culture is a fascinating one, sometimes tragic, often heroic, always funny, and never less than urgent beneath a quiescent surface. It is time we told it. We should be more interested in ourselves as English Jews.
>
> ENGLISH ... JEWS (46)

So, whereas for Cheyette, writers such as Harold Pinter and Anita Brookner, have chosen to efface or codify their Jewishness, and others, such as Clive Sinclair and Elaine Feinstein, have succeeded by 'transcending and transfiguring their Britishness', Jacobson has arguably set the tone for a new generation of British-Jewish writers by confronting the interface between Jewishness and 'Englishness' in his work.[29]

British-Jewish writers today are, then, shaking off a culture of reticence and self-censorship which arguably inhibited previous generations of Anglo-Jewry. From Jeremy Gavron's experimental literary fiction in *The Book of Israel* (2003) and *An Acre of Barren Ground* (2005) to more popular texts such as Giles Coren's *Winkler* (2006) or Charlotte Mendelson's *When We Were Bad* (which was shortlisted for the Orange Prize in 2008), to Francesca Segal's Costa prize-winning *The Innocents* (2012), British-Jewishness is being represented in diverse ways in contemporary writing.[30] Indeed, in 2007 Donald Weber suggested that this wave of new Jewish writing in Britain might represent the 'flowering' of 'an Anglo-Jewish literary "revival"'.[31] He argued that 'Anglo-Jewish writers... are getting mouthy, raising their Jewish voices unabashedly – and in public'. Weber cites as further evidence of this 'revival' cultural events such as Jewish Book Week, The Jewish Film Festival and the high profile given to new writers such as Naomi Alderman (winner of the Orange prize in 2006).[32]

Moreover, established writers who have not previously foregrounded their Jewishness, such as Mike Leigh, have recently engaged more explicitly with Jewish themes. Commenting on a 'new world in which we [Jews] are another ethnic, cultural faction', Leigh notes that, 'some of us are old enough to remember what it was like when you didn't say you were Jewish'.[33] His play about the complexities of contemporary Jewish family life, *Two Thousand Years*, sold out within days at the National Theatre in 2005. However, there is another side to this, as Weber terms it, 'stunning burst of productivity' in British-Jewish literature. Perhaps, some would suggest, it was a little premature to hail a new wave of British-Jewish writing based on the emergence of a handful of potentially invigorating writers. In Autumn 2006, David Herman, writing in *The Jewish Chronicle*, bemoaned the 'apparent absence of Jewish novelists in the highest echelons of contemporary fiction'.[34] His complaint focused on the dearth of British-Jewish writers included in shortlists of major literary prizes and, in particular, a poll in *The Observer* Sunday newspaper that had charted the most significant novels of the past 25 years and excluded British-Jewish writers.

Although the issue of Jewish authors and shortlists for literary prizes has shifted somewhat in recent years, Herman's overview still perhaps signals a need for caution: whilst celebrating the vibrancy of British-Jewish culture at present, we might also have to acknowledge the ambivalent attitudes towards Jewishness which are deeply engrained within British culture. On the one hand, we have what seems to be a glittering explosion in British-Jewish writing, a new confidence; but, on the other, a lingering sense of exclusion from the mainstream of British life. Certainly, the situation today is complicated. Whilst Jews in Britain are relatively secure and integrated it is also true that antisemitism still surfaces in some more or less subtle ways and that antisemitic attacks are reportedly rising.[35] Clearly world politics, most notably the Israel-Palestine situation, impacts significantly on attitudes towards Jews in Britain. Moreover, given the complex debates about religious and ethnic identities that have preoccupied Britain in recent years, representations of Jewishness are in many ways more charged than they have been for some time. But, this seemingly contradictory picture is not necessarily an inhibiting or creatively constricting issue. The profound ambiguity about Jews that can be traced back throughout the history of Anglo-Jewry is central to the work of contemporary British-Jewish writers. It produces a rich generative tension that is not always easy to digest. And this is the point. It is what gives this writing edge.

This paradox is perhaps best exemplified in discussions about the status given to the work of Jacobson. Jacobson's acclaimed and highly publicized novel *Kalooki Nights* won the 2007 *Jewish Quarterly* Wingate Literary Prize but it failed to make the Man Booker shortlist. This novel presents an uncompromising, robust and challenging exploration of Jewishness. Jacobson has described it himself as 'the most Jewish novel that has ever been written by anybody, anywhere'.[36] This is not a Jewishness located at a distance. It is set in 1950s Manchester and present-day London and presents a head on confrontation of what it means to be a British Jew of the post-war generation. *Kalooki Nights* is funny and disturbing, audacious and bitter. It expresses an insecurity and rage at the heart of Anglo-Jewry. It is not a comfortable read. So, does this, what we might term, *hyper-Jewishness*, account for Jacobson's exclusion from the Booker? Possibly not. We could argue that he missed out on the prize for another reason entirely: that is, because he writes within the comic novel genre, a form that has never been especially popular with Booker juries.

In 2010 Jacobson did, at last, win the Booker. *The Finkler Question* is also a comic novel but in its reflection on issues of aging, love and loss it has often been described as elegiac.[37] I shall draw from Jacobson's representation of contemporary British-Jewishness in *The Finkler Question* in later chapters. For now, it is worth noting that the novel which finally won the Booker for Jacobson is narrated from the perspective of Julian Treslove, a non-Jewish philosemite. In private, Treslove thinks of Jews as *Finklers*. He had settled on this nomenclature on meeting Sam Finkler, the first Jew he had ever knowingly encountered. Treslove reflects that 'it took away the stigma...The minute you talked about the *Finkler Question*, say, or the *Finklerish Conspiracy*, you sucked out the toxins'.[38] Whereas in *Kalooki Nights* the word Jew was deployed with ferocious excess, the joke in *The Finkler Question* is that, although Jewishness is the focus of extreme and even obsessive interest, it cannot quite be spoken.[39] Jacobson has come to popular success with a novel that codes and decodes Jewishness for a non-Jewish readership in an adroit manner. Does this suggest that the British literary establishment might still prefer its Jewishness served up at a slight remove? Perhaps. But the *Finklers* in Jacobson's novel articulate many of the conflicts, ambiguities and insecurities that lie at the heart of contemporary British-Jewish life. It is a very Jewish novel.

British Jews today: who do we think we are?

Jacobson's Booker triumph (routinely depicted as a singular act of British-Jewish heroism within the Anglo-Jewish press), along with the high-profile given to other contemporary British-Jewish writers such as Linda Grant, Naomi Alderman, David Baddiel and, most recently, Francesca Segal, has then arguably opened up British-Jewishness to a wider readership than ever before. But if it is the case that British Jews are gaining a new visibility in contemporary writing, what issues are raised by such exposure? Are all representations of Jewishness necessarily welcome? It is clearly problematic to expect any one writer, or even a handful, to represent an increasingly diverse Anglo-Jewish population. Issues of identity, difference and visibility are undoubtedly complex and touch some raw nerves among British Jews. In the final part of this introductory chapter, I want to provide a context for reflecting on the literary material that will be discussed throughout the rest of the book by considering the ways that these issues of representation are being debated within Anglo-Jewish life.

Jews in Britain are generally viewed as being highly assimilated, affluent and influential but it is still hard to explain exactly what is meant by British-Jewishness. As David Baddiel explains, in his contribution to the *New Statesman* discussion of Jews in Britain, attempts to define Anglo-Jewishness are intrinsically unsatisfying:

> Anglo-Jewishness: you see it even sounds woolly – is not really a clear identity. As immigrant, you have two possible destinies: either you come to dominate your culture, as Jews to some extent have in the US, or you become an important underground voice. But Jews in the UK occupy neither one position nor the other. Most of them arrived here before it was considered fashionable or important to proclaim your ethnicity.[40]

In identifying the anomalous position of Jews in Britain, Baddiel echoes numerous other attempts to sum up British-Jewishness. As we have seen, in relation to literature, comparisons to the American experience do not quite hold. Debates about multiculturalism subtend this confusion. Jews are a minority group, but they do not have the same presence in the public consciousness as other immigrant communities in Britain. It is not clear whether Jewishness is a religion, an ethnicity or a cultural identity. Jews are, in general, viewed as being economically and socially privileged rather than being especially deprived or marginalized. These ambiguous identifications, combined with an innate wariness about attracting attention, have meant that British Jews have not generally been involved in developing debates about multiculturalism. As Keith Kahn-Harris and Ben Gidley put it, 'the Jewish community, despite the lessons its diasporic story might have for a multicultural nation, failed to get a place at the table of multiculturalism'.[41]

Kahn-Harris and Gidley argue that Jews in the UK occupy a 'paradoxical position' which 'as both ubiquitous and marginal has had deleterious consequences' (7). So, although the Jewish experience in Britain can in many ways be seen as a success story, the nature of integration and assimilation is inevitably that over time distinct minority identities become absorbed into the majority. Although orthodox Jews tend to live within Jewish communities and manifest obvious distinction in their clothing, diet, and so on, many Jews in Britain today, who might identify with Jewishness in broad cultural terms, are largely secular. These Jews are incrementally coupling with non-Jews and bringing up children who do not necessarily identify as Jewish themselves. Jewishness in this way becomes a trace, an increasingly diluted, almost homeopathic, element of identity.

Anxieties about the future of Anglo-Jewry have exercised the leadership of Anglo-Jewry in recent years. In a strongly articulated argument about retaining particularity, the Chief Rabbi, Jonathan Sacks, stated in 2007 that 'multiculturalism has run its course, and it is time to move on'.[42] In 1993 Sacks had been instrumental in establishing the Jewish Continuity organization in Britain. This was a proactive attempt to move Anglo-Jewry beyond its earlier preoccupation with sustaining security to instead confront and challenge the perceived dilution of Jewish identity in 1990s Britain. An advert in the *Jewish Chronicle* for Jewish Continuity characterized the current situation in dramatic terms. It set out the statistics of the dwindling Jewish population (less than 300,000) and, invoking the spectre of extinction, reached the bleak conclusion that 'Jews are not dying but Judaism and Jewish identity are'.[43] In 1994 Sacks summed up this sense of existential crisis by asking the provocative question: 'will we have Jewish grandchildren?'[44]

In 2004, a study of Jewish identity in Britain was undertaken by UIJA (United Jewish Israel Appeal), an organization whose stated mission is 'to be the catalyst for Jewish renewal across the community'.[45] The authors of the study's findings, *Beyond Belonging: The Jewish Identities of Moderately Engaged British Jews*, conclude that:

> Ethnic sentimentality and the thick network of personal ties to other Jews may continue to sustain Jewish group life and the distinctiveness of Jews from the wide society. However, the emerging younger generation – one more highly educated and culturally cosmopolitan than its parents and grandparents – may need an explicit rationale for Jewish involvement and commitment. To be compelling and effective, the rationale will need to be more developed and more articulated than those offered in the past. Ethnic attachment for ethnic attachment's sake, continuity for continuity's sake, runs the risk of being seen as meaningless. (24)

Such concerns perpetuate an impulse to protect and sustain a fragile sense of collective identification. The continuity argument is powerful, but the extent to which it represents the priorities of many British Jews is not evident. As David Cesarani points out in his *New Statesman* contribution, 'Who Speaks for British Jews?' despite being routinely characterized as 'clannish', 'Jews in this country have always been fractious and unruly'.[46]Certainly, debates about representation and leadership within current Anglo-Jewish life are often pugnacious and it is hard to conceive of any unified or singular sense of British-Jewish identity. But questions of who speaks, and what is spoken, are also rather subtle matters, and, I would argue, not quite articulated in the public debates and declarations of Anglo-Jewish communal bodies.

The UIJA report by its own definition does not address the many 'unengaged' Jews in Britain, stating that they 'were too hard to reach to merit precious communal resources' (xi–xii). In the screening questionnaire for the study only those who scored between 5 and 16 were eligible to be interviewed. Arguably, then, the nature of unengagement means that such Jews are rendered invisible within such contexts. I tested my own eligibility and scraped a score of three points, which included a point for reading 'one or more Jewish books in the last year' (p. 99). This make me officially 'unengaged'. I am not suggesting that this is erroneous. The report is coherent and rigorous within its own framework. I am, however, interested in asking how someone such as me, technically distanced, but nevertheless connected to Jewishness through family, history, culture and work, might identify as a twenty-first century British Jew?

Contemporary British-Jewish writing begins to answer this question. It does not speak *for* British Jews, but instead engages with fragments *of* British-Jewishness. In presenting a rather messy and imprecise picture of Jewish identity, the texts that I look at in *Writing Jewish* show that such modes of identification are finely nuanced, indeterminate and often contradictory. This multiplicity, I would argue, characterizes much contemporary British-Jewish writing. Inevitably, the 'contemporary' is a somewhat sliding term but, for the purposes of this project, I am reading texts produced from 1990 onwards in terms of what I see as these contemporary tendencies. Drawing from this context, the book focuses on the ambiguities that are generated by being both British and Jewish and the ways in which these tensions have informed recent critical debates, memoirs and fiction. Many of the writers that are discussed throughout *Writing Jewish* are journalists, academics and cultural commentators but they often also publish more explicitly literary writing such as novels, poetry and drama. In many cases these modes are combined in the form of self-reflexive memoirs. So, although life-writing and fiction are, of course, generically distinct, some of this material overlaps in its deployment of tropes as well as its thematic concerns.

I want, throughout this study, to develop an emphasis on ambiguity to consider the ways in which British-Jewish writers are becoming increasingly interrogative about notions of exclusion and perhaps more alert to the possibilities, as well as the perils, of diffuse forms of identification. In the immediate post-war context, British-Jewish writing expressed a recurring anxiety about Jews being perceived as rootless foreigners who could never belong fully in Britain. Contemporary writing reflects back on these anxieties and continues to circle around these issues of belonging and not belonging. However, in recent writing, especially since the 1990s, we see a subtle shift in focus. As I shall discuss more fully in relation to 'half-Jewishness' in Chapter 8, increasingly the emphasis becomes not so much on being Jewish, and therefore not quite British, but on being British and perhaps not quite Jewish. Some of this uncertainty is deployed rather playfully, but, as we shall see, it is also presented as a point of tension. Woolf's statement, which I quoted in the epigraph to this chapter, 'the Jewish writer is *not* particularly different', is intriguing in this context. Perhaps, then, it is a *lack* of distinguishable difference, rather than the perception of difference, that has become the disquieting matter.

A history of ambiguity, uncertain identification and a culture of muted antisemitism have informed the contemporary field in a number of ways. These themes will be developed throughout *Writing Jewish*. Issues of belonging and alienation, location and dislocation, identities and stereotypes, will all be explored in more depth as the book progresses. An understanding of the way that memory informs a sense of British-Jewish identity forms the basis of these discussions and so the following chapter looks at issues of remembering and forgetting to ask how memory shapes British-Jewish writing today. As the trend in Jewish celebrities tracing their Jewish pasts on the BBC television programme *Who Do You Think You Are?* demonstrates, that which is forgotten sometimes seems to be as significant as that which is remembered. So, in terms of individual and collective British-Jewish identities, the next chapter looks at some of the ways that we forget, as well as remember, who we think we are.

Notes

1. Michael Woolf, 'Negotiating the Self; Jewish Fiction in Britain since 1945', in A. Robert Lee, ed., *Other Britain, Other British: Contemporary Multicultural Fiction* (London: Pluto Press, 1995), pp.124–141 (129).
2. Howard Jacobson, *Kalooki Nights* (London: Jonathan Cape, 2007), p.56.
3. *New Statesman*, special issue 'Who Speaks for British Jews?' 28 May 2012.
4. For a text of Blair's speech see: http://www.sefard.org/opening.htm. Accessed 21 June 2012.
5. In a 2007 article on British-Jewish writing Donald Weber also makes this point. See 'Anglo-Jewish Literature Raises Its Voice', *JBooks.com*, 12 July 2007. http://www.jbooks.com/interviews/index/IP_Weber_English.htm.

6 'Loyalty, Identity, Belonging', *New Statesman*, p.5.

7. Cecil Roth, 'Why Anglo-Jewish History?' (1968). Quoted in Todd Endelman, *The Jews of Britain 1656–2000* (Berkeley: University of California Press, 2002), p.1.

8. David Cannadine, 'Cousinhood', *London Review of Books*, 1989. Quoted in Endelman, p.271.

9. The question of how one defines a Jewish writer is the focus of much debate. For a useful overview of such discussions see David Brauner, *Post-War Jewish Fiction: Ambivalence, Self-Explanation and Transatlantic Connections* (Basingstoke: Palgrave, 2001), chapter one, pp. 1–37. In *Writing Jewish* I have tended to focus on writers who identify themselves as British-Jewish and on texts that address themes of British-Jewishness.

10. Bryan Cheyette, 'British-Jewish Literature', in Sorrel Kerbel, ed., *Jewish Writers of the Twentieth Century* (New York: Fitzroy Dearbon, 2003), pp.7–10 (p.7). Cheyette's forthcoming, *Diaspora's of the Mind: British Jewish Writing and the Nightmare of History* (New Haven: Yale University Press, 2014), promises to make a substantial contribution to the development of British-Jewish literary studies, especially in terms of postcolonial theorization.

11. For a useful collection of essays on British-Jewish Studies see 'Whatever Happened to British Jewish Studies?' special issue of *Jewish Culture and History*, 12.1–2 (2010). I am grateful to Vallentine Mitchell for permission to reproduce some of my contribution to that volume here. See Ruth Gilbert, 'Displaced, Dysfunctional & Divided: Contemporary British Jewish Writing'. *Whatever Happened to British-Jewish Studies?* special issue of *Jewish Culture and History*, ed. by Tony Kushner and Hannah Ewence, vol. 12, 1–2, Summer/Autumn (2010), 267–280.

12. David Cesarani, *The Jewish Chronicle and Anglo-Jewry* (Cambridge: Cambridge University Press, 1994), p.2.

13. See, for example, Tony Kushner, *The Jewish Heritage in British History: Englishness and Jewishness* (London: Frank Cass, 1992).

14. See Tony Kushner, *The Holocaust and the Liberal Imagination* (Oxford: Blackwell, 1994) and Anthony Julius *Trials of the Diaspora: A History of Anti-Semitism in England* (Oxford: Oxford University Press, 2010).

15. Quoted in Endelman, p.247.

16. Howard Cooper and Paul Morrison, *A Sense of Belonging: Dilemmas of British Jewish Identity* (London: Weidenfeld and Nicolson, 1991), p.9.

17. Anne Karpf, *The War After* (London: Minerva, 1996), p.215.

18. Although there are, of course, significant distinctions to be made between Englishness and Britishness, the terms are often conflated in the writing on which this study focuses. Throughout *Writing Jewish* I generally use the term British to encompass an idea of Englishness except where there are specific issues relating to other identifications.

19. Howard Jacobson, *Roots Schmoots: Journeys among Jews* (London: Penguin, 1993), p.3.
20. Jonathan Freedland, *Jacob's Gift: A Journey into the Heart of Belonging* (London: Penguin, 2006), p.14.
21. Linda Grant, *Remind Me Who I Am Again* (London: Granta, 1998), p.71.
22. Linda Grant, *The People on the Street: A Writer's View of Israel* (London: Virago, 2006), p.5.
23. Linda Grant, 'It's Kosher', *Guardian*, 20 September 2005.
24. Linda Grant, 'Background Noise', *New Statesman*, 28 May 2012, 50–51 (51).
25. Bryan Cheyette, 'British-Jewish Literature', p.7.
26. Jacobson, 'Now We are 350', *Jewish Quarterly*, 20 (2006), 41–46, (45).
27. Jacobson, 'Now We are 350', 44.
28. Similarly the title of Barnet Litvinoff's memoir, *A Very British Subject*, (London, Vallentine Mitchell, 1996) signals a somewhat ironic relationship to British identity. Following in this tradition of family narratives that explore the often compromised processes of anglicization for Jews, see Andrew Miller's *The Earl of Petticoat Lane* (London: Heinemann, 2006).
29. Bryan Cheyette, 'British-Jewish Literature', p.10.
30. See Jeremy Gavron, *The Book of Israel* (London: Scribner, 2003), *An Acre of Barren Ground* (London: Scribner, 2005); Giles Coren, *Winkler* (London: Vintage, 2006); Charlotte Mendelson, *When We Were Bad* (London: Picador, 2007); Francesca Segal, *The Innocents* (London: Chatto and Windus, 2012). Segal won the 2012 Costa first novel award, the 2012 National Jewish Book award for fiction and was longlisted for the 2013 Women's Prize for Fiction (the Orange Prize).
31. Donald Weber, 'Anglo-Jewish Literature Raises Its Voice'.
32. Naomi Alderman, *Disobedience* (London: Viking, 2006).
33. Mike Leigh, 'Mike Leigh Comes Out', Interview with Golda Zafer Smith, *Jewish Renaissance*, 4 (2005), 6–8 (8).
34. David Herman, 'Where Are the Novelists?' *Jewish Chronicle*, 20 October 2006, p.43.
35. See for example, *Report of the All-Party Parliamentary Inquiry into Antisemitism*, 7 September, 2006, http://www.thepcaa.org/report.html; and *Community Security Trust Report*, 2008: http://www.thecst.org.uk/docs/Incidents_Report_08.pdf. Accessed 10 June 2012.
36. 'Howard Jacobson Talking', 21 January 2006, interview by Cara Wides, http://www.somethingjewish.co.uk/articles/1730.
37. As Nicholas Lezard puts it: 'Although it's true that *The Finkler Question* has its moments of high comedy, it also has moments of heartbreaking sadness; the two are, indeed, intertwined.' 'Is Howard Jacobson the only person writing British Jewish novels?' *Guardian*, 15 October 2010.

38. Howard Jacobson, *The Finkler Question* (London: Bloomsbury, 2010), p.17.
39. Lezard notes that 'Jacobson told me, when *The Finkler Question* made the Booker longlist, that its success might have something to do with the fact that, for once, its Jewishness is being approached from the outside, by a non-Jew', *Guardian*, 15 October 2010.
40. David Baddiel, 'My Identity is in My Bones – But Let's Not Make a Big Deal Out of It', *New Statesman*, 28 May 2012, 70.
41. Keith Kahn-Harris and Ben Gidley, *Turbulent Times: The British Jewish Community Today* (London: Continuum, 2010), p.7.
42. Jonathan Sacks, *The Home We Build Together: Recreating Society* (London: Continuum, 2007), p.3.
43. *Jewish Chronicle*, 17 December 1993, 8–9.
44. Jonathan Sacks, *Will We Have Jewish Grandchildren? Jewish Continuity and How to Achieve It* (London: Vallentine Mitchell, 1994).
45. Steven M. Cohen and Keith Kahn-Harris, *Beyond Belonging: The Jewish Identities of Moderately Engaged British Jews* (London, UIJA/Profile Books, 2004), p.viii.
46. David Cesarani, 'Who Speaks for British Jews?' *New Statesman*, 28 May 2012, 23–27 (23).

2

'Two Thousand Years of Memory': Memory and British-Jewish Identity

In *I Dreyfus* (1999) Bernice Rubens explores what she calls the 'Dreyfus syndrome'.[1] Rubens does not attempt to directly rewrite the story of the nineteenth-century Dreyfus affair (a French cause célèbre centred on the fate of a Jewish army officer who was wrongly accused of treason), but instead revisits some of the issues that the episode raised about Jewishness, identity and belonging. As I suggested in Chapter 1, contemporary British-Jewish writing presents a new confidence among Jews in today's Britain, but it also reveals the effects of a less secure past. Rubens draws from this underlying insecurity for British Jews by relocating the Dreyfus narrative to a 1990s English public school. This bastion of establishment values is presented as a kind of time capsule which contains a muted, but deep, seam of antisemitism. Sir Alfred Dreyfus, a self-confessed 'closet Jew' (18), has been raised in an atmosphere of lies and ignorance about his Jewish origins and he manifests a complex relationship to Jewishness throughout the story. His strategic denial of Jewishness enables him to become headmaster of the school. However, when he is framed for the murder of a child (invoking a deep cultural association with Jews and the blood libel), he begins to reconstruct a growing sense of his Jewish identity. The repressed, it is implied, will always return. In this way the narrative presents a rather odd proposition, suggesting that Jewishness, however much disavowed, denied and even unknown, remains a constituent part of identity and is somehow stored within

19

the deep memory of every Jew. This chapter sets out to interrogate the terms of this proposition.

At one point, Dreyfus, who is uneducated in Jewish tradition, stands by his father's grave in an English village churchyard and recites 'the *Shema* in full, that prayer, never knowingly learnt but planted at birth in every Jewish heart' (68). Such moments recur throughout the novel. As Dreyfus' carefully constructed identity, as an 'Englishman', unravels, so his apparently innate Jewish self surfaces. In an unsettling process of mystification, Rubens relates how he is inordinately drawn to the services that are held for the few Jewish boys at the school. He explains that although 'the songs they sang were entirely unknown to me, they were strangely familiar' (91). This sense of the already known accelerates as his crisis intensifies. So, when he is imprisoned for child murder, the distraught Dreyfus recounts that:

> I decided to sing to myself to allay my fears. And out of my mouth, as from nowhere, except from out of two thousand years of memory, came a tune that my mother had sung to me when I was a baby. Her own mother had sung it to her. That Yiddish song was the sole Jewish legacy my mother could not deny... I imagined her face as I sang it to myself, and with her I mouthed the odd Yiddish word that I could remember and for some reason that recollection gave me so much joy that for a moment I forgot where I was and why. (213–214)

The (re)construction of a tender memory provides a moment of comfort and he is able to temporarily forget his present condition by remembering this joyous formative moment. However, although he yearns to repeat this sensation of infantile plenitude, Dreyfus cannot again reinhabit the memory until finally he is exonerated of the charges against him. When that day comes, and he hears the cheers in the court, he tells the reader, 'I don't recall any detail. Only one thing I remember. I was singing my grandmother's song and the Yiddish slid like silk off my tongue, as I recalled every single word' (265).

In these ways, the narrative implies that what Dreyfus had been most guilty of was trying to forget that he was a Jew. When he remembers who he really is, the reconciliation provides a kind of mystical resolution, an epiphany of connection. On his release from prison the final stage of his journey towards remembering his Jewishness is realized as he takes his family to revisit their European past. At the site of a gas chamber in Auschwitz-Birkenau he recites the prayer for the dead. Here memory is presented as complete and Dreyfus's identity crisis is fully resolved. As Rubens puts it, this is his, 'Day of At-Onement' (276).

Rubens' writing elsewhere on the Jewish condition is incisive, but this novel seems to endorse a problematic view of Jewishness as an ineffable essentialism. It is worth looking at this underlying premise of *I, Dreyfus* to consider the issues it raises more generally about the construction of memory in Jewish identity. The narrative perpetuates a sense that Jewishness is a never entirely forgotten trace that resides within the collective memory. In the following discussion I want to explore further the ways in which the relationship between history, memory and identity is figured in relation to Jews in Britain today. The past, for most British Jews, is as L.P. Hartley famously put it, quite literally 'a foreign country'.[2] That is to say, that the majority of Jews in Britain have family origins elsewhere. Today's Jews might be the third or fourth generation of immigrants, or their roots in Britain might go back further, but the sense of not quite belonging, which as we have seen can be both troubling and thrilling, permeates contemporary British-Jewish writing. In this chapter I explore how memory might form a bridge between the past and the present, but I also suggest that such bridges can create some unsteady crossings.

Whilst, as *I Dreyfus* demonstrates, it is unwise to make assumptions about the existence of an innate Jewish memory, this chapter will suggest that ideas about memory have had a particular resonance for Jewish writers and theorists, especially in the post-war years. As Yosef Yerushalmi has observed, for Jews, 'Zakhor', the command to remember, is both a repeated biblical command and a structuring cultural principle.[3] But remembering is never a simple process.

In the following discussion, I shall outline different aspects of memory, considering the ways in which individual, familial, collective and cultural memory all inform the representation of contemporary British-Jewish identities. This will also provide a context for the next chapter, which looks specifically at how the Holocaust is remembered in British-Jewish writing, particularly in relation to the concept of postmemory in the second generation of Holocaust survivors. The final section of this chapter draws together ideas about memory, and its effect on identification for contemporary British Jews, by focusing on representations of Passover, a festival that foregrounds issues of food, ritual and memory. Ideas about memory and amnesia, presence and nostalgia, continuity and loss, place and dislocation are not, however, confined to these chapters of *Writing Jewish*. They underpin the book as a whole.

Memory: models, metaphors, meaning

Edward Casey has claimed that we are 'made of memories', and this seems at an intuitive level to be right.[4] But what does such an assertion really mean? What are the implications of placing memory at the centre of ourselves? As Anne Whitehead has argued, memory is not an ahistorical concept.[5] It is understood differently, given different meanings and values, within different times and cultures. From the philosophical musings of the ancient Greeks, to the development of psychoanalytical theories of the unconscious in late-nineteenth century Europe, to the scientific models developed by contemporary neuroscientists, memory is imbued with cultural meaning.

In some respects, it might be easier to think about *how*, rather than *why* we remember. Neuroscientists have focused their attention in recent years on understanding the biology of the brain, identifying and charting the physical processes by which memories are made. But the fascination with memory remains a wider cultural issue, as well as a subject of scientific enquiry, and developments in neuroscience have intrigued artists and cultural commentators as well as scientists and medical researchers. Indeed debates that seek to locate memory in a physical region of the brain have provided suggestive, even poetic, images of, for example, the seahorse-shaped hippocampus and the almond-shaped amygdala. Arguably, what neuroscientists have been really trying to find out in their explorations of chicken's brains, engrams, synapses, circuits and neurotransmitters is how, in fact, we think we know who we are. In a personal reflection on the ontological impact of memory loss, Deborah Waring explains:

> We are all the sum of our memories, both recent and long ago. They are what make us who we used to be, who we are, who we become. The ancient Greeks understood. They had two rivers in Hades: Mnemosyne and Lethe, memory and oblivion.[6]

Similarly, as the neuroscientist Steven Rose puts it, 'memory defines who we are...Lose your memory and you, as you, cease to exist'.[7] Rose's research into the biology of memory, which extends scientific exploration to think also about metaphorical modes of interpretation, has been influential in recent literary explorations of the ways in which the past shapes contemporary identity. It is perhaps not surprising that given the ruptures and repressions of Jewish history this work has been of particular interest to Jewish writers.[8]

For Linda Grant, seeking to understand her mother's memory loss and the way in which that connects to a wider issue for the children of immigrant Jews, the neuroscientific explanation provides an appropriately dynamic model for exploring the complexities of memory and identification at both a personal and cultural level. 'There are many metaphors for the memory' Grant notes:

> – we used to think of it as a great warehouse, then a filing system, then a computer with its hard and floppy drives...But memory isn't any of these things. Above all, it isn't a place, a storehouse or a machine for recording events. What the scientists now know is that it's 'an intricate and ever shifting net of firing neurons and crackling synapses, distributed through the brain'. It's a labyrinth, 'the twistings and turnings of which rearrange themselves completely each time something is recalled'.[9]

This model makes sense for Grant in terms of her own experience of shifting and sometimes contradictory cultural identifications. As the child of Eastern European immigrant Jews, brought up in post-war Liverpool, she finds that, 'I like this idea very much. Memory, unlike people, doesn't dig itself into the soil and claim territory, it's rootless, the Wandering Jew of our physical selves' (289). Grant's ideas about memory, subjectivity and collective identity are resonant, bringing together scientific and cultural interpretations to develop an understanding of Jewish identity as encompassing collective as well as personal histories.

As Nicola King has argued, memory is imbued with meaning and given particular value within certain emotional and epistemological contexts. 'It is not only the *content* of memories, experiences and stories which construct a sense of identity', she explains, but 'the concept of the self which is constructed in these narratives'.[10] But personal memories, the stories that form the sinews of subjectivity, derive in large part from family narratives, the context in which the self is formed. And, in turn, family memories are formed within wider social and cultural contexts. In his influential study of collective memory Maurice Halbwachs argued that, rather than recalling memories in isolation, we remember in relation to the groups in which we function as social beings, contending that 'no memory is possible outside frameworks used by people living in society to determine and retrieve their recollections'.[11]

Halbwachs' theorization draws a distinction between memory and history. For him, collective memory is primarily concerned with events that have occurred within living memory and it emphasizes continuity, whereas history is focused on the past and tends to chronicle change. Other theorists, however, have questioned such a clear distinction and have developed ideas about collective memory that engage with the more distant past. Paul Connerton's key text, *How Societies Remember* (1989) focuses particularly on 'habit memory', in terms of bodily performance (postures, costume, gestures and so on) in the process of inter-generational transmission. Drawing from a sociological and anthropological perspective, he argues that 'images of the past and recollected knowledge of the past...are conveyed and sustained by (more or less) ritual performances'.[12] Building on such thinking, Jan Assmann has developed an idea of 'cultural memory', exploring the ways in which memories are transmitted by way of commemorative ceremony and ritual through generations.[13]

This extension of Halbwachs' collective model into 'habit' and 'cultural' memory is important in thinking about Jewish identity. Jewishness is arguably embedded in a sense of collective identification, whether specifically religious or familial and broadly cultural in nature. However, collective memory is not only about what surfaces; it also pertains to that which subtends the cultural group. As Gemma Romain explains:

> Collective memory does not have to stand for biological personal memories, it can relate to historical knowledge and beliefs that are explicit or silent in society. These do not necessarily have to be articulated by an individual on order to exist and function. Collective memory represents the ways in which history, myths, ideas, personal experiences and personal memories are publicly verbalised, commemorated, memorialised, articulated in folk tales and fables, or forgotten, revised and repressed.[14]

Here Romain signals the importance of forgetting, as well as remembering, in thinking about collective memory. So, returning to Albert Dreyfus, we can see that the dichotomy between memory and forgetting that the novel suggests, is perhaps not so distinct. The broken bridges between the past and the present, the personal and the collective, cannot simply be repaired by transcendental moments of recollection. Memory operates at a more subtle level.

'Remind Me Who I Am Again': memory and Jewish identity

For Jews, and other diasporic peoples, the balance between remembering and forgetting is especially delicate. David Roskies has discussed the ways in which many 'memory veins' (in terms of communities, geographies, languages) have been severed as a result of the displacements that many Jews experienced in the late-nineteenth and early-twentieth centuries. In his study of the Jewish search for a 'usable past' he has argued that 'in times of crisis, the function of Jewish memory was to transcend the ruptures of history'.[15] And this, perhaps never more so than in the crises of the twentieth century. Roskies points out that 'collective memory and collective amnesia' are inextricably linked (13), but, as Jonathan Boyarin argues, memory and forgetting are not terms representing simple opposites suggesting an equal relationship between presence and absence.[16] Rather, forgetting has its own weight, and indeed presence, in its symbiotic relationship to memory. By demonstrating the ways in which forgetting as a process and oblivion as a state come together in the French concept of *oubli*, Boyarin considers the complex interplay of memory, forgetting and the production of Jewish nostalgia for a metaphorized past.[17] This interaction between remembering and forgetting is felt acutely within families, especially when the weight of a parents' forgetfulness comes to bear on the next generation.

Linda Grant, writing about her mother's disintegrating memory makes the point that, for diasporic communities, memory has an especially significant function. It provides connections to the past that cannot be taken for granted:

> If you lose your memory in Yorkshire, Yorkshire is all around you. You can go to the parish church and there are the records of births and marriages and deaths. That's not to say your experiences are commonplace, it's just that they are easier to replicate ... But what was particular in my mother's case was that in her brain resided the very last links with her generation. And what a generation it was – those children of immigrants who had in their heads two worlds, the one they lived in and a partial, incomplete place that their parents had handed on to them. (31)

There is a real sense here that those memories, passed on from parent to child, can somehow stem the flow of loss produced by repeated displacement. But, once individual memory function falters, so too does that delicate balance between the 'two worlds' of the past and the present in the familial and collective context. As Grant notes, 'It did not matter to my mother, but it did to me, that with her memory, that vast house, was passing away a whole world which when it was gone would be finally beyond any recall' (24). Similarly, Lisa Appignanesi observes this intensification of interest in the past, in generational and cultural terms, at precisely the point that it seems to be in danger of slipping away: 'it can hardly be coincidental', she notes, 'that I want to remember, to uncover, to know, at the moment when my last gateway to family memory – my mother – is losing hers'.[18]

Grant quotes John Bridgewater, of the welfare organization Jewish Care, who asserts 'without memory we don't exist'. He goes on to make the point that 'when a member of the family starts to lose their memory it turns everything up because not only are they losing their recall of you, your recall of them is challenged. It's almost a challenge to your own existence' (268). Bridgewater recognizes that this has particular implications in relation to Jewish culture. 'So the whole thing about memory', he explains, 'is that',

> It's not just one member of the family losing their memory. And for the Jewish community it's even more complex because while all cultures are to do with memory, none more so than the Jewish community in which everything is about what was. (269)

The implication is that Jews need memory, transmitted through families, to substitute for the breaks and fissures resulting from a collective history that has been marked by repeated geographical and cultural displacements. What has been lost, these accounts remind us, are not only personal relationships and generational continuity, but cultures that cannot be excavated or reclaimed. There is no return.

As Pierre Nora has argued in his study of *lieux de mémoire* (sites of memory), focusing on the decline of French peasant culture, the ruptures between the past and present create a self-consciousness which lead us to 'speak so much of memory because there is so little of it left'.[19] The Jewish emphasis on remembering 'what was' might, in these terms, also be seen as a compulsion to mitigate a condition of amnesia. When Grant wonders, towards the beginning of her memoir, 'if it is a tragedy or a blessing when Jews, who insist on forgiving and forgetting nothing, should end their lives remembering nothing' (15), she perhaps recognizes a fundamental tension within the Jewish collective psyche.

The French writer, Henri Raczymow's, conceptualization of 'memory shot through with holes' is also useful in thinking through this interplay between memory and forgetting.[20] In a talk given in 1986 Raczymow reflects on the sense of displacement, the profound disconnection from the past, experienced by European Jews of the post-war generation, explaining that for them 'Jewish identity was not nothing, it was nothingness, a kind of entity in itself' (99). His observations about memory and nostalgia signal complex issues of absence and loss for contemporary Jews. Discussing the tendency of Jews in 1990s France to mythologize the lost world of their of grandparents he argues that 'we are submerged in mythology, and in their case even their nostalgia is mythical, for it is something that they never knew, that no longer exists and that will never again exist. Their nostalgia is devoid of content' (101). Such nostalgia for a Jewish past, which only really exists in the traces of imagined memory and partially represented moments, emerges as a key theme in contemporary British-Jewish writing and this negotiation of past and present, history and myth, memory and forgetting, is something that I shall return to throughout *Writing Jewish*.

Within a collective context of discontinuity and loss, individual stories about Jewish experiences are often poignant in the ways in which they engage with ideas about memory. Memory, is in this respect, a way in which to memorialize, in the sense of commemoration, both collective and personal losses. As Appignanesi puts it, signalling the complex balance necessitated by remembering, 'the dead are lost. But maybe, none the less, it makes a difference if by remembering them we lose them properly' (7). So, remembrance and loss are inextricably linked. One does not negate the other. We can see this interplay in an oral history collected by the London North-West Reform Synagogue (2003). The stories told here recall the ruptures of the twentieth century as they were experienced by Jews who live in Britain today. It is a rich and evocative record of the effects of war, displacement, immigration, adaptation and survival. In one account, Eva Graham, born in Czechoslovakia (Slovakia) in 1938, describes a childhood marked by trauma and loss. Her tone is remarkably lacking in self-pity as she explains:

> I don't remember my parents as people – I can't put a face to them. I was twenty-two before I actually found some photographs of them. My theory is that if you can't personally remember someone, you can't really mourn for them, because you can't recall – 'This is what my mother looked like, what my father looked like'…I simply don't remember.[21]

Here, the loss is irrecoverable and Graham does not try to fill this void with memory. Instead of everything being 'about what was' the words 'I simply don't remember' express absence with stark precision.

Photographs in Graham's account mark loss rather than substitute for past presence and this raises a theme that runs through many explorations of memory and is perhaps especially resonant for

Jews. In *Camera Lucida* Roland Barthes explores the fundamentally elegiac quality of photography and this is something picked up on by Marianne Hirsch in her study of postmemory. As Hirsch explains 'the referent haunts the picture like a ghost; it is a revenant, a return of the lost and dead other'.[22] In her discussion of Holocaust photographs she goes on to explain that:

> Photography's relation to loss and death is not to mediate the process of individual and collective memory but to bring the past back in the form of a ghostly revenant, emphasizing, at the same time, its immutable and irreversible pastness and irretrievability. (20)

When the past fades from living memory there is an increasingly urgent generational imperative to reconnect with what has passed, but, as commentators repeatedly remind us, memory is unreliable, mediated, shot through with holes. In Grant's account of her struggle to make sense of unexplained family photographs and incoherent scraps of the past, she recognizes the fundamentally fragile nature of the project. Her quest takes on an increasingly desperate and fatalistic quality:

> Perhaps the distant past that was slipping away into darkness was not gone forever and if I knew how to look I could find it and it would be there, if only for the moment it took to pass it from one generation on to the next. (137)

This sense of the precarious nature of personal, familial and collective memory is a recurring theme in contemporary British-Jewish writing. As identities are increasingly seen as in process, constantly under construction and open to reconstruction, a knowable sense of cultural identity, which could be either remembered or forgotten, cannot be assumed. In this way the imperative to 'remind me who I am again', has become a resonant question for our times.

The collective identity of any group is understood, and in a sense, remade with each remembering. *Beyond Belonging*, the 2004 study that set out to encourage Anglo-Jewish continuity, which I discussed in Chapter 1, identifies 'critical moments' in the lifecycle (such as bar/bat mitzvah, marriage, birth of a child, death of a parent) when possibilities for engagement with Jewish tradition are heightened. These occasions are by their very nature ritualized and as such both reiterate and consolidate collective memory. It is in these moments that continuity seems to be most meaningful. However, continuity depends on an *a priori* connection to one's heritage. Jonathan Freedland's memoir *Jacob's Gift* exemplifies the importance of collective memory in terms of such ritual, familial and cultural connection.

It begins when Freedland's son, Jacob, is born. Freedland recounts how he had looked in his newborn's eyes and heard 'a string of words I had not expected'.[23] It transpires that the words, a manifestation of deep memory, were a Hebrew prayer of thanks and the voice that he heard was his own. Like Alfred Dreyfus, in Rubens' novel, the prayer surfaces at an intense point of emotion. It is, undoubtedly, a moving moment. I would, however, want to pause to question its underlying premise.

When he prepares to have his son ritually circumcised Freedland notes that 'this was a tradition which every Jewish male had obeyed for thousands of years…It was inconceivable that Jacob would be different' (5). Freedland is right to identify this as a determining moment in perpetuating a sense of Jewish identity within the family, the community, and the collective context. However, his Jewishness is both anchored in family history and continuous, in that he has married a Jewish woman, and he has fathered Jewish children. In thinking about issues of memory, particularly how identities are remembered and forgotten, one wonders about those Jews in Britain who have more uncertain and dispersed identifications with their Jewishness, whose knowledge of Jewish ritual and tradition may be limited, and whose sons may not be circumcised. In other words, those Jews in Britain today who might identify as Jewish in some ways, but who have forgotten, or perhaps never known, any prayers.

The final section of this chapter looks at some examples of the ways in which contemporary British-Jewish writers have represented such moments of connection and disconnection to their Jewish pasts by focusing on the motif of food in general and the festival of Passover in particular. Here Jonathan Safran Foer's somewhat artful enquiry, 'what does it remember like?' becomes increasingly suggestive.[24]

'What Does It Remember Like?': eating the past

Food holds many symbolic associations with the past and is often seen as a way of remembering collective identities within diasporic cultures. As Grant puts it:

> In our family, as in every Jewish family, food was part of our ancestral memory. In her kitchen my mother cooked recipes for cheese blintzes and *matzoh brei* that her own mother had brought with her from Kiev, and the dishes that came to the table were our link to the vanished communities of earlier times; they traced the wanderings of the Jewish people across the world. (77)

This is a compelling idea and is reiterated throughout many reflections on Jewish identity. As the cookery writer Claudia Roden explains, Jewish dishes 'are a link with the past, a celebration of roots, a symbol of continuity. They are that part of an immigrant culture that survives the longest'.[25]

Mr Rosenblum's List (2010) by Natasha Solomons draws from this idea of food as a way of connecting to the past for diasporic Jews. The novel explores ways of being, or becoming, British for a German-Jewish émigré couple in post-war England. Sadie, a character subsumed by the losses of *'before'*, is living in a Dorset village with her husband Jack in 1952. She turns to her mother's recipe book. In the category of 'cakes to help you remember' she finds the recipe for 'Baumtorte' (tree cake), in which each layer represents a memory. 'Sadie', we are told, 'like her mother and grandmother before her, had baked a Baumtorte whenever she needed to remember'.[26] As she bakes the cake, she recollects all the previous occasions when she had baked it, from when she was a girl and it was at its thinnest, to the day that she received her exit visa and left behind her family in Nazi Germany. As she recalls all these memories and 'everyone she needed to remember' (140), Sadie bakes through the night. 'When dawn came, there was a cake towering many feet high with a thousand layers of rings; every layer holding a memory' (141). The local women are overwhelmed by the scent of baking, noticing that 'it had a strange smell, not merely dough or sugar but the fragrance of unbearable sadness' (142). The cake, it is suggested, is a bridge between past and present. It is redolent of an acutely painful past and allows, through the repetition and re-enactment of memories, a process of healing to begin.

Such writing might be critiqued. It could be seen to present a somewhat sentimental invocation of a complex chapter of history for Jews in Britain. Yet, far more overtly cynical British-Jewish writers also draw from images of Jewish food in their work. In fact, rare is the contemporary Jewish writer that does not at some point throw in a bagel, or a bowl of chicken soup, to underscore (with more or less irony) their connection to a remembered Jewish identity. Jewish food memories are deployed in various ways: to signify nostalgia for childhoods and cultures that have passed; or, more satirically, to suggest an awareness of the clichés that Jews can fall into when caught in the mists of memory. So to take just one example, we see how in Adam Thirlwell's ultra-knowing novel, *Politics* (2003), that Moshe, the distinctly detached half-Jewish hero, when in crisis, is drawn to the comforts of the *Kosher Knosherie*. In this setting, this restless and disconnected child of the twenty-first century consumes a salt-beef bagel and feels a passing sense of connection to his Jewish heritage: 'Now that he was sad, it made him feel happy. It made him believe he liked salt beef'.[27] As a product of postmodernism, Moshe's relationship to Jewishness through food is of course self-conscious. He does not just like salt beef, he observes himself believing that he does so.

Howard Jacobson's commentary on 'Dinner in the Diaspora' mediates these poles of popular sentimentality and arch detachment. Taking a simultaneously teasing and thoughtful approach, Jacobson explains that:

> The suggestibility of Jewish food extends beyond the juices of the stomach to the juices of the mind...Not a particle of Jewish food can pass a Jew's lips...without his tasting the soupy bitter-sweet of exile...Where do you go to get the original smetana and kez with Bismarck herring on a poppy-seed bagel with a side serve of *latkes* and *chrain*? ...Nowhere, is the answer. Smetana and Kez Land exists no more, and probably never existed in reality in the first place...But if we are recreating a mythology, we also know it is one we cannot do without.[28]

Jacobson recognizes here the empty nostalgia that so often attends Jewish memory culture, but he also embraces the diasporic mythologies that such disconnection suggests. It is a shrewd and yet knowingly romanticized figuration.

Within Jewish ritual, food functions at an even more fundamental and structural level. As Rabbi Lionel Blue has observed, 'in Judaism you don't study theology, you eat it'.[29]Grant, like many others, places this thought in specific relation to Passover. 'Our religion', she recalls, 'was embodied in our cooking, like the Passover meal on *Seder* night where everything we put in our mouths symbolizes the slavery of the children of Israel under the terrible rule of the Egyptians, and their flight to freedom' (78). The Passover story is remembered each year through a highly ritualized series of symbolic and narrative enactments, many of which are centred on food. As Yerushalmi notes, the Seder (the ritual dinner) is the 'quintessential exercise in Jewish group memory':

> Here, in the course of a meal around the family table, ritual, liturgy, and even culinary elements are orchestrated to transmit a vital past from one generation to the next. The entire Seder is a symbolic enactment of an historical scenario...Significantly, one of the first ritual acts to be performed is the lifting up of a piece of unleavened bread (*matzah*) before those assembled, with the declaration:...'*This is the bread of* affliction which our forefathers ate in the land of Egypt'. Both the language and the

gesture are geared to spur, not so much a leap of memory as a fusion of past and present. Memory here is no longer recollection, which still preserves a sense of distance, but reactualization. (44)

The symbolism of the Seder meal, which as Yerushalmi suggests is reactualization, is enacted through the tropes of metaphor and metonymy. So, for example, salt water is a metaphorical signifier of tears and the bitter herbs are a metonymic symbol of pain and suffering. This symbolism is both poetic and blunt. It has a dreamlike quality that suggests the intense and overdetermined nature of such remembering.

Michael Kenny has argued that 'memory needs a place, a context. Its place, if it finds one that lives beyond a single generation, is to be found in the stories that we tell'.[30] Passover presents a particularly resonant story of exile, dispossession, and a desire for the promise of a home. Even among relatively disconnected Jews, memories of Seder nights often invoke nostalgia for childhood family gatherings and a sense of Jewish belonging. Indeed, there is a sense that for many 'moderately' engaged Jews this may be nearly all that remains of a connection to Jewish identity. Bernice Rubens, for example, notes in her sharply observed memoir that although she had shed many aspects of Jewishness throughout her life, she generally sustained the rituals of Passover. She recalls on one occasion:

> I had cooked a traditional meal with all the symbols that feature in the Seder-night service of Exodus. The wine, bitter herbs, the parsley, the salt water, the lamb bone, the matzos, the boiled eggs, and *charoset*, a sweet paste each with a particular meaning in relation to the Seder meal. ... I had Grandma in mind. Every year of my childhood, she and my Auntie organised the Seder table, and as far as I was able I faltered in their footsteps.[31] (162)

The sense here of ritual as recollection is key. For Rubens, as for many other British Jews, the event is inevitably linked to personal family reminiscence as well as more general cultural memory. These are evocative memories of memories and the recounting of such memories often reveal, as the tellers bask in a warm glow of nostalgia for a Jewish past, an underlying sense of disconnection. As Rubens suggests, the repetitions involved in such rememberings become, potentially, ever more faltering. Moreover, with its emphasis on the suffering and bitter tears of the Jewish past, and the emotive aspiration to return to the mythical Promised Land ('Next year in Jerusalem'), Passover can remind British Jews that they might still be strangers in a strange land.

Julia Neuberger in her 1995 exploration of Jewish identity in Britain is interesting in this respect. She recalls fondly how Pesach was celebrated in her family of exiled German Jews in 1950s North London, describing the festival as a joyous and celebratory occasion. But she also notes that it was 'tinged with sadness' reminding them that 'we were fortunate enough to be free and safe, but others had perished'.[32]The ritual enactment of historical oppression recalls the persecutions of the recent past into the present and, as Jewish identity is concentrated, so British identity is diffused. Neuberger describes a 'strong sense of being emotionally Jewish, with the festivals setting a pattern for the year', but notes also that 'Passover, with the memories it evoked, gave us our strongest sense of not being wholly English' (17). Memory here works in at least three different temporal moments: the remembering of the distant Jewish past that is enacted within the Seder ritual; the evocation of painful recent memories in the aftermath of the Holocaust; and Neuberger's recollection of her 1950s childhood from her adult perspective within 1990s Britain. In such accounts we see, inevitably, a series of conflations and slippages between these realms of memory. Memory, in this way, does not provide a secure sense of identity. It suggests instead the difficulties inherent in understanding oneself within both personal and collective frameworks.

Again, Grant's account of her mother's memory loss illustrates what might be seen as a wider cultural anxiety about disconnection among British Jews. Grant identifies how when ritual is disconnected from family, home and the collective memory of a community, it is potentially emptied out of meaning. In the Jewish care home in which her mother is resident the care workers are almost all non-Jewish but it falls to them to perform rituals for the residents, such as lighting the Shabbat candles on Friday evenings. In this way, these mostly Caribbean and Africa workers stand in for the traditional Jewish family and, within an environment marked by dementia and memory loss, ritual replaces memory. As Grant observes:

> In the home it's non-Jews who are the transmitters of memory and of our culture. The link has been broken with the past, there's a gap in recollection and it's filled in by words and rituals learned by rote. It forces me to wonder what it means to be Jewish. (223)

Grant ponders this question, searching for a way in which to anchor herself within this context of drifting and dissolving identities. She comes to reflect on Passover:

> Those memories we resurrect on the feast of Passover of our days of slavery in the land of Egypt, are they personal memories or just as parroted

as the ones the Jamaicans and Ghanaians say when they light the Sabbath candles for the old Jews, who watch the flames and try to remember where they've seen something like them before? (223)

Here the understanding that the ritualization of memory might have become, through an inescapable processes of dilution and dissipation, no more than the 'parroting' of increasingly empty repetition, is poignant yet potentially astute. As Grant had noted earlier in the book:

> It is my fate now...to scramble among the ruins of my mother's memory in search of my past, of who all of us are. To have grown up as a Jewish daughter into an insistence of the importance of memory...without the past we're nothing, we belong to nobody. (28)

This powerful lament on memory, belonging and identity, is not limited to the specific circumstances of memory loss and generational disconnection that Grant narrates. It impacts on 'who all of us are' and suggests a far more widespread cultural condition for many Jews in contemporary Britain.

'Who All of Us Are': conclusion

In his novel, *The Book of Israel*, Jeremy Gavron presents a subtle consideration of the ways in which Jewish identity mutates in one family. As the family line extends through generations, spanning Lithuania in 1874 to London in 2001, the narrative explores issues of increasing disconnection. The reader is led in and out of different perspectives, places and characters, but the role of memory in terms of cultural identity is a continuous theme. Towards the end of the novel, a chapter set in London in 1978 focuses on Julia, the thoroughly anglicized child of acculturated German refugee parents, who is married to Jack (originally Israel) Dunn (Dunsky). Jack, a disavowing Jew, is away from home and Julia, attempting to reconnect with her Jewish identity, has decided to host a Seder dinner. The event, recounted in a somewhat breathless first-person narrative, is both risible and painful.

Julia is an excited and ignorant hostess. From the moment she opens the door her insecurity is apparent: 'Happy Passover: Do you say that? Happy Passover? Isn't it terrible that I don't know? Have you done this before? If you have it's more than me'.[33] Here, as Julia stumbles through an embarrassing and alcohol-fuelled evening, we see a clear contrast to Rubens' romanticized depiction of Jewish memory in relation to Alfred Dreyfus. Julia does not have any innate repository of Jewishness memory from which she can draw, however much she may desire to do so. The implication is that she has not just forgotten a way of being Jewish; she has never known it. Her reconstruction of Jewishness now is dependent on 'mugging up' from the 'armful of books' she has recently acquired at *Jerusalem the Golden*, a shop in Golders Green (259).

The final chapter of *The Book of Israel*, 'Circumlocution', is set in 2001 and presents a yet more tenuous and garbled recollection of Jewishness. This is narrated by Julia and Jack's daughter-in-law and focuses on how when she was pregnant she and her husband debated whether or not they would have a hypothetical baby son circumcised. The fictional monologue reflects a loose sense of Jewish identity. 'It all seems so simple at the beginning. You're Jewish', she says. 'Your husband is done and you want your child to be the same' (278). But 'God', she explains, 'it's not as though we do anything else … I mean the only Jewish ritual we perform is going to see the new Woody Allen film when it comes out' (276). For Freedland the judgement to have his son circumcised was never in doubt. As he explains, 'even the Jewish man with the slackest link to his heritage was marked by it' (5). But for Jews such as this fictional couple, connections to Jewish ritual and tradition are increasingly flimsy. Again, as Grant put it, above, in relation to the culture of forgetting that characterized her mother's care home, 'the link has been broken with the past, there's a gap in recollection'. As it turns out, the circumlocuted modern couple have a baby girl.

Such narratives demonstrate that remembering for British Jews today is complex. Memory, which is individual and intimate, also connects Jews to a shared past and a collective history; but, as I have suggested throughout this chapter, such connection cannot be taken for granted. Many texts present self-conscious attempts to remember what it is to be Jewish and underlying this is a concurrent anxiety about what might be forgotten. From the mystification of Rubens in her characterization of Sir Alfred Dreyfus' innate Jewish memory, to Grant's poignant reflection on the cultural implications of memory loss, to the sequences of disconnection charted by Gavron and others, we see how writers have been drawn to map out the often circuitous routes of memory. For Jews today, living in the relatively calm environs of contemporary Britain, memory might offer some powerful connections to tradition and perhaps also to nostalgic forms of identification. Memory may provide some comforts, but it might also invoke anxieties about the fragile and sometimes fraught nature of the relationship between past and present. In particular, for Jews today, a consideration of memory might well necessitate a confrontation with difficult questions about the ways in which we remember the Holocaust. The following chapter develops this discussion. For contemporary British Jews, thinking about the Holocaust crystallizes many of the issues of connection and disconnection that this chapter has explored. It is hard to forget. But perhaps it is equally hard to remember.

Notes

1. Bernice Rubens, *I Dreyfus* (London: Abacus, 2000), p.viii.
2. L.P. Hartley, *The Go Between* (London: Penguin, 2004), p.7.
3. Yosef Hayim Yerushalmi, *Zakhor: Jewish History and Jewish Memory* (Seattle and London: University of Washington Press, 1982; 1996).
4. Edward S. Casey, *Remembering: A Phenomenological Study* (Bloomington: Indiana UP, 1987), p.290.
5. Anne Whitehead, *Memory* (London; Routledge, 2009).
6. Interview with Deborah Wearing by Louise France, Observer, 23 January 2005. http://www.guardian.co.uk/books/2005/jan/23/biography.features3
7. Steven Rose, *The Making of Memory: From Molecules to Mind* (London: Vintage, 2003), p.1. Rose was born into an East End Jewish family.
8. Appignanesi's novel, *The Memory Man*, which presents the story of a neuroscientist specializing in memory studies, specifically acknowledges Rose's contribution to her understanding of this area. See Lisa Appignanesi, *The Memory Man* (London: Arcadia, 2004), p.257.
9. Linda Grant, *Remind Me Who I am Again* (London: Granta, 1998), p.289.
10. Nicola King, *Memory, Narrative and Identity: Remembering the Self* (Edinburgh: Edinburgh University Press, 2000), pp.2–3.
11. Maurice Halbwachs, *On Collective Memory*, ed. and trans. by Lewis A. Coser (Chicago, University of Chicago Press, 1992), p.43.
12. Paul Connerton, *How Societies Remember* (Cambridge: Cambridge University Press, 1989), pp.3–4.
13. Jan Assmann, 'Collective Memory and Cultural Identity', trans. by John Czaplicka, *New German Critique*, 65 (1995), 125–133.
14. Gemma, Romain, *Connecting Histories: A Comparative Exploration of African- Caribbean and Jewish History and Memory in Modern Britain* (London: Kegan Paul, 2006), p.171.
15. David G Roskies, *The Jewish Search for a Usable Past* (Indiana University Press: 1999), p.1.
16. Jonathan Boyarin, *Storm from Paradise: The Politics of Jewish Memory* (Minneapolis: University of Minnesota Press, 1992).

17. Boyarin, pp.3–4.
18. Lisa Appignanesi, *Losing the Dead* (London: Vintage, 1999), p.7.
19. Pierre Nora, 'Between Memory and History: Les Lieux de Mémoire', trans. Marc Roudebush, *Representations*. 26 (1989), 7–12. Quoted from Michael Rossington and Anne Whitehead, eds, *Theories of Memory: A Reader* (Edinburgh: Edinburgh University Press, 2008), p.144.
20. Henri Raczymow and Alan Astro, 'Memory Shot Through With Holes', *Yale French Studies,* 85, Discourses of Jewish Identity in Twentieth-Century France (1994), pp.98–105.
21. David Stebbing and Evelyn Kent, *Jewish Memories of the Twentieth Century* (London: Evelyn Kent Associates, 2003), p.80.
22. Hirsch, Marianne, *Family Frames: Photographs, Narrative and Postmemory* (London: Harvard University Press, 1997), p.5.
23. Jonathan, Freedland, *Jacob's Gift* (London: Penguin, 2006), p.4.
24. Jonathan Safran Foer, *Everything is Illuminated* (London: Penguin, 2002), p.199.
25. Claudia Roden, *The Book of Jewish Food: An Odyssey from Samarkand and Vilna to the Present Day* (London: Penguin, 1996), p.11.
26. Natasha Solomons, *Mr Rosenblum's List* (London: Sceptre, 2010), p.140.
27. Adam Thirlwell, *Politics* (London: Vintage, 2006), p.247.
28. Howard Jacobson, 'Dinner in the Diaspora', *Jewish Quarterly*, 193 (2004), 87–8 (88).
29. Quoted from Grant, p.78.
30. Michael G. Kenny, 'A Place for Memory: The Interface between Individual and Collective History', *Comparative Studies in Society and History,* 41 (1999), 420–437 (421).
31. Bernice Rubens, *When I Grow Up* (London: Abacus, 2006), p.16.
32. Julia Neuberger, *On Being Jewish* (London: Heinemann, 1995), p.13.
33. Jeremy Gavron, *The Book of Israel* (London: Scribner, 2003), p.259.

3

'An Impossible Task': Remembering the Holocaust

In the pit at Babi Yar lie the remains, I assume, of my Haft relatives, per-haps of the two young women in the photograph, and their children and grandchildren. That history breathed down our necks as we were growing up, a constant reminder that where there were suburbs and houses and trees and allotments and W.H. Smith and Tesco and Marks and Spencer, a kind of mental chasm yawned beneath our feet into which we were always fearful that we could fall.

Linda Grant (1998)[1]

We have an impossible task: to hold onto something at the same time as letting it go. The fact that it's impossible doesn't mean it's not worth try-ing. Remember. And at the same time, remember that it's over.

Naomi Alderman (2012)[2]

This chapter develops Chapter 2's analysis of the role of memory in British-Jewish culture by looking at representations of the Holocaust in contemporary texts. As the above epigraph from Grant suggests, even within the relatively benign conditions of 1950s suburbia, the Holocaust subtended the lives of British Jews at a deep and sometimes unconscious level. This sense of history as 'breathing down our necks' is a key theme in accounts from the immediate post-war generation. For Alderman, who is a further generation away from the war, the Holocaust was still a pervasive presence throughout her childhood.[3] Noting the difficulties of having been educated to 'imagine myself in a camp', she is aware of an ongoing sense of anxiety about the potential re-emergence of anti-semitism: 'the Holocaust is right here', she says, 'it could happen at any moment' (30). So, like Grant, she grew up with a consciousness of the 'mental chasm' into which post-war Jews were always 'fearful that we could fall'. But Alderman also recognizes the paranoia that accompanies such fear. 'Except it's not here', she acknowledges; adding that, 'right now, right here, life is about as good for us as life has ever been for anyone in the history of the world. Probably better' (30). She thus sums up a disparity that informs much contemporary British-Jewish writing on the Holocaust. This tension, between remembering a traumatic collective past, whilst living fully in the present, is the focus of this chapter.

Britain, unlike mainland Europe, did not (with the exception of the Channel Islands) experience Nazi occupation and, although Jews in twentieth-century Britain encountered some antisemitic prejudice, they were not actively persecuted. However, as Grant and Alderman suggest, the impact of the Holocaust on British Jews is complex and in many ways still unresolved. It is, however, important not to oversimplify what are often divergent connections and differing experiences. British Jews who may not have been overtly affected by the Holocaust were nevertheless reminded that the position of Jews might always be precarious. Many others, who had lived in Britain for a generation or more, but who had origins in the European regions that came under Nazi control, lost family members. Such knowledge would be absorbed in complex ways through the post-war period. For other Jews in Britain, those who had fled Nazi Europe in the 1930s and the survivors who came to Britain after the war, the traumas of the Holocaust were acute and immediate.

Jews living and writing in Britain today are affected by these experiences, directly or indirectly, as they negotiate their British and Jewish identities in a post-Holocaust world. Most are the children, grandchildren or great-grandchildren of people who had to reconcile this history in far more pressing and meaningful ways. Some chose never to speak about the Holocaust, others spoke of it often and in many modes. For some it strengthened identification with Britain, for others it revealed a profound insecurity about issues of belonging. For some it intensified and accelerated processes of assimilation, for others it marked a realization of inassimilable otherness. So, whilst it would be ill-judged to exaggerate the effects of the Holocaust on British Jews today, it would also be an oversight to minimize the impact that the Nazi genocide has had on British Jews, in the past and in the present.

In this chapter, I shall begin by outlining the British response to the Holocaust during the war, and in the post-war period, exploring the ways in which this has been remembered or misremembered within the British national consciousness. I shall then go on to think about the experience of the 'second-generation' in Britain, the children of Holocaust survivors and refugees, and the ways in which the concept of 'postmemory' can be used to discuss the representation of their experience. This section draws in the main from memoirs written by the children of survivors and European refugees who, although not necessarily born in Britain, have made their home in Britain today. Finally, I shall consider recent fictional treatments of the Holocaust by contemporary British-Jewish writers, exploring how these texts confront the elisions that imbue the British experience of the Holocaust, in order to interrogate notions of history, truth and coherent identity. A consideration of memory, in relation to the construction of Jewish identities, which was outlined in Chapter 2, is threaded through the following discussion. It is driven by the dilemma that Alderman outlined: the 'impossible task' of remembering the Holocaust whilst living in the contemporary moment.

The Holocaust: British contexts

As National Socialism took hold in Germany and the threat of Nazi persecution spread throughout Europe, an increasing numbers of Jewish refugees attempted to flee to Britain. Only a small number were admitted. For British Jews this was a period of insecurity and their response to the plight of the Jews of Europe was underpinned by fear, anxiety and equivocation. As a consequence, the established Anglo-Jewish community was divided about how to react to events in Europe. Some were initially acquiescent with attempts to limit immigration, but many others were active in helping refugees escape from Europe. After Kristallnacht in 1938 some restrictions were relaxed and around forty thousand European refugees did come to Britain. Among the successes of refugee activity was the Kindertransport scheme of 1938–1939 in which ten thousand Jewish children were rescued from Nazi Germany and given refuge in Britain. Memoirs and literary texts that explore the refugee experience suggest that, whilst acknowledging the many acts of generosity and welcome offered in Britain, it is also necessary to recognize that exiles from Nazi Europe received a mixed reception from the Jews already resident in Britain as well as the wider British population.[4]

In general, this was a frightening and uncertain time for British Jews. As knowledge of the Holocaust filtered through to Britain, British Jews were gripped by, as Anne Karpf has put it, 'a feeling of overwhelming powerlessness, paralysis and despair'.[5] In retrospect, the apparent passivity of Anglo-Jewry in this period seems bewildering but, as Tony Kushner has argued, the Jewish community at that time 'had neither the moral energy, vision and self-confidence nor the financial resources to confront the horrors facing the Jew of Europe'.[6] Howard Cooper and Paul Morrison have documented the ways in which knowledge of the Holocaust permeated the collective consciousness of Anglo-Jewry. They note that during the war, when reports of death camps and gas chambers were reaching Britain, this knowledge was 'unbelievable, inassimilable', and they go on to explain how, as the gradual realization of the horrors that had taken place in Europe was absorbed, British Jews were left in a state of repressed grief and guilt which led, in some cases, to a 'strange selective amnesia'.[7] As one British Jew explains, 'it was too much to face, the Holocaust, and we didn't talk about it afterwards. It was a freezing of the emotions' (89).

Perhaps unsurprisingly, given the immobilizing effects of such a collective trauma, as well as the already ambiguous position of Anglo-Jewry, the post-war experience for Jews in Britain was mixed. On the one hand they were grateful to have escaped the horrors experienced by European Jews, but Britain in the late forties was not an entirely comfortable home for Jews.[8] Mass observation reports from the post-war period reveal an undercurrent of antisemitic sentiment which manifested itself in a variety of ways. Jewish immigration from Europe was discouraged. Holocaust survivors were not wholeheartedly welcomed to Britain and the German-Jewish refugees who had fled to Britain were often treated with particular suspicion and hostility. Moreover, Jewish terrorist action against the British Mandate in Palestine led to increased antisemitic feeling and there were anti-Jewish riots in a number of British cities throughout 1947. As I shall explore more fully in Chapter 5, the response of Anglo-Jewry to the founding of the nation State of Israel in 1948 was complex, reaching to the heart of those issues of belonging and alienation which shape so much of the British-Jewish experience.

Despite knowledge to the contrary, there was, in the aftermath of war, an implicit refusal to acknowledge that Jews had been the victims of Nazi policy. In Britain the war was represented primarily in terms of British heroic triumph in a mythologized narrative that elided the reality of the Nazi genocide. In a country that had suffered profound losses throughout the years of war, and continued to experience economic deprivation and hardship for some years to come, this was an understandable ideological strategy. But for British Jews, and those Holocaust survivors who did find refuge in Britain, the silence about the fate of European Jews and the underlying antisemitism that continued to circulate at the time was bewildering and painful. The word Holocaust, to describe the genocide, did not come into usage until the late 1950s and it was not until much later (arguably the 1990s) that consciousness of the Holocaust really impacted on Britain.[9]

This period of history is not just a Jewish issue. It touches on a raw nerve in the construction of the British national identity. World War II, which is still within living memory in Britain today, is a key component in the self-definition of British identity. Values of fair play, pluckiness and liberal tolerance have created a compelling national narrative but, as historians such as Tony Kushner and David Cesarani have demonstrated, Britain's role was far more equivocal than this mythology suggests.[10] The Allied cause was, of course, motivated by some worthy principles but, far from acting unambiguously as the liberal champions of Jews in Europe, the British drew routinely from their own deep pool of antisemitic ideology throughout and beyond the war years.

In his important study, *The Holocaust and the Liberal Imagination* (1994), Tony Kushner makes the point that British culture had not, even by the early 1990s, addressed the Holocaust with the same energy as had been seen in the US context. He argues that:

> In Britain the battle to achieve a presentness for the Holocaust has been much harder. Until recently the limitations and strength of a mono-cultural liberal ideology provided a less favourable atmosphere for consideration of the Holocaust. Britain perhaps still has a long way to go. (268)

However, British consciousness of the Holocaust has been refocused in recent decades and throughout the 1990s there were several key developments which contributed to raising awareness. So, for example, The Holocaust Educational Trust, which was established in 1988, played a key role in ensuring that in 1991 the Holocaust was made a mandatory subject within the secondary school National Curriculum for 11- to 14-year-olds.[11] In 1993 the Jewish experience of the Warsaw Ghetto uprising was marked by a small but landmark exhibition in the Imperial War Museum and in 2000 the Imperial War Museum opened the first permanent Holocaust exhibition in the UK. In 2001 Holocaust Memorial Day was established.[12]

For Jews in Britain, perhaps still lacking the evident confidence of their American counterparts, remembering the Holocaust requires a consideration of a troubling collective past. It raises complex themes relating to memory and identity that relate to the domestic context in Britain but also connect to wider issues of trauma and transmigration. A number of recent memoirs, written by children of European émigrés and Holocaust survivors, have explored some of the ambiguities and difficulties inherent in remembering such a painful and fractured past. The next section of this chapter looks at some of this material.

'Transgenerational haunting': post-memory and the second generation

In *Tales of Innocence and Experience* (2003), the German-born writer Eva Figes presents a lyrical meditation on memory and knowledge.[13] Figes, who came with her parents to Britain in 1939, explores the complex relationship between past and present. Reflecting on becoming a grandmother, she recalls her early childhood and the loss of her grandparents in Nazi Germany. On the surface, she had lived through the English war experience, but her consciousness was infused by a muted knowledge that was located in the Europe of her early childhood. She recalls a jolting point of realization when, aged 13, she watched the news reels which were screened in British cinemas at the end of the war. Seeing footage from Nazi concentration camps projected on to a screen, whilst sitting in a suburban English cinema, creates a profoundly destabilizing effect. Figes relates the memory in a powerful passage:

> I sit by myself with the black and white images flickering on the huge screen and realize that everything has changed for ever ... I came down the steps of the Odeon, blinking in the too-bright light of a Saturday afternoon, and everything was suddenly distant, alien, the quiet English streets, everything uneventful under an empty sky.
> I had lost my tongue. I could not speak a word of the language I had learned so assiduously. I felt it was all a lie, the bank on the corner, the municipal flowerbed, the bus stop opposite the haberdasher. What had I to do with this pretence of normality? (122–123)

As the Englishness that she has learned, in terms of language and behaviour, begins to unravel, Figes experiences an intense sense of disconnection from the national narrative of wartime Britain. Instead, she begins to glimpse her connection to a deeply held trauma that cannot be normalized.

> This is not war as I have understood it, living with it for six years, air
> raids, news bulletins of soldiers wading ashore, tanks rolling, happy women
> throwing flowers. This is a secret at the heart of darkness opening up, a
> yawning stinking pit....
>
> Something opens, something shuts. A hidden wound opens, a dark pit,
> deeper than any bomb crater I have peered into up till now. But human lips
> shut. That which cannot be spoken must be left unspoken. (124)

This realization fundamentally impacts on the development of Figes'
identity. As she ponders this formative moment, she writes in the
present tense: 'remember' she says, 'this is not yet history: this is now'
(124). Memory here does not just connect the past to the present in
a direct way. As Figes notes, 'the journey of memory is not a regular
trajectory from now to then' (43). It is a far more jagged matter. The
disjunction that Figes experiences in the cinema is related to geographical and generational connection as well as estrangement. With after-
knowledge, 'many years later', it occurs to her that her mother had
probably already seen the newsreel, but a mutual silence infused both
mother and daughter's confrontation with trauma: 'Struck dumb', she
remembers, 'I never asked, she never said' (126).

Victor Jeleniewski Seidler explores similar issues of assimilation and
alienation, memory and silence. In *Shadows of the Shoah* he reflects on
Jewish identity and belonging and the particular difficulties of remembering for the children of European refugees and Holocaust survivors.[14] Seidler was born in England in 1945 and he discusses how his
Polish and Austrian parents named him Victor both to celebrate and
to share in the English victory. However, he recalls a childhood that
was characterized by an atmosphere of ambiguous identification, invis-
ibility and silence. Noting the difficulties his parents found in articulating what had happened to them in Nazi Europe, he explains that:

> To speak was to make it real and to expose themselves to a pain and sense
> of loss they often did not want to be reminded of...Even though we grew
> up in the shadow of the Shoah, we were not taught to name our experience.
> Rather, the past was to be passed over in an anxious silence. (6)

Again, as Figes puts it, 'that which cannot be spoken must be left
unspoken' (124). Within a climate of more widespread British reticence, and a general refusal to acknowledge the specificities of the Nazi
persecution of Jews, such silence created a troubling dissonance.

Seidler's parents, like many immigrants who had fled the Nazi
regime, attempted to protect their children from the pain and losses
of the recent past by encouraging them to thoroughly assimilate

into British life: 'to fit in', 'to keep your head down', to learn ways of 'becoming English' (4). But this understandable drive towards assimilation for refugee Jews involved a complicated negotiation of Jewishness. The potential for 'double consciousness' that resulted from such negotiation was often transmitted to the next generation, who were of course already more English than their parents.

Anne Karpf, in *The War After*, recalls a similar sense of 'being an alien' (48), remembering 'a permanent struggle between Jewish and English, inside the home and outside' (49). Whilst their Jewishness was often a source of pride for these children of immigrants, it was also a hidden, private and essentially domestic identity. This was partly an effect of the tacit antisemitism that infused British culture at the time, but also a consequence of the unprocessed trauma that these European parents had experienced. As Seidler puts it, England was supposed to be a place in which 'the past could be left behind' (5). In a personal reflection on his own background, Jon Stratton presents a similarly combined sense of rupture and silence, asking a question that underpins other accounts of this experience. 'What was it like', he writes,

> To grow up ... in England in the 1950s and 1960s, the son of a fearful assim-
> ilating Jew who had no way of talking about her own fears brought about
> by what the Nazis had done and, indeed, no discourse in which to concep-
> tualize what had happened?[15]

Stratton, the child of a Jewish mother and non-Jewish father, imagines his mother watching the footage of the concentration camps after the war, and realizes that she 'would have had no language' through which to articulate her response, and nobody who would understand what it had meant. 'Certainly not my father', he notes, 'the man she had married for, among other things his Englishness, his situatedness as English within England, his certainty of place' (152–153). The tension recalled here, between expression and silence, connection and isola-tion, Englishness and Jewishness, is defining. As Stratton terms it, this is the 'traumascape' of the second generation (154).

Memoirs by Figes, Seidler and Karpf, as well as those by Lisa Appignanesi, Eva Hoffman and others in recent years, explore the ways in which the experiences of the children of refugees and Holocaust survivors are formed in relation to memory.[16] *Shadows of the Shoah, The War After, Losing the Dead, Lost in Translation, After Such Knowledge, Tales of Innocence and Experience*, each title suggests loss: loss of family, home, history, language, innocence, the

self. These losses are at the core of these texts. But, in finding wholeness within fragmentation, home within exile, presence within loss,
these titles also invoke continuity and search for ways in which to
move beyond the past into the present. An exploration of the role of
memory within collective, familial and personal narratives is central to
the ways in which these texts reflect on the subtle effects of displaced
experience and belated knowledge.

As the children of survivors grow into middle age many of this
generation begin to explore the role of the past within their families.
Certainly, for Karpf and Appignanesi, the death of a parent and the
effects of memory loss on the older generation, brings a particular
emotional intensity and urgency to their stories. These accounts are
often highly self-reflexive. As Stephen Wade has suggested, there is
perhaps a 'natural Jewish affection for mixing memoirs with cultural
assessment'.[17] In this way, these second generation reflections create
narratives of the self that recognize the often provisional, unstable
nature of both memory and subjectivity.[18] In developing a consideration of the delicate interplay between family history, memory
and identity these memoirs engage with what Marianne Hirsch has
termed, 'postmemory'. 'Postmemory', Hirsch argues, 'characterises
the experience of those whose stories are dominated by narratives
that preceded their birth, whose own belated stories are evacuated by
the stories of the previous generation shaped by traumatic events that
can be neither understood nor recreated'.[19]

In negotiating their way through layers of family memory these
writers show that memory can be unreliable, inconsistent, fickle and
dangerous. As Appignanesi puts it:

> Memory, like history, is uncontrollable. It manifests itself in unruly ways.
> It cascades through the generations in a series of misplaced fears, mysteri-
> ous wounds, odd habits. The child inhabits the texture of these fears and
> habits, without knowing they are memory. (8)

What Appignanesi signals here is an understanding that memory does
not present a straightforward narrative. It surfaces insistently within
the lives of the children of Holocaust survivors, such as Appignanesi,
but it is 'uncontrollable', 'unruly' and essentially unknowable. Memory,
these texts suggest, is an intensely flawed map to the past. It is, instead,
a far more organic entity. Appignanesi makes the point that 'mine is
the last generation for whom the war is still a living tissue of memory
rather than a dusty and barbaric history of facts and statistics' (5–6).
The image of 'a living tissue of memory' is evocative. Karpf similarly

describes the Holocaust as 'part of the family tissue' (96), explaining that as knowledge about the Nazi atrocities emerged during the 1960s, for her it was 'biography' as well as history, the 'living matter' of her family. For these writers, post-memory is not just knowledge. It is something altogether more vital and intimate.

The subtle transference of fears, tastes, values and so on occurs in all families. Karpf explains it in this way: 'Family stories', she writes, 'are a kind of DNA, encoded messages about how things are and should be, passed from one generation to another' (17). The narratives of children of refugees and Holocaust survivors resonate with a sense of memory passed between the generations that is especially charged, often painful and sometimes almost somatic in its effect. As Seidler puts it:

> We lived with death and with murder, even if at the same time we remained numb to their realities. We learned to know, but at some level not to feel or to talk about. We learned not to ask questions... They did not realize how much they passed on to the second generation, through not really sharing their experiences. We took it into our bodies, as if it were food. (109)

A pattern emerges in these accounts, in which memory, as Seidler's words suggest, is nebulous, perhaps silent, but nevertheless absorbed at a deep level. Hoffman, for example, writes of 'that most private and potent of family language – the language of the body' (9). She discusses the ways in which her parents' memories of wartime trauma erupted through 'nightmares', 'sighs', 'illnesses' and 'tears' (10), explaining that 'the pain of their psyches reverberated in my body almost as if it were mine' (14).

In a sustained reflection on the somatic nature of memory and trauma, Karpf explores further the subtle ways in which such memories, for the second generation, might be written on the body suggesting that, even in early childhood, 'outlawed feelings' (sadness, depression and discontent) 'erupted' through her body in a number of ways (10). In a revealing section of her narrative she describes how, as an adult suffering from debilitating eczema, she scratched her skin raw in a cycle of brutal self-punishment. This is experienced as a literal disintegration of the frontiers of her body.[20] As deeply repressed feelings of anger and despair surface, she explains that 'my skin no longer seemed able to keep what was inside in' (103). The illness, she suggests, may have been partly instigated by her confusion about a romance with a non-Jewish man. Her mother had figured the affair as a betrayal of Karpf's Jewish identity, and, by implication, a rejection, or perhaps an even a more fundamental forgetting, of the trauma and of her parents' wartime experiences.

The figuring of memory at this bodily level is one example, among many, of the profound and indeed primal nature of such remembering. As Hoffman argues, her parents' experience of the Holocaust had been 'transmitted to [her] as [her] first knowledge, a sort of super-condensed pellet of primal information'. She continues that it 'seemed to be such an inescapable part of my inner world as to belong to me, to my own experience. But of course [it] didn't' (6). And it is in this 'elision, that caesura' (6) that she summarizes the source of the second generation's identity crisis. Their memories of trauma are powerful, affecting, defining even; but they are not their own. This uncanny feeling of closeness to, but distance from, their parents' earlier lives is common to all these texts. It constitutes, in Appignanesi's phrase, a kind of 'transgenerational haunting' (8). 'My reality and my parents' wartime realities are worlds apart', she acknowledges. 'But psychic states float about in families and can land wherever there's space for them' (16). These ideas complicate a mechanistic understanding of memory. It is not, as we saw in Chapter 2, a filing system, however complex; a hard drive, or an intricate storehouse of experiences that may or may not be lost or found. It is a far more haunting and visceral phenomenon than those models suggest.

Karpf tells a story about the experience of cold that operates on all these levels. She opens her book with the observation 'my family was big on coats' and she discusses how for this family 'cold wasn't just a meteorological fact but almost a psychic state... The air outside was a polluting miasma, a kind of alien non-chicken soup' (4). She learns early in life that the outside is a dangerous place. This knowledge seeps into her like some 'peculiarly mobile fog' (4). But Karpf ends the book with an anecdote that presents a slightly different perspective: 'It's a windy day and I'm going out with B [her daughter]. "Put your coat on," I plead, "you'll be cold." "No, mama," she replies. "I'm not cold you are"' (317). This story has a strangely timeless, fairy tale, quality about it as the mother tries to protect the child from the cold and whatever other dangers might lie ahead. The old-world address, 'mama', as well as the eternal bite of the cold contribute to this effect. But this is not a tale of endless repetition. Karpf's experiences and fears reflect those of her parents, but they are not the same. She has lived 'the war after', not the war itself. She does not elaborate further on this exchange between herself and 'B'. She does not need to. There is a sense here that post-memory is a process, 'a living tissue', rather than a fixed condition. The third generation might not experience the cold in quite the same way as their parents. It is almost a happy ending.

'Belonging Nowhere': Jewish refugees in Britain

These accounts, from children of survivors and those refugees who have lost relatives in the Holocaust, are personal and intense. I want now to turn to fictional writing about the experience of Jewish refugees in Britain. A number of recent literary texts have represented the experience of Jews migrating to Britain, particularly in relation to the *Kindertransport*. Such writing explores some repressed aspects of Jewish memory as well as prompting a reconsideration of British identity. Works such as Diane Samuels' play *Kindertransport* (first staged in 1993) have contributed to a growing interest in the more ambivalent aspects of this history, focusing on the losses and silences that assimilation into British culture demanded for these displaced Jewish children.[21]

The play is set in a present day London home, as a mother (Eve/ Evelyn) and adult daughter (Faith) sort through an attic, a symbolically resonant memory space. In so doing they confront the hidden story of Eve/Evelyn's original identity as a German Jew, her migration to Britain with the Kindertransport and her painful assimilation into Britishness. Until she discovers documents and photographs in the attic, Faith is unaware of her mother's history of exile, loss and complicated identification. This leads to a confrontation between mother and daughter which pivots on the complex relationship between remembering and forgetting. Samuels explains in her 'Author's Note' to the play-text that:

> Past and present are wound around each other throughout the play. They are not distinct but inextricably connected. The re-running of what happened many years ago is not here to explain how things are now, but is a part of the inner life of the present. (vii)

As part of this enactment of the 'inner life of the present' the child version of Eve/Evelyn and her mother, Helga, are also on the stage throughout the play. The juxtaposition of the nervous child, who must learn to repress her foreignness in order to assimilate into British life, and the neurotic adult that she has become, implies the potentially damaging effects of constructing such an identity.

As the drama unfolds, so Faith discovers the repressed aspects of her mother's past, a history that Eve/Evelyn's adopted mother has colluded in silencing. Eve/Evelyn tells her daughter that the past is, 'over and done with', 'it's forgotten' (72). When Faith discovers that papers relating to this part of her family history have been torn up, she is horrified. 'Who's going to take care of their memory?' she asks; and adds: 'Did they die for you to forget?' (73). A generational tension between remembering and forgetting is thus dramatized. However, as the encounter unfolds, it becomes apparent that perhaps Faith's generation can afford to encounter the past in ways that the trauma-tized Eve/Evelyn's generation cannot. Eve/Evelyn claims that the past is a blank; but she also acknowledges, in the overdetermined nature of such matters, that it is more than just a void. Memories, she recognizes, are displaced by processes of substitution as much as by amnesia. Recalling her parents, she reflects that: 'I think I must have loved them a lot at one time. One forgets what these things feel like. Other feelings displace the original ones' (74). So, it is in this ontological sense that Eve, the German-Jewish child, substitutes or reinvents herself as Evelyn the baptized English-Christian adult. But, as the omnipresent and menacing story-book figure of the Ratcatcher (a leitmotif throughout the play) implicitly reminds us, such substi-tutions are rarely complete. At the end of the drama the past has been revealed but not resolved and, as the curtain comes down, the Ratcatcher casts his shadow. He represents a history that has not been fully remembered, but that cannot, either, be forgotten.

This history encompasses not only the horrors of Nazi genocide, but also the ambiguities that permeated British responses to those Jews who escaped the Holocaust. Phyllis Lassner focuses her reading of Samuel's play on the deep-rooted culture of British antisemitic ambiv-alence. She explains that in these terms:

> Eva has to be Jewish or British; she can't be both. Within Evelyn's hysterical hold on her British identity lies the Jews' placelessness, their wandering, their designation as a nowhere people. The result in this play is a construction of the modern history of Anglo-Jewry as irremediably unstable, veering between accommodation and assimilation in a state of understated suspension. (92)

As, for example, the title of Eva Tucker's semi-fictional memoir *Becoming English* suggests, assimilation for these exiled Jews in Britain was an ongoing negotiation rather than an attainable end point.[22] As Lassner argues, such processes of becoming, create an 'irremediably unstable' condition and, undoubtedly, much of the liter-ature that draws from this history reveals the painful and labyrinthine nature of these historical negotiations.

This moment in Anglo-Jewish history has been the focus of a number of recent fictional texts by British-Jewish writers. David Baddiel's *The Secret Purposes* (2004), Natasha Solomons', *Mr Rosenblum's List* (2010) and *The Novel in the Viol*a (2011), as well as Jake Wallis Simons', *The English German Girl* (2011), all explore, from slightly different perspectives, the difficulties of assimilation and the equivocal treatment of Jewish refugees by the British in the war and post-war years.[23] This wave of writing by contemporary British-Jewish writers could be viewed, perhaps rather cynically, as exploiting recent Jewish history in order to construct or reinstate the Jew as a marginalized other and thus serving both creative and commercial ends. However, conversely it could be argued that the history of Jews in Britain is a story that has not yet been fully told. As British-Jewish identities are becoming increasingly more visible, then this history is perhaps hard to ignore. In these terms, such fictional reworkings of the Jewish past contribute to a growing awareness of the distinct backgrounds of British Jews. Moreover, these British-Jewish writers, who are often two generations away from the Holocaust, are arguably well placed to articulate difficult issues in British as well as in Jewish histories. Like Faith in Samuels' play, they are able to confront a painful past, despite, or perhaps even *because*, that past is not directly theirs.

Indeed a number of contemporary British-Jewish writers have turned to the life-stories of their grandparents as a starting point for fictional writing. Baddiel, for example, drawing from his German-Jewish grandfather's experience, tackles the overlooked history of the wartime internment of German-, Austrian- and Italian-born Jews. He also depicts the culture of antisemitism that was prevalent in the British establishment in this period, focusing, in particular, on the documented memo from the Ministry of Information which stipulated that anti-German propaganda should 'deal with the treatment of indisputably innocent people ... and not with Jews' (64). Much of the narrative is driven by the efforts of a fictionalized Ministry translator, June Murray, to produce irrefutable evidence that Nazi atrocities against Jews were occurring in Europe. Baddiel's novel epitomizes a recent trend within contemporary writing in general, and Jewish writing in particular, in the way that it combines family history, fictional narrative and documentary source material. As it focuses on issues of memory and truth, the novel presents a perhaps surprisingly nuanced exploration of identity and the ways in which knowledge might be compromised in relation to historical record.

The Secret Purposes includes an excerpt from, 'Helpful Information and Guidance for Every Refugee', the pamphlet that was issued by the German Jewish Aid Committee, advising new refugees about what constituted 'proper' behaviour in England. This document also provides the thematic focus of Solomons' *Mr Rosenblum's List*, subtitled *Or Friendly Advice for the Aspiring Englishman*. Solomons, like Baddiel, bases her fiction on the experience of her German-Jewish grandparents who came to England in 1936. However, whereas Baddiel's communist hero, Isaac Fabian, is determinedly resistant to being reconstructed as an Englishman, Solomons' titular character, Jack Rosenblum, is an 'aspiring Englishman' who embraces reinvention. 'Assimilation was the secret', he thinks:

> *Assimilation.* Jack had said the word so often to himself, that he heard it as a hiss and a shibboleth. He was tired of being different; he did not want to be doomed like the Wandering Jew to walk endlessly from place to place, belonging nowhere. (2)

So, Jack, unlike his wife Sadie, who as we saw in the last chapter in relation to food and memory, struggles to shed the past, is an enthusiastic convert to Englishness. He studies the advice in Helpful Information assiduously. He only speaks English, he works hard, he learns how to finish *The Times* crossword in less than two hours and he does not engage in any activity that could be construed as politically subversive. He is 'an almost-Englishman' (9). When he is released from a brief spell in prison, having been categorized as a 'class C alien' (considered the most minimal threat to national security), he studies the 'Helpful Information' even harder, annotating and expanding it until it becomes his own personal compendium of Englishness. Item 150 on his list of essential English attributes is that an Englishman must be a member of a golf club (21). When, as a Jew in post-war Britain, he is refused entry to any existing clubs he takes action. He moves to rural Dorset and sets about building his own golf course.

The conflict between assimilation and the preservation of Jewish identity, especially in relation to the losses of the Holocaust, is played out in the different approaches demonstrated by husband and wife in relation to memory. Jack builds his golf course, looking to the future as a way of mitigating the ruptures of past, whilst Sadie, who is attached to the Jewish calendar because 'it was all about memory' (33), fixates on the few remaining photographs she has of her family and the recipes passed on to her by her mother. Jack's pursuit of Englishness is fervent, but it stems from his fear of being exposed as a 'fraud and a foreigner' (99). He tries hard to forget, but Sadie works equally hard to remember: 'the only thing worse than remembering, she decided, was starting to forget' (33). By the end of the narrative, they each find a way to reconcile this tension and the novel reaches a point of wistful resolution.

The commercial success that the novel has achieved might be attributed to the ways in which the Jewish immigrant experience is presented in a poignant, but essentially heart-warming, tale. In her follow-up book, *The Novel in the Viola*, Solomons again draws from the history of Jewish refuge from Nazi Germany to Britain, telling the story of a young woman's transition into English life in terms of a conventional romance narrative between the Jewish servant girl and her English master. Again, the fictionalization of exile is made palatable for a contemporary mainstream readership. The Ratcatcher does not exactly cast a dark shadow over these narratives. However, Solomons' readership is not necessarily the same as the audience for Samuel's play, or as the readers of more overtly literary explorations of trauma, memory and identity. These narratives, alongside other more sombre reflections on the Jewish past, contribute to a wider, and perhaps more popular, understanding of the difficulties experienced by Jewish refugees throughout and beyond the war.

In 2011, the same year as Solomons' *The Novel in the Viola* was published, Jake Wallis Simons' *The English German Girl* also came into print. This is a novel that again centres on a romance, but this time between a young German-Jewish woman and the son of the Anglo-Jewish family who have somewhat grudgingly given her refuge. Simons' novel is carefully researched. The afterword cites a range of credible sources and demonstrates an obvious commitment to representing the seriousness of the context from which the fiction draws. His final words merit some attention. To avoid 'historical travesty', he writes:

> I wanted to make it as accurate and realistic as possible; at the same time, I did not want to stand accused – as Peter Hall memorably put it – of 'bumming a ride on the Holocaust'. This phrase haunted me in the writing process. (369)

Simons' work self-consciously avoids this charge of exploitation but it raises wider questions about issues of entitlement and authority in representing, or indeed claiming, a connection to the Holocaust for contemporary British Jews in general.[24] As I bring this chapter to a close, I want to explore this idea a little further.

'It Is Not Nothing': vicarious victimhood in the post-Holocaust world

As Simons' afterword shows, sensitivities about how to present Holocaust history can haunt the thoughtful contemporary British-Jewish writer. Questions about whether one is exploiting a history that is not one's own or claiming a vicarious victimhood are challenging. This is an issue that has been addressed in the controversial French work, *Le Juif Imaginaire/The Imaginary Jew* (1980), by Alain Finkielkraut.[25] Finkielkraut, the child of Holocaust survivors, like other writers of the second generation, recognizes the fundamental disparity between his parents' experience and his own. He also writes frankly about the potential appeal of martyrdom for the post-Holocaust generation, explaining that: 'I inherited a suffering to which I had not been subjected, for without having to endure oppression, the identity of the victim was mine... Without exposure to real danger, I had heroic stature' (7). This acknowledgement of the potential thrill produced by second-hand suffering makes for uncomfortable reading; but it also raises some important questions.

Howard Jacobson's *Kalooki Nights* grasps this issue for those British Jews, like him, for whom the Holocaust was relatively distant in geographical terms but rather close in temporal and emotional ones.[26] Jacobson's character, Max Glickman, recalls a childhood in which his 'uncle' Ike would repeatedly declare, 'and for this... apropos anything, Jewish, the Nazis tried to exterminate us' (4). Max's father's stock response: 'Since when did any Nazi try to exterminate *you*, Ike? You personally?' (4), contributed to a strangely charged atmosphere, a form of repeated 'jousting' between the two men, that the boy worked out was 'a sort of magic, to ward off evil' (4). Like Grant's awareness of the mental chasm [that] yawned beneath our feet', which I discussed at the beginning of this chapter, these post-war children lived in a unsettling environment that combined the apparent comforts of Anglo-Jewish life with the dawning realization of the horrors that had beset European Jewry. 'Thus', Max explains, 'did I grow up in Crumpsall Park in the 1950s, somewhere between the ghettos and the greenery of North Manchester, with "extermination" in my vocabulary and the Nazis in my living room' (5). When his friend introduces him to Lord Russell of Liverpool's *The Scourge of the Swastika: A Short History of Nazi War Crimes* he finally locates the source of his angst:

Over *five million*! So that was what being put an end to meant! The figures conferred a solemn destiny upon me. For it is not nothing to be one of the victims of the greatest crime in world history.

By any of the usual definitions of the word victim, of course, I wasn't one. I had been born safely, at a lucky time and in an unthreatening part of the world, to parents who loved and protected me. I was a child of peace and refuge... But there was no refuge from the dead. For just as sinners pass on their accountability to generations not yet born, so do the sinned against. (5)

Max, like Finkielkraut, realizes that there is perhaps some kudos in being connected, albeit somewhat distantly, to the victims of the Holocaust. 'It is', as he sees it, 'not nothing'. But, as he ponders the double negative of his claim to suffering, he understands that this is an awkward appropriation. If his actual lived experience has been safe and uneventful what really connects him to the 'over five million'? And, in the unremarkable environs of post-war Crumpsall Park, what makes him special? As Finkielkraut, who was in fact far closer to the realities of the Holocaust, put it: 'I was safe, but I had a remedy for the anguish that arises from excessive security: I was Jewish' (8).

For Max, an early fascination with Holocaust atrocity (especially when perpetrated by women) shared with his friends, Manny and Errol, provides a compelling form of identification. When they tire of 'playing concentration camps' (33) he and Manny go on to produce *Five Thousand Years of Bitterness*, a cartoon history of Jewish suffering. In Chapter 6 I shall discuss the inner world of sado-masochist fantasy that Max constructs in relation to this interest, but for now, I want to think about the status that Max gives to the role of collective memory in relation to the Holocaust and his self-fashioning as a British Jew. In a fanciful tale of having once uttered the words, 'Jew Jew, Jew Jew, Jew Jew' (16), as a baby travelling on a train, Max concludes that: 'I am one for whom a train can never again be a train' (17). Instead, with innate suspicion, he claims to insist on knowing everything about it and 'its ultimate destination' (17). As the word 'Jew' is repeated relentlessly throughout the novel, especially in these opening pages, Jacobson presents Max as being caught in the clutches of an extreme, hyper-identification with Jewish victimhood. This constitutes not so much a failure to remember but, instead, a refusal to forget. 'Jew Jew, Jew Jew...', he repeats over and over again, creating the structural and thematic rhythm of the novel:

The Auschwitz Express.

I could not have known anything about Auschwitz at the time ... But footfalls echo in the memory, and who's to say what footfalls, past or future, a child's memory contains?

For what it's worth, I believe we would be able to hear Adam's tread if we knew which part of our memory to access. And Abraham ... And Moses ... And the Jews of Belsen and Buchenwald crying out to be remembered. (17)

As he satirizes Max's excessive identification with Jewish suffering, Jacobson also creates an insistent interrogation of how history and collective memory interact.

The novel is a challenging meditation on post-war British-Jewish identity. Despite his Uncle Ike's constant reminders of Nazi extermination, Max's parents, typically of their generation, did not generally favour too much reflection on the past. As his weary mother says to a middle-aged Max, 'Camps, camps, camps – where did you get all that stuff from? The only camp you ever went to was Butlin's' (427). Such a statement nicely undercuts the affectation that marks Max's appropriation of Holocaust suffering. But, for many contemporary British Jews, who may well feel a strong connection to the Holocaust even if they have not been directly affected by it, Max's insistence on memory, raises some rather serious questions. What is remembered in Britain about the Holocaust? How are these memories processed by British Jews? Where does one draw the line between respectful commemoration, self-indulgent appropriation and morbid fascination?

For Jews in contemporary Britain, living in the shadow of the shadow of the Holocaust, Alderman's injunction to, 'remember. And at the same time, remember that it's over', is a difficult balance to find. Recent writing which explores this complexity allows the reader to face the discomforts and disorientations of such remembering. Themes that have been explored here, and in Chapter 2, about memory and post-memory, history and identity, collective identities and individual subjectivities, will be returned to throughout *Writing Jewish*. They impact on the construction of British-Jewish identities in a number of ways. The following two chapters develop ideas about collective identity, remembrance and loss in particular relation to issues of location and displacement. For contemporary British Jews, many of whom identify, in implicit as well as explicit ways, with a culture of dispossession, ideas about home are charged. Chapters 4 and 5 interrogate some of the beliefs and assumptions that underpin these identifications to think more closely about where and how British Jews belong.

Notes

1. Linda Grant, *Remind Me Who I am Again* (London: Granta, 1998), p.33.
2. Naomi Alderman, 'Anne Frank and So On', *Jewish Quarterly*, 221 (2012) 27–30 (30).
3. Alderman was born in London in 1974.
4. For a full discussion of this material see Phyllis Lassner, *Anglo-Jewish Women Writing the Holocaust: Displaced Witnesses* (Basingstoke: Palgrave Macmillan, 2008), chapter three.
5. Anne Karpf, *The War After* (London: Minerva, 1996), p.185.
6. Tony Kushner, *The Holocaust and the Liberal Imagination* (Oxford: Blackwell, 1994), p.132.
7. Howard Cooper and Paul Morrison, *A Sense of Belonging: Dilemmas of British Jewish Identity* (London: Weidenfeld and Nicolson, 1991), p.87, p.88.
8. This has been well-documented by Tony Kushner. See *The Holocaust and the Liberal Imagination* and *Karpf*, part two, pp.165–245.
9. David Cesarani has recently argued, however, that 'we are mistaken if we look in the past for representations of what we recognise today as "the Holocaust".' See David Cesarani 'How Post-War Britain Reflected on the Nazi Persecution and Mass Murder of Europe's Jews: A Reassessment of Early Responses', in Hannah Ewence and Tony Kushner, eds, 'Whatever Happened to British Jewish Studies?', special issue of *Jewish Culture and History*, 12.1–2 (2010), 95–130 (98).
10. See David Cesarani, *The Making of Modern Anglo-Jewry* (Oxford: Basil Blackwell, 1990).
11. See Kushner, p.262. See also the Holocaust Educational Development Programme, Institute of Education, University of London, which was established in 2009 in order to 'transform teaching and learning about the Holocaust' in the UK: http://www.hedp.org.uk/ (Accessed 28 June 2012).
12. See http://www.hmd.org.uk/ (Accessed 28 June 2012).
13. Eva Figes, *Tales of Innocence and Experience* (London: Bloomsbury, 2004).
14. Victor Jeleniewski Seidler, *Shadows of the Shoah: Jewish Identity and Belonging* (Oxford: Berg, 2000).
15. Jon Stratton, *Jewish Identity in Western Pop Culture: The Holocaust and Trauma through Modernity* (Basingstoke: Palgrave Macmillan, 2008), p.152.
16. Lisa Appignanesi, *Losing the Dead* (London: Vintage, 1999), Eva Hoffman, *Lost in Translation* (London: Vintage, 1989, 1998) and Hoffman, *After Such Knowledge* (London: Vintage, 2005). I am grateful to Vallentine Mitchell for permission to reproduce here material from an earlier article on these memoirs. See Ruth Gilbert, 'Ever After:

Postmemory, Fairy Tales and the Body in Second-Generation Memoirs by Jewish Women', *Holocaust Studies*, 12.3 (2006) 23–39.

17. Stephen Wade, *Jewish American Literature Since 1945: An Introduction* (Edinburgh: Edinburgh University Press, 1999), p.193.

18. For a useful analysis of these issues see Nicola King, *Memory, Narrative and Identity: Remembering the Self* (Edinburgh: Edinburgh University Press, 2000).

19. Marianne Hirsch, *Family Frames; Photographs, Narrative and Postmemory* (Cambridge, MA: Harvard University Press, 1997), p.22.

20. Seidler also recounts a metaphorically suggestive skin condition that caused his head to swell up: 'I could not look myself in the mirror without feeling a sense of revulsion because my features had become almost monstrous. I could not recognize myself' (p. 152).

21. Diane, Samuels, *Kindertransport* (London: Nick Hern Books, 1995; revised ed., 2004).

22. Eva Tucker, *Becoming English* (London: Starhaven, 2009). See, for another example, Zvi Jagendorf, *Wolfy and the Strudelbakers* (Stockport: Dewi Lewis, 2001).

23. David Baddiel, *The Secret Purposes* (London: Abacus, 2004), Natasha Solomons, *Mr Rosenblum's List* (London: Sceptre, 2010) and *The Novel in the Viola* (London: Sceptre, 2011), Jake Wallis Simons, *The English German Girl* (London: Polygon, 2011).

24. Sue Vice presents a useful discussion of issues of entitlement and authority in her 'Introduction' to *Holocaust Fiction* (London: Routledge, 2000).

25. Alain Finkielkraut, *The Imaginary Jew*, trans. by Kevin O'Neill and David Suchoff (Lincoln: University of Nebraska Press, 1994).

26. Howard Jacobson, *Kalooki Nights* (London: Jonathan Cape, 2006).

4

'Rootsie-tootsie': (Re)locating Jews in Contemporary Britain

> How sad that I have found nowhere,
> that I have found no dream,
> that I come from nowhere and go nowhere.
> This is a land without dream;
> an endless landscape.
>
> Bernard Kops[1]

This chapter builds on the previous discussion of memory and British-Jewish identity in order to reflect on the Jewish diasporic experience. In particular it focuses on a perceived lack of rootedness which is reflected in the above quotation from Bernard Kops' poem 'Diaspora'. This sense of disconnection is a recurring motif in contemporary Jewish literature. The following discussion explores the diasporic experience but focuses also on the ways in which ideas of displacement might be interrogated in relation to the lives of Jews in Britain today. So, whilst it looks at themes of place and displacement, belonging and longing, sites of origin and of destination, the chapter will also reflect on more local and contemporary *re*locations within Britain's cities, suburbs and countryside.

First, the chapter considers the connections and some of the disconnections that the diasporic condition raises for contemporary British Jews. It then moves on to explore some of these issues in relation to Howard Jacobson's *Roots Schmoots* (1993). Here Jacobson presents a shrewd and, at times, moving account of a search for Jewish identity as he travels through Britain, America, Israel and Lithuania in order to address what he describes as 'the problem of how it felt not to feel Jewish'.[2] The chapter then moves on to a close analysis of Rachel Lichtenstein and Iain Sinclair's *Rodinsky's Room* (1999), a text that raises critical ideas about memory, myth and self-definition for contemporary British Jews. The connection between location and identity in terms of a sub-textual concern about, again, not feeling quite Jewish, is both raised and repressed in Lichtenstein's story. My reading of this text focuses on the ways in which Israel, Eastern Europe and London's East End feature as key loci in both understanding and establishing a hold on what appears to be a tenuous sense of Jewish identity. The chapter concludes with a few thoughts about Brick Lane, in terms of how it has come to symbolize the flux and flow of different migratory waves.

'I Come From Nowhere': the Jewish diasporic imaginary

Although the experience of Jews in Britain has been relatively tranquil, the process of acculturation and assimilation has not been seamless. As I have suggested so far in *Writing Jewish* there has been, and perhaps still is, an underlying ambivalence towards Jews in Britain and this has inevitably shaped the experience and self-perception of British Jews. So, as we shall see, some contemporary writing about Jewishness and belonging presents painful moments of marginalization, and these are important. As the poet Lotte Kramer writes in 'Diaspora':

> Not for us:
> The constancy
> Of roots, of black trees
> Charcoaled in deep clay;[3]

Kramer, who came to England from Germany as part of the Kindertransport, presents here a powerful image of loss and impermanence. The poetic form here allows a lyrical exploration of exile. It is, in its evocation of exclusion, a bleak iteration of the ruptures of migration and the realities of dislocation.

However, whilst earlier formulations of the Jewish diaspora often focused on themes of forced exile and dispossession, many theorists now tend to present a more gradated understanding of the Jewish diasporic experience. As Bryan Cheyette has put it 'the experience of Diaspora can be a blessing or a curse or, more commonly, an uneasy amalgam of the two states'.[4] Reflecting on the wider Jewish diasporic picture, Robin Cohen explains that:

> The tapestry of Jewish diasporic experiences becomes more nuanced, but more accurate, when we accept a dual model, with the warp of the Jewish diaspora being one of creativity and achievement and its weave being one of anxiety and distrust.[5]

An understanding of the Jewish diaspora in this way, as a potentially positive dispersal, rather than a fundamentally tragic displacement, makes sense, especially when looking at the relative comforts and successes of Jews in contemporary Britain. Such a view also has profound and potentially contentious implications in deconstructing a Zionist ideology that is based on a belief in Israel as the autochthonous homeland for Jews.[6] If, as some recent commentators argue, Israel is not necessarily an absolute locus of origin, and thereby implied return, for Jews, then the relationship between home and exile in the diaspora is far more unstable than might be figured within a traditional Zionist model.

In 'The Diasporic Imaginary' Vijay Mishra has suggested that the idea of a homeland is often, in fact, a mythologized construction. As Monika Fludernick explains:

> People who identify themselves as part of a diaspora are creating an 'imaginary' – a landscape of dream and fantasy that answers to their desires. The term 'imaginary', moreover, implies that this landscape is stocked with a variety of perhaps contradictory landmarks and that, when dreams of a diasporic identity congeal, they sometimes do so around some of these landmarks rather than others. Nobody has the same dream entirely; and nobody's diaspora therefore looks wholly like their neighbour's. [7]

This sense of the 'diasporic imaginary' as a discontinuous and fluctuating dreamscape is exacerbated for British Jews, many of whom are of Ashkenazi, Eastern European, descent. In this respect, diasporic identities are based on an idea of an original homeland that is already split between what might be a fantasy of shtetl roots in Eastern Europe, and an imagined Zion to which there may or may not be any direct connection. Since, in the post-Holocaust world, many sites of Jewish inhabitation in Eastern Europe no longer exist, and because Israel is such highly politicized territory, neither site presents a straight-forward fantasy of home for the diasporic Jew. Again Kops' words are suggestive of this sense of identification in terms of absence, 'I come from nowhere', he writes, 'and go nowhere'.

The Polish born writer Eva Hoffman who, having migrated to America as a child has now made her home in Britain, articulates the subtle translations that occur in the diasporic condition. However, she also reflects on the fact that this is in many ways a more generalized state of being in the contemporary world. 'The weight of the world used to be vertical', she writes:

> It used to come from the past, or from the hierarchy of heaven and earth and hell; now it's horizontal, made up of the endless multiplicity of events going on at once and pressing at each moment on our minds and our living rooms. Dislocation is the norm rather than the aberration in our time ... In a decentered world we are always simultaneously in the center and on the periphery.[8]

Hoffman's memoir, *Lost in Translation*, presents a sensitive account of the pains and pressures of migration, but it also underscores the point that, in an increasingly dispersed world in which 'dislocation is the norm', all ideas of home are in some sense imaginary.

So, rather than focusing on fixed ideas of home and exile, perhaps it is useful to present an interrogation of the idea of the diaspora as, in Cheyette's words, 'a place without beginning or end'.[9] Such a perspective seems to inform Howard Jacobson's 1993 memoir/travel book *Roots Schmoots*, a text that was tied into a television series for Channel 4.[10] The book, which combines cultural commentary with personal reflection, sets out to deconstruct any sentimental attachment to ideas of an original homeland for British Jews. 'I had', Jacobson explains at the beginning of his journey, 'been feeling rootsie, I don't deny that. Aggressively rootsie. Rootsie-tootsie'. He insists, however, that this journey to various sites of Jewish significance is not motivated by a desire to find a sense of belonging. 'There is, he explains, 'a giddying romance in the idea of homelessness' (7). Jacobson, a British-born Jew, has not experienced the direct losses of rootlessness that were articulated by Kramer in 'Disapora'. His middle-aged exploration of roots is instead framed in terms of a post-war British perspective. He recalls how, for his generation, the Jewish past was of little immediate significance:

> Our grandparents, or our parent's grandparents, had come over with chickens in their baggage fifty year before, fleeing the usual ... some libel or pogrom or another- that was as much as they cared to remember to tell us. And in truth that was as much as we cared to know. We had been Russian or Poles or something – why split hairs? And now we were setting about becoming English. Roots we didn't think about; tendrils we needed. You don't look down when you're climbing. (2)

In this context, roots, or the lack of them, are no cause for sorrow; they are instead an irrelevance for a generation of British Jews who were looking upwards to an assimilated future. So, in approaching his 'rootsie' voyage of self-discovery, Jacobson knowingly undercuts a tendency towards lazy nostalgia in framing such journeys. But there is also a serious point underlying his merciless interrogation of the romance of homelessness. As Elizabeth Grosz has observed:

> The borderline position of the exile – not at home in one place or another, nomadic, meandering, indirect, yet not necessarily lost or abandoned – has, in spite of its difficulties, some strengths and qualities which the exile may be reluctant to give up.[11]

In the previous chapter, we saw how Jacobson has questioned any simplistic appropriation of Holocaust memory for post-war British Jews. Here he plays with a similar tension, recognizing that for the children, grand-children and great-grandchildren of immigrants, an abundance of comforts can create its own crises and the idea of exile is often rather thrilling. Assimilated Jews in today's Britain might well experience a lingering sense of displacement; but a stubborn attachment to the condition of dispossession is perhaps underpinned by a desire to define oneself in relation to otherness which is, as Grosz suggests, 'hard to give up'.

Jacobson narrates complex feelings of connection to Israel and as I shall discuss more fully in Chapter 5, the story he tells in this section of his travelogue is vivid, energetic and conflicted. However, as the memoir progresses it becomes apparent that for Jacobson, along with many British Jews, it is Eastern Europe, not Israel, that is the more significant and painful site of origin. Jacobson's search for an imaginary homeland is in many respects paradigmatic of all such journeys. It demonstrates the compelling and profoundly ambiguous nature of the concept of return. Other memoirs, by Anne Karpf, Victor Jeleniewski Seidler, Lisa Appignanesi and Eva Hoffman each present some subtle reflections on this experience and in popular culture we can also see such ambiguities being played out in recent genealogy television programmes. The format, in which a celebrity (accompanied by a camera crew) traces their roots, is fairly blunt, and episodes tend to either climax in a flood of emotion or end on a more subdued note of disappointment. For subjects with Jewish backgrounds, these searches frequently present particularly complex and confusing narratives. Since many sites of Jewish origin in Eastern Europe no longer exist in any recognizable form, such journeys mark a Jewishness that cannot really be revisited, let alone recovered.

Jacobson's reflections on return, which were also televised, to some extent follow this format. When he finally reaches Lithuania, the shtetl home of his ancestors, and a place to which he does have a direct familial connection, Jacobson finds, in contrast to his travels in America and Israel, a grey and haunted post-Holocaust Eastern European landscape. It is a melancholy tale. 'All that is left', he writes, 'is a cemetery' (97). Although he had anticipated a journey in which he would repossess 'nothing' (perhaps the diasporic 'nowhere' of Kops' poem), he had not been prepared for the emotional impact of such a bleak discovery. The 'romance of homelessness' is, in the end, not so much 'giddying' as sobering. However, as he wanders around the neglected gravestones, he admits to, 'feeling that it is something, not nothing, that a Jew descended from this community has come back for an hour or two on a wintry afternoon' (500). It is, for Jacobson, an uncharacteristically muted moment. He is left with an ambiguous understanding of what the experience means. It cannot be dismissed as simple nostalgia. It means 'something, not nothing', to return to this site of Jewish origin. Again, the double negative that we saw in Jacobson's later treatment of the British-Jewish relationship to the Holocaust in *Kalooki Nights* (which I discussed in the previous chapter), 'not nothing', is deployed to suggest a dense weight of meaning, however ambiguous. But *what* it means, even for someone of Jacobson's incisiveness, is not clear. Herein lies a potentially irresolvable tension, and one which is expressed in much British-Jewish writing today: how to be in the here and now whilst respecting the traces of a past which are, more often than not, located elsewhere.

Jacobson's 'journey among Jews' was inflected by irony from the beginning. But by the end of his narrative he suggests that there is, perhaps, even for the cynical, self-aware, post-Holocaust, British Jew, some momentary connection that can be made to a memory site; however empty. In the next section of this chapter I consider the ways in which issues of land, loss and ambivalent identification, inform British Jews, not just when they are in search of imagined roots elsewhere, but when they are at home, at least notionally, in Britain. I want to start with a few thoughts about British Jews in the countryside.

'A Land Without Dream': British Jews at home

There is a stereotypical perception, perpetuated by many Jewish writers themselves, that Jews are temperamentally unsuited to the countryside.[12] The suggestion is that Jews are, in essence, urbanites.

This essentializing is questionable, but it is true to say that whereas cities such as London, Glasgow, Manchester and Liverpool, have traditionally accommodated different waves of immigrants, the countryside has been regarded as far less progressive and flexible terrain.[13] As Anne Karpf explains in relation to her experience in post-war Britain:

> Being Jewish in North London was one thing; when you receded from this epicentre it was quite another. On the rare occasions in my twenties and early thirties when I ventured out of London and into the English country villages whose fulcrum was the church and where Jews were biblical figures, I felt as if I'd pupated into a rabbi, like Woody Allen in Annie Hall. My difference was hanging out.[14]

The image here, of 'difference hanging out', a caricature of visibility, is both humorous and appalling. But, as it speaks of discomfort, so Karpf's account reiterates an idea of Jews as an innately cosmopolitan people who can only belong in the shifting and impermanent environs of a city.

This perception is central to a number of Linda Grant's journalistic essays and her novels, many of which reflect specifically on Jewishness in relation to politics and place in the late twentieth century. In her first novel, *The Cast Iron Shore* (1996), Grant narrates the story of Sybil Ross, the internationally focused, daughter of a Jewish immigrant furrier. Sybil, who (like Grant) has been born and brought up in Liverpool, is preoccupied by transitory, rootless, surface performances of identity. She has, it is suggested, been formed by the perpetual passages and rhythms of the port. 'I understand ports', she says. 'No one who was born in a port knows who they really are'.[15] Towards the end of the novel she describes how she feels when she is obliged to take her Yugoslavian cousin, Nebojsa, on a trip to 'the famous English countryside' (388). Contemplating the Pennines, Sybil and Nebojsa share a sense of bemused disconnection. 'When I look at Nature', she explains:

> I don't really see anything, just the nondescript colours of grass-green and earth-brown and various shapes on the landscape ... I can't identify the name of a tree or a flower and many animals look the same to me unless I can get up close and inspect their fur ... Sheep on distant hills look like maggots ... I don't recognize foxes or mink when they are running around, before they are made into coats and jackets and stoles and hats and trim. (339)

For Sybil, the creatures within the natural landscape only become meaningful when they are denaturalized and fashioned into fur. The implication is that surface appearance and the values of acquisition are more significant than a natural world with which the transitory Jew has no real or deep connection. The Jew here is an eternal exile, a fundamentally rootless being.

In Grant's writing such moments of disconnection tend to lead to an awareness that is sharpened rather than muffled by a sense of not belonging. In a rather different register, Natasha Solomons' novel, *Mr Rosenblum's List*, presents the bucolic setting of post-war Dorset through the eyes of a German born Jew who, as I outlined in Chapter 3, is desperate to assimilate into Englishness. By the end of the narrative, Jack Rosenblum has reached a point of belonging that encompasses, rather than effaces, his Jewishness. His middle-aged daughter contemplates an oak tree, noticing that, 'the roots were thicker than sapling trunks, and plunged deep, deep into the earth', and she goes on to connect the roots of the English oak to another, more distant, landscape:

> In her mind, Elizabeth saw that they formed an inverse shadow tree under the ground, even broader than the great branches above her head. The roots reached down beneath the soil, stretching under the Stour and below the sea. She pictured them surfacing on a forest floor in Bavaria, where an ancient oak tree creaked in a hot summer wind. She inhaled the sudden scent of pinecones and peat, and remembered her mother.[16]

The implication is that as the shadow roots take shape, so the losses of exile are somehow assuaged. This is a satisfying novelistic resolution. It suggests comfort and connection and a sense that the ruptures of the past can, in time, be repaired. However, it does not quite address some of the more complex and contradictory representations of Jews in relation to Britishness, and the English landscape, which are also in circulation.

Alongside a recurrent discourse of alienation within some recent British-Jewish writing, there is also a sense that to connect to the rural landscapes of Britain is to somehow disavow the status of outsider. Ruth Fainlight in 'The English Country Cottage' describes this tension as she writes about the unlikeliness of a Jewish writer being located within the particular setting of rural England. As a New York-born, poet, fiction writer and translator, who has lived in England since her teenage years, Fainlight is well-placed to reflect on the complexities of cultural adaptation and 'transplanted identity'.[17] 'A Jewish poet in an English village', she begins, is:

incongruous and inappropriate
As a Hindu in an igloo, a Dayak in
Chicago, a giraffe at the South Pole.[18]

So the poem starts playfully, describing the absurdity of creatures dramatically out of place. Jews, it suggests, are such creatures. They belong in cities and suburbs, not villages or vales.

The poem goes on to consider the weight of history, suggesting the ways in which 'the shadowy yew in the churchyard' (69) holds memories of deeply embedded English antisemitism from medieval to recent times. Fainlight moves on to present generational differences in relation to issues of alienation and assimilation and, as it explores the subtleties of unsettled identification, the poem becomes increasingly more intense:

Now (though mimicking the locals dutifully),
Thatch and cruck-beams cannot camouflage
The alien. (70)

The sting of mimicry is felt in a stark moment of realization.[19] No amount of traditional English architecture can mask 'the alien' within. Finally, the poem suggests, assimilative compromise must have its limits. 'Sometimes, I wonder if I should have known better', the narrator admits and concludes that it becomes necessary:

To sweetly smile and eat the mess
Of pottage – but never sell my birthright
for an English country cottage. (70)

Jewishness here is a complex birthright. The idea that it can be in anyway exchanged, as the allusion to the Old Testament story of Jacob and Esau makes clear, is a fundamental deception. In a sense, this is the inverse to the resolution offered by Solomons in *Mr Rosenblum' List*. As it actively deconstructs what 'belonging' might mean for a Jew in an English village, roots in Fainlight's poem represent the entanglements of history and the ties of displaced identity as much as any sinews of connection.

It is perhaps not surprising that some of the most intense explorations of diasporic alienation have been expressed in poetry. Poets such as Kops, Kramer and Fainlight, as well as A.C. Jacobs, Jon Silkin and Elaine Feinstein, articulate the complexities of exile, especially for British Jews of earlier generations. Partly, as Peter Lawson has argued: 'Anglo-Jewish poetry tends to follow a Romantic tradition.

This is a universalistic tradition of affiliation with the outsider, the dispossessed and others passed over in silence'.[20] But, although prominent in poetry, this romantic tendency is not just confined to poetic writing. It permeates the ways in which the other British-Jewish writers (of fiction, commentary and memoir) engage in processes of self-construction through a discourse of alienation.

Within many explorations of both estrangement and assimilation is an underlying sense that exile, figured as a perpetual condition of disconnection, also somehow engenders creativity. Bernice Rubens, for example, writing about her childhood in Cardiff, describes a strained holiday to a farm in South Wales. The self-presentation is both sardonic and serious. 'Jews are not countryside people', she explains:

> They don't have the right clothes. They are landless and urban. An English country farmer envisages lineage...Jews are by nature displaced, impermanent, and do not enjoy the privilege of constant legacy...Their true home is exile, and the creative energy that exile engenders. But that does not include the countryside. For that grey area they are ill-equipped.[21]

Alongside this stereotypical play on the innate awkwardness of the Jew in the countryside, we can see that a feeling of dispossession and the claim to creativity have become conjoined in the literary imagination. In these terms, belonging, it is implied, is not entirely desirable. For without exile, where would creative friction emerge? As Jacobson put it 'the romance of homelessness' is alluring. And where better for the contemporary British Jew to feel that thrill of rootlessness than in the English countryside?

The novelist and short story writer Tamar Yellin provides an interesting example of this sense that exile provides a 'true home' for the Jewish artist as she outlines a disjuncture between Jewishness, the English landscape and the English literary tradition. Yellin, who was born in Northern England, describes her awareness that as the Jewish daughter of a Polish immigrant and a third generation Jerusalemite she is in some ways excluded from the traditions of what she terms Brontëland. She recounts a conversation she had with her Polish-born mother on a visit to the Yorkshire Moors. 'I sat gazing at the moors', she writes, 'and turning to my mother, cried: "isn't it beautiful!" and my mother, the Zionist, mournfully replied, "but it isn't ours."':

> Her words ran me through the heart. It was intensely painful to be denied a sense of belonging in the countryside I loved. At worst I was a traitor; at best an oddity...Yet it was in that moment that I began to find myself.
> To be a writer is to be an outsider.[22]

There are several stages to this account: beginning with longing, moving on to a painful realization of alienation, and then claiming estrangement as an epiphanic moment of self-discovery and, as such, the basis of literary creativity. So, as Yellin romanticizes the position of the artist and the Jew (both cast as eternal outsiders), her identity is reformed rather than deformed in this anecdote of dispossession.

Yellin's account demonstrates that whilst the condition of exile might well be marked by material and emotional difficulties, the idea of *not* belonging is also configured as a potentially powerful form of identification for some contemporary British Jews. The next section of this chapter develops this argument further through a reading of *Rodinsky's Room*, a text that brings us away from the English countryside and back to, what has conventionally been seen as a natural habitat for Jews: the city. In so doing, however, it romanticizes the East End of London and, within a topography of repeated and resisted alienations, marginalizes another, perhaps more common location for contemporary British Jews, the suburbs.

'Go Nowhere': *Rodinsky's Room*

As I have suggested so far, although a pervasive sense of exile and exclusion has informed some aspects of the Jewish experience, it is also the case that this is not the direct experience of many second, third and subsequent generation children of immigrants. Here a perception of exile, or an exploration of the role of outsider, may strengthen a sense of Jewish identity for many contemporary Jews, allowing them to connect with a perceived collective history in the face of a more widespread cultural condition of increasing fragmentation and disconnection. Rachel Lichtenstein's story in *Rodinsky's Room* is, I think, a useful text through which to consolidate some of these themes.[23]

Rodinsky's Room by Rachel Lichtenstein and Iain Sinclair (1999) explores the mystery of David Rodinsky.[24] At the centre of *Rodinsky's Room* is David Rodinsky, a character who is only ever glimpsed in the reconstructed remnants of his life. He is an absent presence whose story embodies an ambivalent identification with what Jack Kugelmass has termed 'ethnic memory culture' and a complex tension between remembering and forgetting that is key to the text's exploration of British-Jewish identity at the close of the twentieth century.[25] Rodinsky was an orthodox Jew who lived in the attic above the synagogue in Princelet Street, in the old Jewish East End of London. In the late 1960s he disappeared but his absence went unnoticed for more than a decade. Rodinsky's room was locked and remained untouched until it was opened in the 1980s. Everything appeared to be as Rodinsky had left it: piles of esoteric books, a calendar dated January 1963, an eccentrically annotated A-Z, a half-eaten bowl of porridge, the imprint of his head left on the pillow and rumours of a mummified cat found sleeping in his bed.

The text is co-authored, but the story is primarily Lichtenstein's, a young British artist who investigates the mysterious disappearance of David Rodinsky in order to explore her own Jewish history and identity. Lichtenstein's quest to unravel the mystery at the heart of Rodinsky's life and disappearance is sometimes frustrating, often painful, and ultimately anticlimactic. At points in the narrative her absorption into the Rodinsky story appears to be extreme and self-destructive. Nevertheless, it is Lichtenstein's intense identification with Rodinsky that generates an intriguing tension within the text. It is this tension and the excesses that the text both produces and represses that form the focus of my discussion.

Lichtenstein's story can be described, in David Roskies' terms relating to memory, as 'a dialectic of loss and retrieval'. He argues that 'a memory-site ... is fashioned from the prior awareness of loss'.[26] Lichtenstein's story in *Rodinsky's Room* is predicated on such a dialectic. Her story begins by connecting to the past through memories of her Polish-Jewish grandparents. She presents her grandfather's death, when she was 17, as a profound moment of rupture and in response she recounts an immediate concern with reconnecting 'my past and my present' (19). She starts by 'reclaiming' her name from the recently anglicized, Laurence, to the Jewish family name, Lichtenstein. She then leaves her family home in Westcliffe, on the Essex coast, to study at art school in Sheffield. There she focuses on explorations of Jewish immigration from Eastern Europe to the East End of London and the questions of 'assimilation and integration' (20) that will preoccupy her for years to come.

Location is an important theme throughout this text, and one which reveals a number of significant issues. However, Lichtenstein passes over her upbringing in the hinterlands of Essex with no comment. In a text so much concerned with place and identity this seemingly small detail is significant. Lichtenstein is a grandchild of the ghetto, but a child of the suburbs. As David Cesarani has argued, in relation to post-war patterns of mobility, 'the Jewish route to the suburbs was long, hard, and devious' but this is not an aspect of her family history that Lichtenstein is keen to pursue.[27] The Essex coast represents the various dispersals that leave many third generation Jews feeling dislocated from their origins and, in some cases, longing for a connection to what seems like a more authentic Jewish experience. For many, such authenticity is inevitably located elsewhere, or in the past; or both. So it is that an uninhabited attic in the East End becomes the ideal locus for a journey into ethnic memory culture.

During her first research trip to London, Lichtenstein is advised to visit a heritage centre. In so doing she reverses the journey that her grandparents have made from the East End to Essex and returns to the exact place where they had their first marital home and business. She takes the tube to Aldgate East, walks up Brick Lane into a derelict synagogue at 19 Princelet Street and stumbles into the story of David Rodinsky. Lichtenstein realizes that 'the moment I entered 19 Princelet Street I knew I was meant to be there' (22). However, the past that she looks for in the East End is not directly hers. It is a vague memory that she attempts to recall into an uncertain present. Nevertheless, she takes on the role of custodian of the past and describes how, giving sightseeing tours of the Jewish East End in the early 1990s, she was repeatedly noting sites of absence. So, tours would consist of visiting old Jewish sites that, as newly built car parks covered the remains of the past, were already no more than a memory.

Lichtenstein's preoccupation with the protection of the Jewish past demonstrates an admirable commitment to an ethnic heritage. But, in other respects, especially in the way that she claims the past in order to define herself, it borders on the fetishistic. Inevitably, perhaps, the lost Jew at the centre of Lichtenstein's quest to recover the story of Rodinsky is, in effect, herself. Certainly, at the centre of Lichtenstein's narrative is an ambivalent and overdetermined relationship to her own Jewish identity. Lichtenstein's mission to uncover and recover the story of David Rodinsky is inextricably bound up with her struggle to decide between the orthodox Jewish life that she is drawn to in Israel and the largely secular Jewish life that she inhabits in England. But, conversion to orthodox Judaism involves a painful rejection of her family. As she explains almost in passing: 'My parents are far from orthodox. My mother is in fact not Jewish' (126). This statement illuminates the sense of isolation and estrangement that underpins much of Lichtenstein's narrative. In choosing to identify with her father's parents, the Polish-Jewish part of her family, she implicitly denies her mother's family history. In Jewish law Jewishness is defined through the maternal line. Technically, then, Lichtenstein is not Jewish. This crucial detail is the unsayable fact that haunts the text. It is another absent presence that draws Lichtenstein to Rodinsky; the Jew whose Jewishness had been distilled to such an extent that he could only exist within a reified attic room removed from the world around him.

Lichtenstein feels intuitively that 'Rodinsky had chosen me to tell his story' (286) but, as she takes on the role of Rodinsky's archivist, storyteller and amanuensis, she becomes less a ventriloquist, speaking through Rodinsky, than a double, inhabiting his story as her own.

Ghosts, locked rooms, doubling, remembering, repeating, home and homelessness all contribute to a pervading sense of the uncanny in this text, but the uncanny is far more than just a trope here. The spine-tingling quality of this story is rooted in its evocation of profound uncertainties about memory and identification that run through the narrative. Lichtenstein relates how on a cold November day, 'reading some terrible book about the Holocaust ... I saw him for the first time' (49). She describes a dim vision of a 'dark silhouette' that she pursues into Brick Lane:

> He looked ancient, his skin was so pale and transparent it gave off a blu-ish hue, and hanging majestically underneath his nose was a long trail-ing white beard. His coat and large black hat were tattered and worn but unmistakably the costume of a Hasidic Jew, an unusual sight in the 1990s in Whitechapel. I was beside myself with excitement and fear. (49)

Is this David Rodinsky? Or the ghost of David Rodinsky? The appari-tion disappears and Lichtenstein wonders if she has imagined the whole episode. The blurring of the line between reality and delusion is signifi-cant. In her quest to find Rodinsky, Lichtenstein has entered into the world of the past but it is unclear whether this world still survives in a real shape or form. In chasing shadows she is looking for herself, for a connection with her own Jewishness that exists in the pasts of her paternal grandparents. But this past has been repressed in the literal and metaphorical shift from Lichtenstein to Laurence that her family has enacted. In going back to a previous place, a site of origins, Lichtenstein is attempting to reclaim and indeed remember an identity.

The Hasidic old man that she follows is, of course, not Rodinsky. He is called Mr Katz, the owner of a small shop selling string and paper bags located opposite the mosque in Brick Lane. When Lichtenstein meets Mr Katz and tells him about herself he remembers her grandparents and they share a meaningful moment of connection. She has found, for a time, what she had been looking for. But Mr Katz recognizes the doubling that underpins Lichtenstein's journey into the uncanny. He shows an astute understanding of the ways in which the past and present intersect when he suggests that it is in fact she that is the ghost in this tale. What does she do for a living, he asks, 'apart from haunting old synagogues?' (53).

As strange coincidences and ghostly layerings are repeated throughout the narrative an eerie mood builds and there are many examples of the uncanny in the text's representation of blurred images and fragile histories. But the uncanny is also present at a deeper and more structural level in Lichtenstein's attempt to recover her own Jewish past. As Jon Stratton has argued, in his discussion of the Jewish uncanny, 'Freud's description of the uncanny as the experience of the return of the repressed, can be read as a reworking of the idea of displacement in the terms of personal experience'.[28] He points out two experiences of the uncanny: that of the assimilating Jew and that of the children of assimilated Jews. For the assimilating Jew the attempt to acculturate into a new society leads to repression. But since repression can never be complete an inevitable residue or excess will surface. For the children of assimilated Jews the repression works at another level. Their parents' assimilation leads them to experience a sense of displacement from both their present situation and a Jewish past that is beyond their own experience. As Stratton explains, 'the uncanny is related to their inability to feel at ease, to feel at home in the cultural order in which they find themselves'.[29]

The lines of A.C. Jacobs, a Scottish-Jewish poet, who lived within a variety of diasporas, are resonant in this context. 'Strangers never grow into cities', he writes,

> And their children encumbered with memories
> Are clumsy, and afraid
> They miss too much.
> Sometimes, the strangeness is itself a promise.[30]

This uncanny effect of alienation, homelessness at home, the strangeness of the familiar, characterizes Lichtenstein's experience within her narrative. She describes a recurring sense of suffocation and claustrophobia as she pursues Rodinsky's story. She becomes ill with pneumonia and literally cannot breathe in the 'dusty synagogue' (55) when working on the Rodinsky archive. Whilst an asthmatic disposition is not simply a somatic sign of repression, the motif is metaphorically resonant. It seems that in identifying so closely with Rodinsky, and fixating on the past to such an excessive extent, Lichtenstein has repressed aspects of Jewishness that are located in the present. The twenty-first-century British Jew might well be an orthodox scholar living in holy isolation. But s/he is more likely to be part of a shifting and diverse society living perhaps in the suburbs of London, or Manchester, or Glasgow. Or even the Essex coast.

As she finds out more about Rodinsky's story Lichtenstein realizes that 'his life, particularly the latter part of it, was grim and lonely' (300–301). Rodinsky's mother was traumatised, his sister was mentally ill, and Rodinsky had died a sad and isolated death. So the story does not provide any nostalgic comforts for the postmodern Jew searching for a usable past. There was no real mystery to Rodinsky's life. Only confusing and half-forgotten memories. Most significantly, his story marks the ways in which, for Jews, identity cannot be perpetually fixed in the past. Rodinsky's life, as it emerges through the text, was not confined to the synagogue in Princelet Street. His hand-drawn maps which were inserted into his diaries and books track journeys that he took well beyond the borders of Spitalfields to places in outer London and Essex. He had spent some of his childhood in foster care in Dagenham and ended his days in a psychiatric institution in Epsom. The attic did not contain the whole story.

As the book draws to its conclusion, Lichtenstein's own journey moves away from the past and into the present and future. She describes how in her last days in Poland she becomes overwhelmed by the weight of remembering. Like Jacobson, on his journey to the grave-yard in Lithuania, this is a desolate tale. Significantly, Lichtenstein's journey of self-discovery becomes relocated at this very point. When Lichtenstein returns to London from Eastern Europe it is for less than a day. She goes straight to Israel (the old world made new) to a wedding that is a particularly noisy, colourful and life-affirming event. And it is at this late stage in the book that she mentions Adam, 'the man I was going to marry' (282). The son of an Irish Catholic and a Pakistani Muslim who had grown up within the Jewish community in a suburb of Leeds, Adam represents the hybridized condition of post-colonial culture in contemporary Britain. He is not Jewish but he is Jewish. He looks Jewish. He has been one of the first Muslims in history to be members of a Zionist youth organization. He can break into song in perfect Hebrew. He is, for Lichtenstein, an uncanny mirror image, her 'perfect match' (282). She explains that she had already decided that she could not whole-heartedly complete the conversion to orthodox Judaism that she had considered in Israel. Instead, she chose not to isolate herself from her friends and family; not to reject the pleasures of secular life. In short, she chose to connect with the complexities of the present rather than become mired in the past represented by Rodinsky's empty room. The journey ends as she realizes that she is at home in London 'the city of a thousand cultures' (283) at the break of the new millennium. From this point in the book, the narrative accelerates. She marries Adam, becomes pregnant and gives birth to a son. She names him David.

As she moves into her present, she completes the story of Rodinsky by laying his memory to rest. Significantly, in terms of the unspoken patterning of the book, she moves beyond the triangle that she has constructed between the East End of London, Eastern Europe and Israel and returns to Essex. She reads kaddish by Rodinsky's pauper's grave in Waltham Abbey cemetery. The first edition of *Rodinsky's Room* ends here. The second edition includes an afterword that incorporates responses to the original publication. Lichtenstein creates another end. The success of the book allows her to acquire funds through an arts project to buy a headstone for Rodinsky's grave. David Rodinsky is laid to rest through the inscription of his name on a marble headstone with the words 'May his soul rest in peace'. So Lichtenstein leaves the past behind to live as an assimilated British Jew in the composite, hybridized, shifting conditions of the twenty-first century. 'The strangeness', as Jacobs suggested, 'is itself a promise'.

'An Endless Landscape': diaspora and Brick Lane

It is, in the end, the suburbs, not the city, that become a locus of resolution for Lichtenstein. But, throughout *Rodinsky's Room*, and in a more general sense, it is the East End of London that continues to provide an emotional pull for the disorientated contemporary British Jew. I want to end by returning to this location and looking briefly at some moments that demonstrate the ways in which Brick Lane can be seen as an example of diasporic fluidity and renewal. In many respects this area has been seen, in Lichtenstein's words, in her 2007 book *On Brick Lane*, as a 'mythical landscape'.[31] For third or fourth generation British Jews it figures as, a form of 'diasporic imaginary', a place that was once home to many Jews and which has been romanticized and figured as an East End shtetl, the site of a supposedly authentic Jewish life that has, inevitably, become dispersed and diluted over time. But, as has often been observed, Brick Lane has been the home to many waves of immigrant inhabitation from Huguenots and Jews, to Bengalis.[32] Lichtenstein, whose exploration of the area embraces these cultural differences, but is essentially nostalgic, notes a sign over the mosque, that 'was once a synagogue and before that a church', which reads, 'Umbra Sumus – We Are Shadows' (3). This can be seen as a mark of loss, signifying the ghostly presence of things past but it can also be read as a part of an ongoing process of migratory fluidity.

Jeremy Gavron's lyrical novel, *An Acre of Barren Ground,* presents a series of interlinked stories, all based on the site of Brick Lane.[33] These are subtle narratives of transmigration, displacements and resettlements, which are layered and overlaid throughout time in a series of allusive, stylistically diffuse and poetic moments. Gavron's characters range from boars and pre-history wanderers, to Roman colonizers, Shakespeare's sister, dot-com millionaires, and the seeds that disperse and settle in a post-war bomb site. The same piece of land is thus inscribed and re-inscribed as a palimpsest. The point underlying Gavron's text is suggested by the title, which of course references Shakespeare's *The Tempest*, a play that evokes ideas of displacement and diaspora as it recognizes, within the context of emergent colonialism, that no land can ever be fully possessed, no land is ever barren. Instead land always holds the traces of submerged lives and scattered seeds. In this context, Jacobson's journey in search of roots, Yellin's mother's need to distinguish between land that is 'ours' and land that is not, and Lichtenstein's desire to locate her Jewish identity through a journey into the past, are perhaps all outmoded impulses.

As Daniel and Jonathan Boyarin argue:

> Diasporic cultural identity teaches us that cultures are not preserved by being protected from 'mixing' but probably can only continue to exist as a product of such mixing. Cultures, as well as identities, are constantly being remade. While this is true of all cultures, diasporic Jewish culture lays it bare because of the impossibility of a natural association between this people and a particular land – thus the impossibility of seeing Jewish culture as a self-enclosed, bounded phenomenon.[34]

The Boyarins have been criticized for presenting a utopian and depoliticized view of diaspora and it true that such theorizations can sometimes fail to consider very real conditions of displacement and exile that continue to impact on many people in the world today.[35] However, for contemporary British Jews who are not generally refugees living within an active condition of exile, such thinking does show a way in which Kops' lament on 'a land without dream' can be reconfigured. For British Jews, the diaspora is 'an endless' but not empty landscape that presents some past and some current ambiguities, but also has considerable potential. As Joseph Finlay has recently argued:

We know, as children of modernity, that we can never be fully 'at home', that communities are virtual, free flowing and in flux, and that identities are multiple. We know, from the tradition of post-colonial thought that homelands are always 'imagined'...

In 'coming out' as diaspora Jews we should declare ourselves proud to be inheritors of a tradition that sees the whole world as its zone of concern, rather than limiting its ambition to a narrow strip of land.[36]

For British Jews today, some of whom question the status of Israel as an imagined home and those too who understand that the old Jewish world of Eastern Europe, or even the Jewish East End of London, no longer fully exists, the diaspora is arguably where we belong. Identities are, as Finlay argues, increasingly multiple. So it is that a Jew such as me, with an Eastern European family background, brought up within a Jewish community in an outer London suburb, can feel entirely at home in a stone cottage in Dorset. As I dwell on matters of Jewishness, I look out of my window and see a hill. I have no obvious or deeply rooted connection to this hill; but as I stare at it (which I do often), I feel an unaccountable sense of belonging. 'Roots Schmoots' is a complex phrase. Superficially, it seems to dismiss myths of attachment, but, at the same time, it is assertively and insistently Jewish. And this, as I look at my hill, somehow sums it up.

It is necessary, however, to recognize the tension between belonging and displacement that continues to be a preoccupying theme in contemporary British-Jewish culture. Stone cottages and hills are only part of the story. The next chapter will explore the ways in which Israel is represented in recent British-Jewish writing and we see here that ideas about belonging, even within an awareness of fluid identifications and diasporic potential, are still surprisingly unresolved.

Notes

1. Bernard Kops, 'Diaspora', in Peter Lawson, ed., *Passionate Renewal: Jewish Poetry in Britain since 1945* (Nottingham: Five Leaves, 2001), p.192.
2. Howard Jacobson, *Roots Schmoots: Journeys Among Jews* (London: Penguin, 1993), p.1.
3. Lotte Kramer, 'Diaspora', in Peter Lawson, ed., *Passionate Renewal*, p.215.
4. Bryan Cheyette, 'Diasporas of the Mind: British-Jewish Writing beyond Multiculturalism', in Monika Fludernick, ed., *Diaspora and Multiculturalism: Common Traditions and New Developments* (New York: Rodopi, 2003), pp.45–82, p.45.

5. Robin Cohen, *Global Diasporas: An Introduction* (London, Routledge, 2010), p.35.
6. Caryn Aviv and David Shneer have been particularly forceful in refiguring previously assumed ideas of diaspora and home. See, *New Jews: The End of the Jewish Diaspora* (New York: New York University Press, 2005).
7. Monika Fludernick, p.xi.
8. Eva Hoffman, *Lost in Translation* (London: Vintage, 1998), pp.274–275.
9. Cheyette, 'Diasporas of the Mind', p.78.
10. Gemma Romain suggests that this context is perhaps more important than is made explicit in Jacobson's account, pointing out that 'his reasons for ethnic reclamation are never contextualized into the practicalities of making a living'. See, *Connecting Histories: A Comparative Exploration of African- Caribbean and Jewish History and Memory in Modern Britain* (London: Kegan Paul, 2006), p.154.
11. Elizabeth Grosz, 'Judaism and Exile: the Ethics of Otherness', in Erica Carter, James Donald and Judith Squires, eds, *Space and Place: Theories of Identity and Location* (London: Lawrence and Wishart, 1993), pp.57–71, p.69.
12. David Brauner has explored this in terms of what he calls 'the Jewish anti-pastoral'. See *Post-War Jewish Fiction: Ambivalence, Self-Explanation and Transatlantic Connections* (Basingstoke: Palgrave, 2001), chapter three, pp.74–112.
13. A report on the 2001 census noted that 'Jews lived in all but one of the 408 districts in the United Kingdom, but their distribution was uneven countrywide. Almost a quarter (23.1 per cent) lived in just two places, the London boroughs of Barnet and Redbridge. Over half (52 per cent) lived in a further eight: Harrow, Camden, Hackney, Hertsmere, Bury, Leeds, Westminster and Brent'. See David Graham, Marlena Schmool and Stanley Waterman, *Jews in Britain: A Snapshot from the 2001 Census*, http://www.jpr.org.uk/downloads/2001_census.pdf. Accessed 10 May 2012.
14. Anne Karpf, *The War After* (London: Minerva, 1996), p.51.
15. Linda Grant, *The Cast Iron Shore* (London: Granta, 1998), p.2.
16. Natasha Solomons, *Mr Rosenblum's List* (London: Sceptre, 2010), pp.310–311.
17. Jules Smith, http://literature.britishcouncil.org/ruth-fainlight. Accessed 20 March 2012.
18. Ruth Fainlight, 'The English Country Cottage', *Jewish Quarterly,* Spring 2000, republished in Natasha Lehrer, ed., *The Golden Chain: Fifty Years of the Jewish Quarterly* (London: Vallentine Mitchell, 2002), pp.69–70.
19. For a discussion of mimicry in which the other is figured as 'almost the same but not quite', see Homi Bhabha, *The Location of Culture* (London: Routledge, 1994), p.86.

20. Peter Lawson, 'Otherness and Affiliation in Anglo-Jewish Poetry', in Axel Stähler, ed., *Anglophone Jewish Literature* (London: Routledge, 2007), pp.123–32, p.124.
21. Bernice Rubens, *When I Grow Up* (London: Abacus, 2006), pp.56–7.
22. Tamar Yellin, 'A Jew in Brontëland', *Jewish Quarterly*, 208 (2007) 68–69 (69).
23. I have discussed *Rodinsky's Room* in more detail in 'The Golem in the Attic: Jewish Memory and Identity in Rachel Lichtenstein and Iain Sinclair's *Rodinsky's Room*', *Jewish Culture and History*, 9.1 (2007) 51–70. I am grateful to Vallentine Mitchell for permission to reproduce some of this material here.
24. Rachel Lichtenstein and Iain Sinclair, *Rodinsky's Room* (London: Granta, 2000).
25. Jack Kugelmass, 'Jewish Icons: Envisioning the Self in Images of the Other' in Jonathan Boyarin and Daniel Boyarin, eds., *Jews and Other Differences: The New Jewish Cultural Studies* (Minneapolis: University of Minnesota Press, 1997), pp.30–53 (p.43).
26. David Roskies, *The Jewish Search for a Usable Past* (Indiana University Press, 1999), p.x.
27. David Cesarani, 'A Funny Thing Happened on the Way to the Suburbs: Social Change in Anglo-Jewry Between the Wars, 1914–1945', *Jewish Culture and History*, 1 (1998), 5–26 (22).
28. Jon Stratton, *Coming Out Jewish: Constructing Ambivalent Identities* (London: Routledge, 2000), p.71.
29. Stratton, p.75.
30. A.C. Jacobs, 'Alien Poem', in Peter Lawson, ed., *Passionate Renewal*, p.185.
31. Rachel Lichtenstein, *On Brick Lane* (London: Hamish Hamilton, 2007), p.1.
32. See Monica Ali's novel, *Brick Lane* (2003), for an exploration of the area in terms of its Bengali population. See also Tarquin Hall, *Salaam Brick Lane: A Year in the New East End* (2005).
33. Jeremy Gavron, *An Acre of Barren Ground* (London: Scribner, 2006).
34. Daniel Boyarin and Jonathan Boyarin, 'Diaspora: Generation and the Ground of Jewish Diaspora', in Jana Evans Braziel and Anita Mannur, eds, *Theorizing Diaspora* (Oxford: Blackwell, 2003), pp.85–118, p.108.
35. Gemma Romain outlines some of these debates. See *Connecting Histories*, pp.121–123.
36. Joseph Finlay, 'There's No Place Like Home', *Jewish Quarterly*, 213, (2009) 2–3 (2).

5

Belonging and Division: British-Jewish Reflections on Israel

> As a teenager growing up in what I would have called 'diaspora', I felt torn. I was connected to my fellow Britons, of course. I was (and remain) sentimentally patriotic for the land of my birth. But I felt bound too, in ways I could not always explain, to my fellow Jews. It was tiring when these two ties pulled in different directions, to feel I could not give to one without inching away from the other. A Jewish state seemed to offer an answer.
>
> Jonathan Freedland (2006)[1]

Like Jonathan Freedland, I am a forty-something British Jew. I have never felt exactly 'torn' between Britain and Israel but I do remember some long evenings in the 1970s when the family gathered together to watch the Eurovision Song Contest. As we sat in my grandparents' Gants Hill semi, we didn't think to root for any other country but Israel. That was just how it was. A few years on, I would have serious misgivings about the politics of Israel. So, despite a family context in which support for Israel was largely unquestioned, my feelings now about Zionism are marked by doubt and discomfort. Reading the reflections of other British Jews on Israel, it is apparent that this, perhaps more than any other issue, elicits deeply equivocal responses for many Jews in Britain today. Israel is, for some, a fantasy of a homeland, a place of ultimate belonging; but for others it casts an uncomfortable shadow over Jewish identity in the contemporary world. It is this ambivalence, and the ways in which it impacts on a sense of British-Jewish identity, that provides the focus for this chapter.

Freedland's words quoted above signal the identity crisis that a sense of split loyalties can engender. His memoir *Jacob's Gift*, which is subtitled *A Journey into the Heart of Belonging*, reflects on key ideas about belonging and place in relation to Jewish identity. As the previous chapter demonstrated, these are powerful themes in contemporary British-Jewish literature. The word 'belonging' recurs with striking regularity in titles across a range of recent texts on British-Jewish identity and, as we shall see in the following discussion, the role of Israel in shaping an emotional landscape of belonging and not belonging for British Jews is profound.

In order to address this intense set of associations, the chapter focuses on the issues of doubled and divided identifications that Freedland's quote suggests. It looks firstly at memoirs by writers such as Howard Jacobson, Linda Grant, Victor Jeleniewski Seidler and Freedland, to reflect on the ways that ideas about Israel inform issues of belonging for the post-war generation of British Jews. It then shifts the focus from first-person reflection, to explore how highly charged recent debates about Israel have been articulated in literature by Howard Jacobson and Mike Leigh. I argue that these writers, who appear to be presenting diametrically opposed ideas about Zionism and anti-Zionism, in fact draw from a quite similar lexicon of shame and disillusionment in order to articulate the complex signification of Israel for British Jews. The chapter ends with an exploration of two Mandate novels, by Jonathan Wilson and Linda Grant. The discussion suggests that in returning to a particularly sensitive period of British-Jewish tension, these narratives signal some of the ambiguities that are perhaps still present in contemporary British-Jewish life. In these terms, Israel has become an imaginary landscape on to which far more domestic anxieties and fantasies are projected.

Belonging: Israel and British-Jewish identity

For many British Jews, the establishment of the State of Israel in 1948 was a momentous and moving occasion. In *A Sense of Belonging* Howard Cooper and Paul Morrison note that in the immediate aftermath of its creation Israel was an idea around which a shaken Anglo-Jewry population coalesced. They explain that in the post-war years, as British Jews mourned the losses of the Holocaust, they were 'also ever-mindful of

Israel's fragile birth, its blossoming development, its confident death-defying resurrection of Jewish optimism'.[2] Similarly, Linda Grant, reflecting on her immigrant parents' experience, explains that:

> It was the place that made them feel they could stand proud in the world, that took their victimhood and fear away from them, the country that turned their eyes away from the past towards the future for the first time in two millennia.[3]

This understanding of the creation of Israel as representing a move away from a painful and fractured past towards a confident future is a potent and repeated theme in writing by British Jews. However, this sense of renewal, even in the aftermath of war, was not without its tensions. Tellingly, *A Sense of Belonging* is subtitled *Dilemmas of British Jewish Identity* and it is perhaps in looking at the hopes and conflicts expressed about Israel that give us particular insight into some of those dilemmas. As Freedland puts it:

> To grow up in Anglo-Jewry in the 1950s was to grow up in a frozen community, which had not discovered ways of meaningfully coming to terms with the complex histories it gathered together. In some ways we learned not to think about the past, but to face Israel as the embodiment of a different, more heroic future ... We were brought up to take Zionism for granted, for this was the way that Jewish identities were now to be constructed.... it felt as if there was a place where we were no longer 'tolerated' and where we could feel a sense of belonging. It was only later that we learned to ask questions about the histories and rights of Palestinians and the possibility of sharing land and living in peace. (49)

Here 'a sense of belonging', the same phrase that Cooper and Morrison use in their title, recurs. It signals a preoccupation with the subtle feelings of alienation and displacement that run through post-war British-Jewish writing. The emergence of the new Jewish state, located in the sun and heat of the Middle East, provided (at least symbolically), some much desired warmth for this 'frozen community'. It came to represent a renewed faith in Jewishness. 'Almost without our being aware of it', Cooper and Morrison explain, 'long-distance support for Israel became the unifying factor in our changed Jewish condition.... The old era's formula "I believe in God" was replaced by the new incantation of Anglo-Jewry: "I believe in Israel"' (113).

However, even from its inception there was a particular friction for British Jews about the history of British colonial enforcement in Palestine. I shall explore some fictional representations of this history towards the end of this chapter. In terms of non-fictional reflections on this tension we can see how issues of divided loyalties played into deep-rooted uncertainties about whether Jews could ever really belong in Britain. Grant, for example, relates how her parents' joy in relation to Israel's creation was undercut by a sense that the British, who had abstained in the UN vote, had once again failed to fully endorse support for Jews. She explains that 'their *exultation*, the idea that the world had done something right for a change' was accompanied by fundamental doubts relating to issues of belonging. So, the moment of Israel's creation, whilst not exactly making them Israeli, also somehow 'made them even more not British than they were already'.[4]

A complex dynamic thus emerged for Jews in Britain in this period. For these families, many of whom had lost relatives in Europe, and who were both grateful and proud to be British, a powerful seam of division opened up to expose a split identification. As Grant observes, her parents' experience of the traumas and deprivations of wartime Britain evoked simultaneously a sense of connection and of disjuncture: 'the war which made them like everyone else', she notes, 'also made them feel different'.[5] Despite their enthusiastic support for emblems of Britishness, such as the royal family, Grant's parents' deep perception of their 'not British[ness]' was a powerful motivation towards Zionism. So, as they supported Zionist terrorist activities against the British in Palestine, they became, as Grant succinctly puts it, 'patriots...with divided hearts'.[6]

For the post-war generation, such as Grant, who had been born and brought up in Britain, feelings about Israel were equally, if not more, complex. For this generation, rejecting Zionism was often bound up with familial tension as well as political conviction. Grant recalls how as a young woman she deployed blunt anti-Zionist rhetoric as weapon against her father, admitting that: 'My anti-Zionism was a form of cruelty...It was sound and fury: cheap, fake Sixties ideology, choosing the arguments that would hurt my father most'.[7] The conflict being played out here is not then between the rights of Palestinians and Jews. It is closer to home. Israel functions as contested territory on to which other, far more intimate and domestic, struggles are relocated. As Grant comes to understand, these arguments had little to do 'with a real place or real people, except in that they were shadows, outlines to be filled in with what we brought to them from our own unspent needs and urges'.[8]

In *The People on the Street* Grant presents a more mature and nuanced exploration of the ways in which, even for a politically left-leaning British Jew such as herself, Israel might still evoke an uncanny sense of connection. 'Despite the millennia of wandering', she notes, 'Judaism also contains a sense of place, but in a kind of negative equation, the longing for a return from exile' (27). Such collective longing, within a condition of perpetual exile, might well create a convergent sense of belonging in an imagined homeland of Israel. In explaining the rationale behind her decision to spend four months living in Tel Aviv, Grant draws from this sense of located familiarity. She writes that:

> I found myself in my forties, drawn to Israel, not out of Zionism or interest in the Middle East conflict, but because the moment I put my foot down there, everything was half familiar. I had half the story already in my head, and was avid and eager to learn the rest. (5)

Here we find that issues about belonging and location explored in the previous chapter take on a particular resonance. There I looked briefly at Howard Jacobson's *Roots Schmoots*. I want now to return to this text to explore the ways in which he too signals a strong connection, albeit strained and mocking, to this terrain.

Jacobson, the ever-sceptical traveller, is unsettled by the unexpectedly powerful emotions he experiences as he arrives in Israel. He explains that:

> As we came off the plane, she [Jacobson's gentile wife] clasped my hand and whispered 'Welcome home, Howard'. ... This is how deep the idea of return runs. This is how much of a foreigner she thinks I have been in England.[9]

So, like Grant, the moment Jacobson sets foot on Israeli soil is strangely defining. As a British Jew he is ambivalent about Israel but he describes, nevertheless, an unexpected bond with this country; a bond which is predicated on the commensurate sense, which he hears in his wife's whisper, that he does not quite belong in England. He thus feels both the sting and thrill of being cast in the role of 'foreigner'. Again, like Grant, he seems almost to surprise himself in his ineffable sense of identification with Israel. Jacobson is left wondering if, in this land of Jews, he has found a resolution to a fundamental contradiction within his own identity. 'So now it's all explained', he declares, toying with an idea of an essential ethnic identity, '– my love of aubergines and falafel ... I am a Middle Easterner. Forget Poland and Russia and Lithuania and the ghetto and Yiddish. We are Bedouins. Tent – and oasis-dwellers who like to festoon our pavilions with cloths that sparkle' (301). As Grant puts it, 'half the story' was already there.

However, Jacobson's other experiences in Israel are not so jaunty. He relates some encounters that are humorous, life-affirming and familiar; but others that are disappointing, suffocating, confusing and alarming. However, it is within this intense and clashing environment of the Middle East that Jacobson's understanding of himself as a British Jew becomes more clearly defined. One episode is particularly telling. Although he expresses many doubts about various aspects of Israeli ideology, Jacobson is equally infuriated by what he views as the mindless sanctimony espoused by a pro-Palestinian couple he meets at the American Colony, an Arab-owned hotel in Jerusalem. This experience allows him to pinpoint a troubling internal conflict. On the one hand his decision to stay at this hotel is a deliberate attempt to challenge his own innate hostility towards Arabs, which he describes as 'the ball of violence that has been lodged in my chest all my adult life' (332); but, in encountering the blunt anti-Zionism of 'Philip from Tunbridge Wells', he identifies what in many respects is a more complex sense of enmity. And, one that has a deeper bearing on his identity as a British Jew. 'It has gone cold in the vicinity of my heart', he explains:

> We are past dealing with rights and wrongs, truths or untruths. I smell the enemies of my soul. Forget the Palestinians. With them we are just having a family quarrel. The enemies of my soul come from Tunbridge Wells. (339)

So, again, it is not necessarily in the elsewhere of the Middle East that the conflicts between self and other are played out with most intensity. For Jacobson, these differences run deep, but they are variations on the family quarrels that Jews know so well. He suggests, in the end, that the most highly charged associations and disassociations are experienced in the impasses of identities that, for British Jews, take place at home.

In its complex political reality and its potent symbolic signification, Israel is then the terrain onto which many such, as Morrison and Cooper put it, 'dilemmas of identity', have been projected. In *Shadows of the Shoah*, subtitled *Jewish Identity and Belonging*, Victor Jeleniewski Seidler once again signals that for many British Jews, especially those of the immediate post-war generation, belonging is a complex process of negotiation rather than a fixed point of identification. In this sense, Israel functions as a testing point for issues of allegiance. In its mildest form this might equate to my memories of Eurovision nights or a version of Tebbit's 'cricket test', reducible to which side one would one support in a direct contest, but in the long shadow cast by the recent

war, these issues took on a far more burdensome significance.[10] As
Seidler recalls, Jewish children growing up in the 1950s:

> Were also aware of issues of loyalty to Israel as opposed to England, and
> what we might do in an imaginary situation of a war between the two
> countries. We wanted to feel that we would resolve this clearly in favour
> of England, but we also wanted to declare the possibility of multiple
> loyalties.[11]

Such intricate questions of identity are not easily reduced to an
either-or dichotomy. But, as Seidler recognizes, 'the possibility of
multiple loyalties' was a vexed proposition.

Freedland explains that, for him, Zionism had once seemed to offer a
resolution to an ontological paradox, a way in which 'to end, once and
for all, the neurosis that comes from being split: man in the streets and
a Jew at home. Zionism said there could be a place, far away where
this self-division would end' (361). Again, the key point here seems to
be that Zionism offered a fantasy of Jewish completeness which was
located 'far away' rather than confronting the realities of complex
identifications closer to home. Like Seidler, Freedland also recalls
playground interrogations focused on what he would do if Israel and
Britain were at war. With the pressure on issues of allegiance that such a
question raises, Freedland imagines a hypothetical scenario, 'a thought
awful to contemplate', in which Israel would became the military target
of Britain. This idea becomes an irreconcilable double bind: 'I know',
he writes, 'that I could not regard the Jewish state as my enemy, but nor
could I turn against the country that has raised me. Bothness would be
impossible; I would have to divide myself in two' (311).

Freedland's relationship with Israel, which he describes as 'simultaneously tied and torn' (22), is deep but also troubling. His mother was
born in British-ruled Palestine and he recalls how as a British youth
he (like Mike Leigh, Sacha Baron-Cohen and David Baddiel amongst
others) was an enthusiastic member of the Habonim, an organization
that 'amounted to the youth wing, among the Jewish diaspora, of Israel's
kibbutz movement' (16). With political hindsight, he reflects back on a
glorious and formative summer tour to Israel as being 'a shameless exercise in Zionist indoctrination' (17), and this was followed by a gap year
which further intensified his commitment to the Zionist cause. When
he returned to Britain, to take up a place at Oxford, Freedland experienced an acute sensation of difference and division. 'I had accepted',
he notes, 'the key Zionist contention that the diaspora could never be
a secure home – that a Jew like me would always feel an outsider in

Britain' (20). So, a fissure in identity, a sense of living in 'two worlds', opened up and Freedland recalls becoming, at this stage of his life, 'an outsider of my own making' (20). This sense of self-division deepened as he became increasingly aware of the Palestinian perspective, and it was compounded when he became a journalist for the *Guardian*, a newspaper known for its critical stance on Israel. Burdened with the task of explaining Jews to the *Guardian* and the *Guardian* to Jews, Freedland describes an especially charged experience in which he was positioned simultaneously on opposite sides of an ideological abyss, whilst feeling that he 'did not belong on either' (27).

Freeland articulates a particularly intense relationship to Israel. This is not necessarily typical but, in its exploration of shifting allegiances and ambiguous affiliations, his account perhaps reflects more widespread internal conflicts within Anglo-Jewry. In *Beyond Belonging* (2004), a report on the 'Jewish identities of moderately engaged British Jews' (once again a title that raises belonging as a pivotal term), we see such tension. The study is sponsored by the United Jewish Israel Appeal, an organization that describes itself as 'the leading supporter of the people of Israel and young Jewish people in the UK'.[12] The authors of the report identify a 'widespread attachment' to Israel by British Jews but, even in this quite particular context, they also note the ambivalence that underpins such attachment. 'Israel is approached with genuine and immutable love', they explain:

> It is seen with familiarity, often appreciated for its strengths and accepted for its shortcomings. If it is to be criticized or reproached, it is to be reproved in the confines of the family, out of earshot of outsiders, let alone antagonists. (50)

The sense that critique of Israel is to be kept quietly within the 'family' of British Jews runs deep, but this is proving to be an uncontainable issue. A 2010 report undertaken by the Institute for Jewish Policy Research concluded that British-Jewish attitudes towards Israel were characterized by 'strong support tinged with concern'. However, the authors sound a warning note, remarking that 'the topic of Israel has the potential to both unite and divide Jews'.[13]

As Geoffrey Alderman has observed, Israel, which once provided a general point of unanimity in British-Jewish life, is becoming an increasingly more schismatic matter. 'Anglo-Jewry is very different today than it was in May 1948', he explains, adding:

> There is no table long enough for all members of Anglo Jewry to sit at ... We've become pluralized and polarized. Maybe that's why some of us experience

an emotional difficulty when talking about Israel. Zionism was at one time the unifying force of Anglo Jewry and is now the most divisive.[14]

There is a realization expressed here that disagreements can no longer be domesticized in terms of a family quarrel. Indeed, the divisions that have been simmering internally within Anglo-Jewry for some time have come to the surface quite dramatically in recent years. In 2002 the campaign group, 'Jews for Justice for Palestinians', was formed to provide a counterpoint to what has sometimes been presented as universal British-Jewish support for Israel. The organization has drawn a number of high profile supporters and triggered acrimonious discussions within the Anglo-Jewish community. More recently, in 2007, a group called 'Independent Jewish Voices' published a 'Declaration' titled, somewhat defiantly, 'A Time to Speak Out'. Signatories included academics and writers such as Anne Karpf, Mike Leigh, Jacqueline Rose, Antony Lerman and Brian Klug. The 'Declaration' provoked some extreme response in what became a highly public and rancorous debate among British Jews.[15] The strength of feeling surrounding these issues demonstrates the uncomfortable, and indeed unresolved, nature of these debates for many British Jews.

I have looked, so far, at the ways in which such tensions have been articulated in memoirs, travel writing and commentary. I want now to shift the focus to explore how these issues are being represented in contemporary fictional writing. As well as highlighting key aspects of the debate, whether through narrative or dramatic enactment, fictional writing is perhaps also able to stand at a slight distance from polemic in order to articulate the subtle emotional complexities of these issues.

Ashamed Jews: recent literary responses to Israel

Two recent works by Howard Jacobson (*The Finkler Question*, 2010) and Mike Leigh (*Two Thousand Years*, 2006), focus some aspects of the argument. These two Manchester-born Jewish authors are contemporaries (Jacobson was born in 1942 and Leigh in 1943) and neither are strangers to controversy. Both have challenged convention in their work. Both have written on controversial topics. Both subject lazy thinking and sentimentalization to robust interrogation. But, in their representation of recent responses to Israel, the two differ. And, it is in this difference that we can perhaps pick up the tenor of a wider debate amongst British Jews. In his journalism and polemical writing Jacobson has been fierce in his attack on knee-jerk anti-Zionism. Leigh is famously outspoken in support of the Palestinian cause. However, in their literary explorations of these issues, both authors have drawn on a nuanced discourse of shame in order to frame their representations of the debate.

Leigh has not often written explicitly about Jewishness, so *Two Thousand Years* provides an interesting insight into this background. In his 'Introduction' to the play text he describes growing up in Jewish Manchester. He explains that his experience was typical, except in two respects: firstly, he was a middle-class child in a predominantly working class area; secondly, he came from a family of long-standing Zionists. His grandfather had edited a Zionist newspaper before the First World War; several members of his family had 'made aliyah' (emigrated to Palestine/Israel); and his parents had met in the Habonim, an organization to which Leigh also belonged in his formative years. So, for Leigh, an attachment to the ideals of Zionism runs deep. In recent years, however, his feelings towards Israel have been defined by disappointment. As he explains: 'Certainly, the confusion and frustration about Israel and Palestine shared by many liberal Jews comes out of once having believed passionately in an enlightened, secular, socialist Jewish State'.[16]

His play places some of these issues within a creative framework. The drama is set in the North London home of Rachel and Danny. In the first scene Jonathan, a family friend, calls and talks about how he had once thought of making aliyah. 'So what happened?' asks Rachel. Jonathan replies: 'Israel happened. It changed. I got disillusioned. I decided I belonged here after all' (14). So, themes of belonging and disillusionment are established from the outset and such disillusionment can only be the product of an original idealism. In turn, Rachel, who was born on a kibbutz, adds to this tone of jaded idealism, reflecting on what she sees as the innate gender inequality of the 'Great Kibbutz Dream'. Later on, Josh, Rachel and Danny's son who to the bemusement of his secular socialist family has recently embraced religion, asks his grandfather, Dave, 'are you proud to be Jewish?' (51). When Dave seems to evade the question, Josh reframes it, asking: 'So what are you ashamed of?' (51). After a pause, Dave embarks on a list, including 'Jewish racists', Thatcherite 'arse-lickers', and finally, Israel. 'And I'm afraid to say', he says:

> I'm ashamed of what's happened to Israel. I'm ashamed of the Lebanon War; I'm ashamed of the illegal settlements on the West bank and in Gaza; I'm ashamed of the way in which they treat the Palestinian people – (52)

At this point his granddaughter, Tammy, interjects

> **Tammy:** You mean you're ashamed of the Zionist state?
> **Dave:** No, no, no, Tammy, don't put words in my mouth. I'm not ashamed of the Zionist state. I'm ashamed of the way that Zionism has been hijacked by a bunch of right-wing religious nutters.
> *Pause.*
> **Tammy:** Yeah...isn't etymology fascinating? I mean, the way words evolve. Take the word Zionism, for example. Once upon a time, it meant something positive and hopeful. But now...well. To some people it's a dirty word. (52)

The play (which by definition does put words in mouths) explores the way in which both Zionism and Israel have multiple significations. Historically, as we have seen, Israel has offered a place of safety and has functioned as a symbol of hope and renewal; but now it represents, for some British Jews at least, a troubling set of associations and a complex sense of affiliation. Leigh's play taps into the power of this internal conflict at a personal and collective level. The discussion that is staged in this North London family home takes in the weary pragmatism of Tammy's Israeli boyfriend, Tzachi, as well as the disillusioned idealism of the older generation. It is specific to the experiences of this particular family situation but can also be seen as dramatizing British-Jewish debates about Israel in a more general sense. Dave recognizes that powerful ideas and words, such as Zionism, can be lost or appropriated and Tammy grasps the imbrication of hope and disappointment that Zionism evokes. It is the genesis for a particular sort of shame; shame that encompasses a sense of a pity, of broken aspiration, as well as dishonour. It has become 'a dirty word' because it signals the complexity of tarnished optimism.

Although stylistically and ideologically quite different, Howard Jacobson's novel, *The Finkler Question*, explores some similar issues. Like Leigh, Jacobson locates the discussion within contemporary London and articulates the tensions about Israel that preoccupy the Anglo-Jewish community. These tensions are seen from the perspective of Julian Treslove, a gentile who is intrigued to the point of obsession by Jewishness. This sideways manoeuvre allows for a humorous faux-naivety in the novel's representation of Jewishness, as the reader, through Treslove's perspective, views Jewishness with an enquiring eye. Early in the narrative he observes, with envious bafflement, the ongoing debate between his Jewish friends, the anti-Zionist Sam Finkler, and the older, less equivocal, Libor Sevcik. Libor who pronounces Israel 'with three "r"s and no "l" – "Isrrrae –", 'a holy utterance, like the cough of God', berates Finkler (who 'put a seasick "y" between the "a" and the "e" – "Israyelis"') for his public disavowal of the Jewish State.[17] As Treslove looks on with the awe of an outsider, the customary argument about this being essentially a 'family matter' is deployed on both sides. Alongside this Jacobson develops an exploration of the place of shame in such debates. So, Finkler argues that 'because I am a Jew I am ashamed', whilst Libor in turn rebukes his friend for 'parading his shame to a Gentile world' (26.)

Finkler goes on to express his views in a highly public manner. As a media academic he uses an appearance on Desert Island Discs to broadcast his support for the Palestinian cause, declaring 'with a falter in his voice', that '"In the matter of Palestine,"'... "I am profoundly ashamed"' (113). He soon finds himself the de facto leader of a group of Jewish academics and media personalities who call themselves ASHamed Jews. In response to this impassioned disavowal of Zionism, Finkler's level-headed convert wife, Tyler, offers a distinctly deflationary perspective. Treslove, who is sleeping with Tyler, is bemused by the ASHamed Jews. '"And is that all they stand for', he asks her, '"being ashamed of being Jewish?"'. '"Whoa!"', she replies,

> 'You're not allowed to say that. It's not Jews they're ashamed of being. It's Israel. Palestine. Whatever'.
> 'So are they Israelis?'
> ...
> 'I don't know about all of them, but they're actors and comedians and those I've heard of aren't Israelis'.
> 'So how can they be ashamed? How can you be ashamed of a country that's not yours?' Treslove truly was puzzled.
> 'It's because they're Jewish'.
> 'But you said they're not ashamed of being Jewish'.
> 'Exactly. But they're ashamed *as* Jews'. (120)

Their conversation continues, circling round what seems to be the illogicality of both the claim and the disavowal. In the end Tyler admits to being sick of the 'self-preoccupation' of Jews, the way they won't 'shut up about themselves', and their 'endlessly falling out in public' (121).

Finkler's experience of the ASHamed Jews bears out this frustration. Jacobson subjects these hollow and publicity-seeking Jewish anti-Zionists to the most savage satire. They are a self-conscious, disparate and disputatious group who meet regularly at the Groucho Club in

Soho to engage in earnest and endless debate. This makes for potentially uncomfortable reading; especially for a non-Jewish audience who are in danger of sitting, like Treslove, on the sidelines as they witness a particularly nasty family spat. However, this potential for discomfort leads the reader to some challenging points of exploration. At one level, the narrative presents a robust satire of self-serving anti-Zionism, but I would argue that the novel moves beyond caricature of such easy targets, to develop a nuanced debate about issues of entitlement, public identification, belonging and attachment. The discourse of shame that is deployed in this context is in fact a rather delicate comic device.

In the end it is apparent that Israel, like the word Jew, in and beyond the novel, is actually hard to say or to interpret in any singular sense. Jacobson has argued that 'for the purposes of my narrative, Israel exists only poetically, in the imaginations of those who cannot adequately describe themselves without it'.[18] This understanding, that more domestic and internal anxieties are routinely displaced on to ideas about Israel, is perceptive. He goes on to explain:

> I happen to think this is largely true outside my novel as well: that Israel performs a function greater than itself, enabling or disabling ideas about belonging and disengagement, fanning the flames of ancient allegiances and animosities. For many Jews and non-Jews in this country Israel has become a figure of speech, the occasion for wild and whirling words, a pretext for bottling up or setting loose emotions which originate somewhere else entirely.

Thinking about Israel as, a 'figure of speech', allows us to develop an exploration of the more subtle dialectic between 'belonging and disengagement' that runs deep in British-Jewish writing about Israel. Responses to Israel are often emotive and explicit but, as Jacobson argues, these responses also articulate more elusive and implicit issues for British Jews.

As Jacobson and Leigh demonstrate, ambivalence about Israel is charged and current, but its roots lie in earlier contexts and draw from complex issues of identification for Jews in Britain. The history of Britain's involvement with Palestine, and the ways that British Jews have been positioned within this history, focuses an exploration of ambiguity and split identifications. The final section of this chapter brings these issues together by looking at recent novels which explore British-Jewish identities in relation to the Mandate period. I want to reflect on the ways in which these narratives present another time and another country in order to provide a setting for tensions relating to the here and now.

Divided identities: mandate fictions

Some recent Mandate fictions include Jonathan Wilson's *A Palestine Affair* (2003), Linda Grant's *When I Lived in Modern Times* (2000) and Bernice Rubens' *The Sergeant's Tale* (2003). Although I shall not be focusing here on *The Sergeant's Tale* it is worth noting that each of these narratives focus on themes of split loyalties and performed identities. In an astute discussion of this fiction Axel Stähler makes the point that 'this particular past is very much part and parcel of the present' going on to argue that:

> British Jewish fictions of the historical colonial encounter of the Jews with the British bring about the convergences not only of English (or British) and Jewish identification patterns, but also of English and Jewish constructions of the past, onto a space that is 'extraterritorial' to both of them. The Mandate in Palestine and the prominence it has achieved in some British Jewish fiction thus appear to demarcate a space in which English and Jewish constructions of the past have to meet perforce. Neither can write itself without the other.[19]

Stähler's discussion of this material examines the notion of 'extraterritoriality', an idea developed by Bryan Cheyette, which posits that British-Jewish writers 'place their narratives elsewhere in order to "sidestep...the hegemony of English, or even British constructions of the past which excluded Jewishness" (29).[20] Setting fictions in the highly charged time and place of Mandate Palestine provokes reflection on issues relating to Britishness and Jewishness, power and identification, which are both historical and relevant to the present day context.

Jonathan Wilson's *A Palestine Affair* (2003) tells the story of a murder that took place in 1920s Palestine and represents the ambivalent position of the Jew who is made to be complicit with the colonial project in the Middle East. It centres on the dilemmas of Robert Kirsch, a British-Jewish investigating officer. At one point in the narrative he is confronted about his potentially split loyalties by Joyce, the American gentile wife of a rootless Jewish artist. When Joyce expresses surprise that Kirsch is Jewish, he replies, 'it's not something that I'm ashamed of'. But the passage continues:

> Was he sometimes ashamed? Kirsch wasn't altogether sure.
> 'Well, no, why would you be? But you're a British policeman. I mean, aren't you, don't you feel that you're on the wrong side of the stockade?'
> Kirsch looked at her and felt his face redden.
> 'I don't know what you mean', he said.[21]

Here the discourse of shame emerges once again. The subtle sense of not quite belonging to one identity or another is enacted in the blush, at precisely the boundary between inside and outside, self and other. It is a manifestation of a particular form of uncertainty that feeds a particular form of shame.

The Mandate context thus facilitates an intense exploration of ambivalent identification. 'British and Jewish captain Kirsch, you're an interesting combination', remarks a rabbi to Kirsch. Kirsch responds by noting that this could be seen as a '*suspicious* combination', and the rabbi sums up the multiple alienations of this conflicted identity: 'To the Jews, British; to the British, a Jew; and for the Arabs, the worst of both worlds. Is that what you mean?' (39). At this point, Kirsch, again faced with what seems to be a fundamental incongruity, reaches a point of discomfort and abruptly changes the subject. But the issue of split and potentially conflicting affiliations remains unsettled. It resurfaces when Joyce berates Kirsch for his lack of obvious sympathy with Zionism. Here the exchange pivots on a fundamental question about how identities are both internalized and performed:

> 'You don't have to lecture me. I *am* a Jew, remember'.
> 'Well, you don't act like one'.
> 'And how does a Jew act?' (130)

This question, 'how does a Jew act' is not something that could easily be asked in contemporary Britain, but it might still be relevant. In theoretical terms it raises questions about whether identities are essential or performative, but it also touches on earlier conceptions of Jews as impersonators, masking their true identities and passing unremarked through gentile society. This cultural history, in which Jews were routinely viewed as suspicious, has contributed to a subtle yet pervasive sense of not quite belonging for many British Jews today. Through historicizing such uncertainties, Mandate novels arguably bring such unease to light, presenting a time in which such a question could be asked, if not answered.

Linda Grant's *When I Lived in Modern Times* (2000) plays on precisely such issues. It is a book about surfaces and depths, mimicry and masks.[22] It tells the story of Evelyn Sert, a young hairdresser from London who sets sail for Palestine as the British Mandate is nearing its end. Against this backdrop, the novel charts the ways in which Evelyn constructs a series of shifting and provisional identities describing herself from the outset as 'a work-in-progress' (50), a spy, and 'an impersonator' (270). In telling Evelyn's story of transience and displacement, Grant explores some of the uncertainties and possibilities that existed for Jews in Palestine as British power under the Mandate disintegrated. Evelyn's position in relation to both Palestine and Britain is complicated. Throughout the novel she searches for a workable identity as a Jew and looks forward to the future within an autonomous Jewish State; but, at the same time, her British background invokes an unstable and uneasy identification with the colonizing administration.

Grant's narrative explores and to an extent embraces the ambiguous position of the Jew at this point of British and Palestinian history. As she narrates the story of Evelyn's splintered identification, Grant also suggests that affiliations and loyalties, like subjectivities, are formed through multiple and sometimes contradictory points of connection. Evelyn is a harsh, brusque and arguably dislikeable character. She is, by her own admission shifty, untrustworthy, and even treacherous. So, in this respect, she embodies many of the things that the antisemitic imagination has feared about Jews and, similarly, many of the things that the colonial imagination has feared about colonized subjects. She cannot be trusted. She might not be what she seems.

As Jon Stratton has noted, fakery and deception have historically been associated with Jewishness within antisemitic discourse. He explains that 'an aspect of the modern stereotype of the Jew is her or his acting ability, and the genius claimed for the Jew as an impersonator and mimic'.[23] But it is also important to acknowledge here (as Stratton does) that the othering of Jews, in particular, has always been marked by a profound ambivalence and that mimicry is by no means a straightforward concept. As Homi Bhabha has argued, the ambivalence of mimicry in colonial discourse is based on the idea of '*a subject of difference that is almost the same, but not quite*'. [24] Jews have often been positioned in this way and this is the role that Evelyn occupies throughout Grant's novel: *almost the same* as the British, *but not quite*. Almost the same as the Jews in Palestine, but not quite.

As her story progresses, Evelyn becomes the figure most dreaded by colonial authorities and one especially associated with the stereotypically duplicitous figure of the 'International Jew'. She takes on the role of a spy, passing on information about the British in Palestine to her Irgun terrorist boyfriend, Johnny and becomes, quite literally, the enemy within. But, her story is not all about artifice and appearance. As the British Empire is poised to collapse so Evelyn sees a moment of potential. The young Evelyn imagines that in Palestine she will somehow experience a sense of belonging that she has never felt in England. She figures her connection to Englishness as a hollow construct:

> No-one I was related to had ever set foot on English soil until forty-five years ago. What could an immigrant child be, except an impersonator? I felt like a double agent, a fifth columnist. And I knew that as long as I lived in this country it would always be exactly the same. I walked among them and they thought they knew me, but they understood nothing at all. It was *me* that understood, the spy in their midst. (27)

Evelyn believes that in Palestine she will find out how the fragments cohere into a whole. This individual desire to be somehow released from a primary condition of displacement is mapped on to diaspora Jews as a whole. Evelyn's fantasy (and the imperative of Zionism) is that in the Promised Land, 'the elemental nature of the Jew, stripped of the accents of foreign language and its customs, was going to reveal itself for the first time since the exile'. 'We would cease', she declares optimistically, 'to be composite characters' (30). So, it is that the imagined subject and the 'imagined community' come together.[25]

However, Evelyn finds a far more confusing landscape of identification in Palestine and there she adopts a series of shifting roles and allegiances. Arabs, for Evelyn exist only 'as invisible men and women, [sinking] into the landscape like the hills and the water and the banana palms' (46), and she soon realizes that she does not fit into the 'new', 'muscular Judaism' of Zionist kibbutz culture. So she moves on to Tel Aviv where she encounters a mismatched grouping of Jews drawn mainly from Eastern Europe and Germany. These so-called Ostjuden and the Yekkes coexist in a state of uneasy tension. They bring with them a jagged consciousness of exile that is based more on pre-existing national affiliations than the overarching sense of Jewish identity that Evelyn imagines will unite them all in Zion. It is perhaps not surprising then that within this 'a raw, strained' society it is the British, who were, she explains 'the only people who did not seem like foreigners to me'. Evelyn is aware of the ambivalence at the heart of this affinity. 'They were the colonial, the oppressive power', she states; but adds, 'they were the enemy and the paradox of my life was that the ways of the enemy were partly mine too' (106).

So, Evelyn leads a double life. She dyes her hair platinum blond and passes as a gentile called Priscilla. She finds work in a hairdressing salon and practises her finely tuned arts of deception on the wives of British colonials. As she witnesses the casual antisemitism of her British acquaintances she worries at the contradiction of her identification: 'Why do I', she wonders, 'not know how to be a Jew in a Jewish land?' (110). One of the conclusions that the novel draws from Evelyn's dilemma is that, of course, there are many ways in which to be Jewish. The irony is that whilst Jewishness might from the British perspective mark Evelyn as other, there is no essential identity as a Jew from which she can draw a sense of self. Again, Bhabha's phrase comes to mind, 'almost the same but not quite'. The lines are blurred.

Evelyn thinks that she finds a way in which to mark that line between self and other in Johnny, her Jewish Palestinian lover. Although (or perhaps, because) she never knows his real name, Evelyn recognizes that he is her double: 'Looking at Johnny' she comments 'was like looking at myself in a mirror. Each of us existed as a reflecting surface' (69). He is, Evelyn admits, the only person in her life with whom she had been completely honest. Johnny, like Evelyn, is adept at disguise and dissimulation. He is, amongst other things, a football fan, a soldier, a tailor and a terrorist. He passes easily as British. She describes him as an 'Englishman in translation' (68). Unlike Evelyn, who sees herself as being a kind of modernist portrait, fragmented, discontinuous and relative, Johnny is confident that he knows exactly who he is. 'He', Evelyn understands, 'merely wore a mask which deliberately set out to deceive, behind which he clearly knew who he was, while I seemed to contain several selves and each of these seemed to me as valid as the next' (140).

Johnny is absolutely clear in his opposition to the British colonial presence in Palestine whereas Evelyn is at some level attracted to and, in many respects, complicit with the colonial power. She is, after all, one of them. Ultimately, however, she finds that her identification with Jewishness triumphs over the familiarity (figured as a kind of nostalgia for Lyon's Corner Houses, wireless broadcasts and warm Ovaltine) that she feels amongst the wives of British policemen. Nevertheless, she struggles still with her ambivalent response to the British: 'When I'm with the British', she observes, 'and they treat me as if I'm British I *feel* British, not a Jew at all' (140).

In a sense, Johnny and Evelyn represent two notions of both subjectivity and of Jewishness: one essential and knowable, the other a series of relative positions. Palestine becomes the arena in which these identities can be explored. It is a fictionalized territory that allows the contemporary British-Jewish writer to transfer questions about belonging and identification to another time and another place. Throughout this chapter it has been apparent that Israel is by no means a straightforward locus of identification for British Jews. The setting of Mandate fictions perhaps enables an oblique, but not necessarily evasive, treatment of more contemporary issues relating to belonging. It could be argued that historicizing themes of divided identities and split loyalties is a way of exploring tensions between British and Jewish identities that have become far more subtle today. In this way, such writing reflects a deep and underlying insecurity in Anglo-Jewry.

I would also argue, however, that Mandate fictions suggest another aspect of contemporary British-Jewish culture: a nostalgic tendency that reflects a growing sense of disconnection from Jewishness in contemporary Britain. In the charged context of the Mandate, especially towards its end, the uncertainty of British-Jewish identity was apparent. Mandate fictions, whilst reminding British Jews of a troubled and divided history, might also appeal to a desire to romanticize, or at least reflect on, a time in which *not* belonging was an accentuated part of the Jewish condition. In less perilous, but also perhaps less exciting, times for British Jews today there is a desire to revisit a context in which Jewishness was a more charged identification. Certainly, there is a sense of relish in the way that Mandate fictions describe impersonated identities, split loyalties and the subtle movements between self and other that existed within this particular colonial encounter. Perhaps also, this relocation and remarginalization of Jewishness circumvents more current tensions within Anglo-Jewry about the situation in the Middle East and Israel's status in the world.

Contemporary British-Jewish writing suggests some of the complex and creative navigations that take place when locating identities and defining belonging for Jews in Britain today. The next two chapters build on issues of memory and identity, place and displacement, connection and disconnection, by focusing on issues of gender and sexuality. The locus of discussion shifts then to that most intimate yet culturally inscribed of territories: the Jewish body.

Notes

1. Jonathan Freedland, *Jacob's Gift* (London: Penguin, 2006), p.361.
2. Howard Cooper and Paul Morrison, *A Sense of Belonging: Dilemmas of British Jewish Identity* (London: Weidenfeld and Nicolson, 1991), p.112.
3. Linda Grant, *Remind Me Who I am Again* (London: Granta, 1998), p.67.
4. Linda Grant, *The People on the Street: A Writer's View of Israel* (London: Virago, 2006), p.17.

5. *Remind Me*, p.67.
6. *Remind Me*, p.68.
7. *People*, p.17.
8. *People*, p.18.
9. Howard Jacobson, *Roots Schmoots: Journeys Among Jews* (London: Penguin, 1993), p.283.
10. In April 1990 the Conservative politician Norman Tebbit discussed issues of loyalty amongst Asian and Caribbean immigrants to Britain in terms of which cricket team they supported. The opening of Clive Sinclair's 1979 short story 'Wingate Football Club' sums up this predicament for British Jews: 'There are some dilemmas it is better not even to think about. I'll give you a for-instance. Suppose England were to play Israel in the World Cup. Who should I support?'. See 'Wingate Football Club', in Bryan Cheyette, ed., *Contemporary Jewish Writing in Britain and Ireland: An Anthology* (London: Peter Halban, 1998) pp.89–99 (p.89).
11. Victor Jeleniewski Seidler, *Shadows of the Shoah: Jewish Identity and Belonging* (Oxford: Berg, 2000), p.45.
12. Steven M. Cohen and Keith Kahn-Harris, *Beyond Belonging: The Jewish Identities of Moderately Engaged British Jews* (London, UIJA/Profile Books, 2004), p.viii.
13. David Graham and Jonathan Boyd, *Committed, Concerned and Conciliatory: The Attitudes of Jews in Britain Towards Israel* (Institute for Jewish Policy Research, 2010), p.36.
14. Geoffrey Alderman, 'Debating the Debate', *Jewish Quarterly*, 213 (2009), 50–54 (52). Alderman's words are transcribed from a conversation that took place in the wake of the Gaza War of 2008–2009. The debate, which was chaired by Jonathan Boyd, involved eight academics, community figures and cultural commentators. The *Jewish Quarterly* transcription explains that the debate was intended to provide a platform for the 'whole swathes of Anglo-Jewry' that had not been represented in more mainstream responses to the bombardment of Gaza (50).
15. See Keith Kahn-Harris, Keith and Ben Gidley, *Turbulent Times: The British Jewish Community Today* (London: Continuum, 2010), pp.154–162.
16. Mike Leigh, *Two Thousand Years* (London: Faber and Faber, 2006), pp.vi–vii.
17. Howard Jacobson *The Finkler Question* (London: Bloomsbury, 2010), p.25.
18. Howard Jacobson, 'Anti-Zionism – facts (and fictions)', *Jewish Chronicle*, 30 July 2010, 22.
19. Axel Stähler, 'Metonymies of Jewish Postcoloniality: The British Mandate for Palestine and Israel in Contemporary British Jewish Fiction', *Journal for the Study of British Cultures,* 16.1 (2009), 27–40 (29–30). I am grateful to Axel Stähler for his generosity in sending me this article.

20. See Bryan Cheyette, 'Englishness and Extraterritoriality: British-Jewish Writing and Diaspora Culture', *Literary Strategies: Studies in Contemporary Jewry*, 12 (1996), 21–39.
21. Jonathan Wilson, *A Palestine Affair* (Nottingham: Five Leaves, 2007), p.30.
22. Linda Grant, *When I Lived in Modern Times* (London: Granta, 2000).
23. Jon Stratton, *Coming Out Jewish: Constructing Ambivalent Identities* (London: Routledge, 2000), p.60.
24. Homi Bhabha, *The Location of Culture* (London: Routledge, 1994), p.86.
25. See Benedict Anderson, *Imagined Communities* (London: Verso, 1991).

6

Bar mitzvah and Balls: British-Jewish Masculinities

I start with what I think is a widespread sensibility that being Jewish in our culture renders a boy effeminate.

— *Daniel Boyarin (1997)*[1]

That's the thing about being Jewish. You haven't got a foreskin, so you need a lot of balls to make up for it.

— *Bernie Rubens (2006)*[2]

In *Unheroic Conduct* (1997), Daniel Boyarin starts from the premise that Jewish men are routinely viewed in terms of effeminacy. For Boyarin this is not just an historic perception. 'The dominant strain within European culture', he argues, 'continues to this day to interpret activity, domination, and aggressiveness as "manly" and gentleness and passivity as emasculate or effeminate' (2). Rather than attempting to dispel this stereotype, Boyarin turns instead to the premodern rabbinical tradition as a way of 'revalorizing and reeroticizing' the Jewish male 'sissy' (19). This argument is suggestive, and forms part of a current interest in rethinking the ways in which Jewish masculinities have been constructed both in the past and in the present. Stereotypes of Jewish masculinity, ranging from the 'Jew-devil' of early modern literature, to the pathologized Jew of modernity, the 'muscle Jew' of Zionist ideology, and the anxious Jew of American comedy, have all been the focus of critical interrogation in recent years. This chapter draws from such work to look more specifically at some of the ways in which Jewish masculinity has been constructed within contemporary British-Jewish writing.

The second quotation cited above is from the character, Bernie
Rubens, in the film *Sixty-Six* (2006). Bernie, on the cusp of his bar
mitzvah in 1960s London, reflects on what it means to be a Jewish
man. He articulates a common cultural perception of a compromised
and thus compensatory type of Jewish masculinity. Circumcision is an
obvious (yet also, of course, generally veiled) focus of difference but, in
many respects, it is just a starting point for exploring more diffuse and
subtle interrogations of Jewish masculinity in contemporary culture.
Bernie, bespectacled, asthmatic and unsporty, is a stereotypically
effeminate Jew. His father, Manny, lugubrious, neurotic and beset by
financial anxieties, is also presented as less than an ideal embodiment
of masculinity. However, Bernie's painfully increasing disappointment
in his father is reconfigured during the course of his bar mitzvah day,
a date that coincides with the English football team's world cup final.
Resolution is achieved when Bernie and Manny share a father-son
moment of exaltation at the English victory. The subliminal message is
that until the boy is reconciled to the spirit of Englishness, on this most
significant of days, he cannot really become a man.

The film ends up presenting a somewhat nostalgic rite of passage
narrative, but it raises some interesting issues about Jewishness and
Englishness, masculinity, belonging and identification.[3] Some recent
novels, which I look at later in this chapter, such as Howard Jacobson's
Kalooki Nights, Giles Coren's *Winkler* and Andrew Sanger's *J-Word*
(2009), draw from similar themes to present more challenging reflections on Jewishness and masculinity within a contemporary mode.
These novels raise potentially disturbing issues relating to male sexuality, violence and belonging; themes that are also developed in Mark
Glanville's memoir, *The Goldberg Variations* (2003), a text that I shall
discuss in the conclusion to this chapter. This exploration of Jewish
masculinity and teenage football hooliganism presents an intriguing
counterpoint to *Sixty-Six*. In Glanville's account, football fandom
leads to the forging of thrilling and dangerous bonds rather than to a
moment of unified national celebration. The narrative suggests that
for Glanville, and many men reflecting on their Jewish identities in
today's Britain, issues of belonging are complicated and potentially
fraught. Allegiances to football clubs, families, religious identities
and nationalities are often, in such accounts, plural, shifting and unresolved, rather than singular and static identifications.

Clever Jews, hyper-sexual Jews, neurotic Jews, wandering Jews,
passing Jews; noses, foreskins, beards, spectacles, money. These associations, and many more, all play their part in creating an idea of the

Jewish man in today's Britain. The first part of this chapter sets out a brief context for thinking about some of these images by looking at the ways in which Jewish masculinity has been constructed historically and culturally. The rest of the discussion focuses on examples from recent texts.

Pathologized, revitalized and analysed: Jewish masculinity in context

From premodern images of menstruating Jewish men, to images of the orientalized Jew of early modern literature, to the racialized and pathologized Jew of modernity, Jewish men have been seen as embodying unstable and somewhat dubious versions of masculinity. Literary studies such as James Shapiro's *Shakespeare and the Jews* (1996), Matthew Biberman's, *Masculinity, Anti-Semitism and Early Modern English Literature* (2004) and Carol Margaret Davison's *Anti-Semitism and British Gothic Literature* (2004), among others, show that the Jewish man has been depicted in highly charged and often contradictory ways throughout English literary history. The depiction of characters as diverse as Shylock, Fagin, Daniel Deronda and Leopold Bloom, demonstrate some of the ways in which English literature has been intrigued and somewhat unsettled by Jewish masculinity. Throughout this history the Jewish man has been presented as both asexual and hyper-sexual, both weakly passive and dangerously predatory, effeminized and grossly monstrous. The Jewish man is, in these terms, an ambiguous, overdetermined and shifting signifier.

Such ambiguity was especially disturbing within an Enlightenment context in which fixing meanings became imperative; an impulse that intensified further as the modern pseudoscientific discourses of race and sex developed towards the end of the nineteenth century. A confusing signifier such as the Jew became a matter for interrogation with a view to classification. If this process of categorization produced an understanding of the Jew as abject, then so be it. As Tamar Garb has explained, 'Jewishness came to be conceived not as a matter of belief but as a racial identity, one which could be observed, measured, understood and pathologized'.[4] Where exactly the Jew fitted into a schema in which 'civilized' values were based on a paradigm of the white Christian male was unclear and so 'he' became, instead a convenient touchstone for defining a norm.

The Jewish body, which could be seen to straddle a boundary between black and white, masculine and feminine, excess and lack,

was a signifier that both challenged and assisted differentiation. As Sander Gilman argues, 'the very analysis of the nature of the Jewish body, in the broader culture or in medicine, has always been linked to establishing the difference (and dangerousness) of the Jew'.[5] In identifying this difference it becomes necessary, as much of Gilman's work has demonstrated, to imagine the Jewish body as essentially and ineffably other. The Jewish woman is often absent at an explicit level from these discussions, but ideas about women fundamentally underpin representations of Jewish masculinity. Garb charts some of the contradictory quality of such evaluations:

> Jewish intelligence and emotionalism could occasionally figure as positive 'Jewish traits', but they could just as easily feed into a mythology of the Jew as excessive, dangerous, and suspect. Indeed, the overriding perception of the Jew's captivity in his own body, his physicality, functioned as a symbol of his baseness in the European imagination. Locked in his body, unable to transcend the flesh, he becomes feminized, castrated, weak. (26)

So, in terms of the Jew's corporeality, 'his' excess, and 'his' threat to 'civilized' values, an idea of embodied femininity is vital to the construction of Jewish masculinity. If Jews were not really men, then they were, by implication, forms of women. These ideas stemmed from medieval and early modern accounts which routinely depicted Jewish men as both dangerously hyper-masculine and simultaneously effeminized. As James Shapiro explains, 'when it came to Jews, the boundaries between male and female were often seen as quite slippery'.[6] Such ideas gained momentum in 1903 when Otto Weininger's *Sex and Character* was published. This notorious pseudoscientific thesis presented Jews as defective beings who were fundamentally lacking in manliness. If, in the terms of the day, Jews were like women, then they were irrational, embodied, insecure, unstable, deceptive, unhealthy, soulless and sexualized. The book became a best-seller.[7]

Boyarin locates this period as the point at which the modern Jewish male was 'invented', arguing that 'the Westernization process for Jews...was one in which *mentsh* as Jewish male ideal became largely abandoned for a dawning ideal of the "New Jewish Man," and "the Muscle-Jew"' (37). A value system in which the exemplar of Jewish manhood had been embodied by the yeshiva scholar thus became reconfigured in relation to other paradigms of masculinity. For Jews, the ideal of muscularity, a more active, physical and vigorous version of masculinity than seen within the rabbinical tradition, can be traced back to the Zionist ideology of the late nineteenth century and in particular the thinking of Max Nordau on 'degeneracy'.[8] From its inception, Zionism had idealized a form of reinvigorated Jewish masculinity based on healthy agrarianism, collective purpose and newly nationalized vitality. As Cooper and Morrison explain, for Zionists, Israel meant that 'Jews would be rescued from their role in the diaspora as hunchbacked, obsequious, dependent, assimilated, backwardly religious traders and moneylenders, to become proud, upright, handsome and secular pioneers, farmers and soldiers'.[9]

Following the losses and trauma of the Holocaust, explicitly macho values such as militarism, toughness and aggression became significant within a new discourse of Jewish masculinity and with the establishment of the State of Israel in 1948 these earlier Zionist discourses of re-masculinization take on a highly-charged tone. As Todd Presner puts it, drawing also from the work of Paul Breines and Warren Rosenberg on 'tough Jews':

> Never again, we are told, will Jews go like lambs to the slaughter. Never again, we are told, can we let down our guard... After 2,000 years of victimization, a regenerated 'muscle Jewry' will fight back and take the land that once was theirs.[10]

This is a powerful blueprint for a new conception of Jewish masculinity. However, this idealization of toughness, although notable, is not the only version of Jewish masculine identity that has developed in the post-war context.

Victor Jeleniewski Seidler recalls his own experience of being part of a post-war immigrant generation in Britain. As Presner noted, this generation had grown up being told that Holocaust Jews had gone to their deaths passively. Seidler recognizes that 'this can create a particular intensity in Jewish men who can feel a need to prove themselves "man enough"'.[11] However, rather than seeing this supposed disempowerment as an impetus towards aggression and military prowess, Seidler instead reflects on the ways in which masculinities have been culturally constructed. In this he follows from the explorations of Jewish masculinity we find in early works in men's studies, such as in *A Mensch Among Men* (1988), a seminal collection of essays edited by the American, Harry Brod.[12] Brod, like Boyarin, Seidler, and others of this generation, is self-reflexive in his approach, admitting that he writes from the experience of being an outsider. In these accounts vulnerability is not necessarily seen as a weakness but is instead a starting point for cultural exploration. 'As a child and adolescent', Brod recalls, 'I did not fit the mainstream male image. I was an outsider, not an athlete but an intellectual, fat, shy and with a stutter for many years' (7). In noting the complexity of his later involvement in the feminist movement, he recognizes how his Jewishness and his masculinity have been imbricated, reaching the realization that 'I must reevaluate what it really means to be a Jew and a man, a Jewish man, in the contemporary world' (8). These approaches to Jewish masculinity, share a genesis and methodology with feminist theory. They have, in recent years, also been developed in terms of queer theory and this work has impacted significantly on current theorizations of Jewish identities.[13]

So, although the 'tough Jew' is a potent image in reconfiguring Jewish masculinity, it is not the only way that Jewish masculinity has been represented within contemporary culture. It coexists alongside other equally pervasive images, such as that of the neurotic Jewish man, which draw from American stereotypes popularized by, for example, Woody Allen in film and Larry David on TV. In a recent British incarnation this can be seen in Simon Amstell's self-characterization in the BBC television sitcom, *Grandma's House*. Here Amstells' self-conscious construction of a gay Jewish sexuality becomes another factor in refiguring a contemporary version of British-Jewish masculinity. Such depictions, which draw from stereotypically familiar Jewish male traits such as anxiety, self-obsession and sexual insecurity, are arguably a response, as well as an antithesis, to the image of the tough Jew. These ostensibly anxious Jewish men are quick-witted, sharp and self-aware. They present what seems to be weakness; but in the ways that they play on and with ideas of inadequacy they suggest an alternative kind of empowerment for the Jewish man.

Contemporary representations of British-Jewish masculinity both draw from and refuse earlier stereotypes. In a literary context we can see the influence of dominant post-war American writers such as Saul Bellow and Philip Roth on British-Jewish male authors such as Howard Jacobson, Clive Sinclair, Adam Thirlwell and David Baddiel, but also the ways in which these writers, and others such as Andrew Sanger, William Sutcliffe and Jeremy Gavron are challenging aspects of that tradition.[14] I start this discussion by looking at Howard Jacobson's *Kalooki Nights*. Jacobson has been cast as 'the English Philip Roth'. But, flipping round the obvious comparison, Jacobson has said that he prefers to think of himself as 'the Jewish Jane Austen'.[15] It is a typically wry repositioning, which, as it wryly feminizes his authorial status, also foregrounds his Jewishness in relation to the English literary tradition. In a perhaps subtle allusion, *Kalooki Nights* even draws in its title and its central theme from a running Austen motif; the card game. However, as Jacobson explains, kalooki 'a version of rummy much favoured by Jews – Jews, Jews, Jews – on account (though not all Jews would agree) of its innate argumentativeness', is far from polite.[16] In his presentation of fraught gender relations, messy family lives and unsettling sexual desires, Jacobson thus rewrites the English novel of manners, turning it instead into a particularly British-Jewish comedy of bad manners.

Sex and sensibility: masculinity in Howard Jacobson's *Kalooki Nights*

In *Kalooki Nights* Jacobson presents a full frontal examination of the interrelationship between masculinity and British-Jewishness. The novel is written from the perspective of Max Glickman, shifting between his complicated present life in London and his childhood in 1950s Crumpsall Park, Manchester. It opens as Max, a heterosexual Jewish cartoonist, reflects on Jewish masculinity. He describes how he once had a job imitating the gay-erotica of Tom of Finland, but notes that he could never quite capture, 'the straining bulge' in the trousers with conviction (3). 'In the end', he confesses:

> I had to admit that this was because I had never worn denim or leather myself, and didn't understand the physics of the pressure from the inside. Jewish men wear loose, comfortable trousers with a double pleat. And maybe, in chilly weather a cardigan on top. It is considered inappropriate by Jews to show strangers of either sex the outline of your glans penis. (4)

Here the Jewish man, safely ensconced in 'comfortable trousers', is presented as modest, serious and distinctly lacking in erotic charge. But Jacobson makes explicit what is implicit within this talk of Jewish trousers, circumcision, explaining that 'the world hates and fears a man who makes a palaver of his private parts. I think that's the issue: not the foreskin, the palaver' (6). Much of Jacobson's writing plays on this idea of loosely contained male Jewish sexuality but, far from presenting conformity to a normative heterosexuality, his novels often explore what could be described as the queer potential of Jewish male sexuality, especially in terms of masochistic erotic desire. A forensic interrogation of Jewish masculinity is central to this.

Kalooki Nights presents a series of opposing and overlapping versions of Jewish masculinity. They range from Max's father, Jack Glickman, 'a boxer whose nose bled easily, an atheist who railed at

God, and a communist who liked to buy his wife expensive shoes' (7); Tsedraiter Ike (one of five 'Uncle Ikes'), 'flabby, one-toothed, wet about the mouth, discoloured, as though he had been dipped in ink at birth' (14); Max's 'genitally besotted' friend, Errol Tobias (6); and the Washinsky family (the father, Selick, and the brothers, Asher and Manny). Manny, who, as it emerges later, will one day murder his parents as they are sleeping in their beds, prompts many of the most difficult questions that lie at the heart the novel.

In their sexual desires, romantic vulnerabilities, ideological assertions, religious affiliations, social hesitations and cultural burdens, these characters describe various and interconnected modes of masculinity. At the centre of this Venn diagrammatic exploration of Jewish masculinity is the father-son relationship, something Jacobson also explores with precision in *The Mighty Walzer* (1999). Selick Washinsky is remembered by Max as 'a stunted growth of perturbations not a man', a pale frummer, wrapped in shawls, hunched over a sewing machine, too miserly to pay for electric lighting. 'Indulge my genius for racial stereotyping', Max declares. 'See him bent, airless, avid' (61). And then, in the exact spirit of the book, he calls into question his own description, modifying but not entirely erasing the excesses of the caricaturist: 'Piffle, all of it, but that's how I was brought up to see him and continue to remember him' (61). But what endures for Max are his memories of Selick as a father. Max envies the Washinsky men for the strong and solemn male bond that, in distinct contrast to his own family, they seem to share. Seeing Manny, he recalls:

> Out with his father on their way to synagogue, both of them spruced up darkly to attend on God, urgent in their errand, two men engaged in what never for a moment occurred to them was *not* the proper business of men, joined as I was never joined with *my* father, bonded in abstraction...I wished my life were more like Manny's. (38)

For the young Max, these Washinsky men recall the 'sissy' Jews that were esteemed within the rabbinical tradition. Max and his own father would never be seen walking to synagogue with such Jewishly masculine purpose. The resolutely secular Jack Glickman is a self-styled new Jew, an atheist who seeks to reinvent the future for post-Holocaust Jews through, 'a kind of muscular Zionism of the mind' (18).

Jacobson expertly both constructs and deconstructs Jack's masculinity, as seen through his son's eyes. In a revealing example, Max spends some time explaining 'epistaxis', the condition that causes his father's nose to bleed easily and profusely, and renders him singularly unsuited to a career in boxing. This debilitating nasal vulnerability is just one detail within a range of suggestive novelistic description but it can also be read as an ironic allusion to old ideas about Jewish male menstruation.[17] The suggestion is of an ambiguous kind of Jewish masculinity and the male Jew is thus effeminized by association. Jack Glickman is both tough and breakable. The epistaxic condition means that he is relieved of active combat duties in the War. Instead he takes charge of the gym.

Max grows up surrounded by his mother's circle of kalooki playing women and his father's friends, a group conspicuous in their rejection of the stereotype of effeminized Jewish masculinity. As I discussed in Chapter 4, the stereotypical lack of affinity between Jews and the English countryside is a stock motif, and one that has been used elsewhere by Jacobson to comic effect. However, these men are vigorous in their robust embrace of outdoor pursuits. They are 'the living proof that Jews too could hike and ramble and love the countryside' (62).[18] As Max recalls:

> What lungs they had, these all-talking, all-walking, un-Asianised, de-Bibled Jews. There was scarcely air left for me to breathe when five or more of them were gathered in our house, so much of it did they inhale. The new Jew, straight of back and undevious of principle, with pollen in his hair. (62)

Again, in a novel in which characters are consistently inconsistent, this group of Jewish hikers rarely leaves the front room of the Crumpsall Park semi: 'it was too comfortable where they were, opening the gates of the ghetto, imagining Jews without Jewishness, dunking biscuits into tea' (68). These characterizations of Jewish masculinity are ironic but also suggest more serious issues relating to the models of Jewish manhood that were available to the young Max. The underlying question for Max, observing these variations on Jewish masculinity, is what kind of Jewish man could he become?

The question structures the novel's account of father-son relationship. By far the most common thread in Jewish explorations of father-son relationships is the bar mitzvah, the rite of passage into Jewish manhood. From Jack Rosenthal's *Bar Mitzvah Boy* (1976) to the film *Sixty-Six* (2006) this is an occasion on which the Jewish boy must reflect on what it means to be a Jewish man. For Max, it does not quite happen. His determinedly atheist father would not allow it, asserting that "'You become a man when you've performed a manly action'" (121). So, instead of initiating his son into the world of Judaic masculinity, he buys Max a pair of boxing gloves. As father and son spar ineffectually, ending up in an uncomfortable bear hug, Max remembers it as 'one of the saddest days of my life' (122). It is from this point that he dates his father's descent into terminal illness.

Alongside this unfulfilling entry into the world of men, and the early loss of his father, the reader learns about Max's sexual development. The writing here is bold, relentless and somewhat disturbing. In what are perhaps the most challenging sections of the novel we read, at length, about Max's masturbatory inner world. These sections present an elaborate erotic narrative based on stories about Ilse Koch, known as the 'Bitch of Buchenwald' and involve in equal measure the repeated humiliations and arousals of a young Jewish man who is subjected to Koch's punishments. In the darkly comic structure of the novel it is not a coincidence that the adult Max engages in a series of painful relationships with cruel, nearly always gentile and, at times, explicitly antisemitic women. His desires, it is suggested, are determined in these early fantasies of abjection. As the novel recounts the ways in which stories and images of Holocaust atrocity were shared with his childhood friends, Errol and Manny, it implies that perhaps this is not just the manifestation of a personal sexual pathology but, potentially, a formative element within the sexual development of many Jewish men of this generation.

On his death bed his father raises the subject of Max's cartoon history of Jewish anguish, *Five Thousand Years of Bitterness* (a work he had started with Manny under the collective name of the Brothers Stroganoff). Jack admits that it was not the sexual fantasy to which he objected, but the way in which his son had drawn every Jew as 'synonymous with suffering' (205). Max, however, has a different understanding. He wants to protest that Jack 'hadn't taken adequate cognisance of their hard-ons', which stood, 'artistically for the virility of the Jewish people in the face of adversity. You know, a cartoonist's way of saying you cannot keep us down. But there are some conversations you don't have with a father' (205). Whether the reader is supposed to trust the reliability of Max's self-justification and read erotic fantasy as resistance is questionable. But there is perhaps in this novel, and throughout Jacobson's work in general, an understanding of the complexity as well as the absurdity of the priapic Jewish man. When such unspeakable desires are spoken, probed and scrutinized, the reader, who is implicated whether through laughter, discomfort or analysis, is placed in an uneasy position. We are forced to consider the relationships between power and sex, history and fantasy, desire and its displacement, that inform many representations of gendered Jewishness.

Jacobson speaks from the point of view of the post-war generation and Max's masculinity is shaped from the particular experience of growing up in the Jewish suburbs of Manchester in the 1950s. The men in and around his family are products of the war. They are formed, in their rejection as well as in their embrace of Jewishness, by their closeness to the Holocaust. As the narrative unfolds, it becomes apparent that even as an adult, living in the cosmopolitan London media world of the early twenty-first century, Max is never far away from these aspects of his past. Giles Coren's novel *Winkler* (2006) explores some similar issues, from a younger and more distant perspective. I want now to look at *Winkler* to think about the ways it asks provocative questions about Jewishness, the Holocaust and the representation of masculinities for an increasingly disconnected generation of British Jews.

Jews who play cricket: Englishness and Jewish masculinity in Giles Coren's *Winkler*

Like *Kalooki Nights*, *Winkler* debunks any facile connection to the past. It presents a dark, witty and potentially offensive exploration of what it means to be a British Jew today. Unlike Jacobson's Max, who is brought up in the relatively insular Jewish community of Crumpsall Park, the antihero of the book, Winkler, (a name that itself connotes a comically diminutive masculinity) is isolated from the outset. The novel begins by placing him within an archetypal scene of Englishness: a public school Fathers' cricket match, raising the issues of identity, belonging and male relationships that will structure the narrative as a whole. It opens with the statement, 'Winkler is an Englishman'.[19] Winkler on the brink of his thirteenth birthday (which, in another example of the un-passed rite of passage, is not marked by a bar mitzvah), is fatherless. He has no parents, just an elderly Jewish grandfather.[20] As he stands in the cricket ground, looking over a quintessentially English churchyard, he muses on his otherness. Where the other boys have deep roots, embedded in the land, the establishment and the traditions of the English upper classes, he wonders: 'What was he entitled to? What could he have?' (3).

Winkler, like Max, is also a kind of caricaturist. He sketches stereotypes in his own crude attempts at self-representation. And, as with *Kalooki Nights*, part of the work of Coren's narrative is to challenge such clichés. As Winkler recalls the summer of 1982, he sees himself as he was then: a short, myopic boy, dressed in his cricket whites, who, at a point of profound disconnection from his immediate surroundings, creates a fantasy of origins. The not quite 13-year old, Winkler thus reimagines an ancestry which is located in a nostalgized Eastern European shtetl, a place populated by bearded, side-locked scholars and heavily-burdened potato farmers. However, faced with the immediate dilemma of needing to produce a father for the Fathers' Match, the young Winkler is jolted out of this reverie. As he assesses it, 'having no parents was marginally better than having Jewish parents' (10). His grandfather suggests a series of father-substitutes ranging from Maurice Mogelbaum (a physically grotesque poker-playing friend), Sammy Patel (who they decide would not be convincing in the role), and English Dave (whose father ran the fish shop, and had lost an arm, or a leg; he's not sure). They decide eventually, on Ginger Bill, a vivacious Jew 'who showed up at weddings and Bar mitzvahs and got very drunk and shouted and danced on tables' (12). The children liked him, Winkler recalls, 'because he behaved so much like a goy that it helped them pretend these occasions were fun and normal in 1970s Britain, and not merely the strange atavistic howling of a moribund race grumbling itself finally to death' (12). Ginger Bill ends up putting in a riotous, but triumphant, performance at the Fathers' Match. It becomes legendary.

The adult Winkler leads a jaded, purposeless and lacklustre life in London. He is a misanthrope; disgusted by the human condition in general and fat people in particular. One night, in the dank and putrid-smelling basement of his shared house, he encounters Wallenstein, 'The Jew Who Lived Under the Stairs'. In a long, rambling chapter titled, 'What Wallenstein Did in the War', the old man tells him his story. As Wallenstein relates a tale of shocking brutality, recounting how he had survived the war by joining a resistance movement in Nazi Poland, Winkler's attention drifts, recalling his early sexual experiences and wondering whether he really looked Jewish. 'His nose was relatively small and very straight', he thinks. 'He did not gesticulate too much when he spoke and he rarely suffered from sinus trouble ... but then of course, there was his cock' (150). When his attention returns to the old man's tale, Wallenstein is explaining the horrific circumstances of his own penis, which had been butchered by 'a bad *mohel*' at circumcision. He goes on to recount how as a vengeful partisan he had enacted gruesome circumcisions on captured Nazis. As Winkler observes, 'the more grim the memory the greater seemed Wallenstein's relish in description' (164).

Wallenstein's story sets off a rage in Winkler and intensifies his latent identity crisis. As he tries to explain the horrors of the Holocaust to his crass work colleagues he is appalled by their insensitivity. However, when one suggests that 'people get a hard-on for the death-porn of it all' (223), Winkler has to admit that he had found Wallenstein's story sexually arousing, recalling 'how many times he had felt an erection uncoil itself' during its telling (223). The ways in which Jacobson and Coren explore the possibly thrilling effect of such sexual thoughts is uncomfortable. As Omer Bartov has written, in relation to growing up in 1960s Israel, 'nothing could be a greater taboo than deriving sexual pleasure from pornography in the context of the Holocaust; hence nothing could be as exciting'.[21] Such taboo-laden territory necessitates a delicate ethical and artistic negotiation in order to raise questions about the complex relationships between desire and identity. Both Max and Winkler have to evaluate their identities in terms of their Jewishness and their male sexualities; but, as British Jews of the immediate post-war generation and the generation after, they have a confused connection to the Holocaust. Winkler's grandfather arrives at a blunt understanding of the younger generation's haphazard approach to the past: 'You were never remotely interested in being a Jew', he points out. 'Never. And now suddenly you're Primo Levi the second' (234). The Holocaust for both Max and Winkler, is, to a greater and lesser extent, close enough to trouble them and far away enough to enter the realms of erotic imagination. When, incidentally, the adult Max watches the 1970s pornographic film, *Ilse: She-Wolf of the SS*, he is disappointed. It fails miserably to live up to his adolescent fantasies.

Following Wallenstein's tale of Holocaust brutality, Winkler embarks on a catastrophic chain of events which include pushing a fat woman under a train, masturbating in front of a blind woman, and being sodomized by an Australian woman called Albuquerque (a scene for which Coren won a 'bad sex' award). As the narrative unfolds, or rather unravels, the veracity of all of these events is called into question. Winkler's grandfather's suspicion that Wallenstein's story was a fiction turns out to be correct. He was, in actuality, a Polish gentile with a dubious war history. And, to add to the sense of increasing uncertainty about all identities within the narrative, it emerges that Winkler's mother was not Jewish. So he is not really Jewish at all.

As his sense of self is called into question, Winkler comes to realize that identifications are complex and often contradictory. The story had opened with a cricket match. Towards the end of the novel, Winkler's Uncle (Ginger) Bill teases out the uneasy relationship between Jewishness and Englishness. The exchange cuts to the heart of the book's exploration of belonging and identity:

'But they didn't really make an Englishman of you, did they?'

'Didn't they?'

'Oh come on'. He says. 'You're a Jew who plays cricket. That's not the same thing at all'. (368)

The book's recognition that identity is a series of shifting positions, rather than the summation of distinct essence, is important, but Bill's statement also reveals an understanding that some identities ('the Jew', the 'Englishman') are culturally charged to such an extent that they are neither comparable nor interchangeable.

The narrative, which has ranged from the puerile to the philosophical, the postmodern to the pastoral, closes with a strange sense of resolution as it becomes a more developed meditation on the interplay between Englishness and Jewishness. Winkler realizes he is both and neither. Reflecting on all these issues, he thinks, perhaps rather hopefully, that 'now everything was resolved. Everything. The legal and the spiritual, the physical and the familial, the social and the sexual' (414). The two texts that I consider next, in the final part of this chapter, also seek reconciliation of such apparently disparate parts. Both Andrew Sanger's *The J-Word* and Mark Glanville's *The Goldberg Variations*, one a novel, one a memoir, circle around similar issues relating to fathers and sons, sexuality, violence and belonging, in order to reach an understanding of the different ways in which one might become a Jewish man in contemporary Britain.

Violence and variation: Andrew Sanger's *The J-Word* and Mark Glanville's *The Goldberg Variations*

The J-Word presents three generations of men, each trying to reconcile their own relationship to their Jewishness, their masculinity and the ways in which these aspects of identity are negotiated in terms of Englishness in the early twenty-first century. They each embody different stages of a process of estrangement, confusion and resolution. And they each ultimately present a sense of excess, signalling that which cannot be absorbed within a singular consideration of identity.

Jack Silver is an 80-year-old, committedly secular, Jew. As the novel opens, Jack is a widower, living in a typically English village on the South coast, trying to come to terms with his increasingly emasculated status as an elderly Jewish man. In many respects he conforms to the stereotype of an aging Jewish intellectual, but his experience of antisemitism as a boy has resulted in an intense discomfort about his Jewishness. In ways that are typical for many of this generation of British Jews, he wants nothing more than for his son, Simon, and grandson, Danny, to escape what he sees as the inexorable taint of Jewishness. With an enthusiasm, stemming from a deep insecurity, which is redolent of Jack Rosenblum in *Mr Rosenblum's List,* 'he embraced England, Englishness and the English language with a mighty passion. He wanted his family to breathe this temperate air and flourish, thrust its roots deeply into this cool nourishing soil and become part of it'.[22]

During the course of the novel Jack undergoes a transformative reconnection to his Jewish past. When Simon, who is working overseas, suffers a nervous breakdown and his wife goes to be with him, Jack is asked to come to their home in Golders Green to look after his grandson. The family represent subtle permutations of Jewish identity. Danny is largely ignorant about his Jewishness. His mother, Penny, is Jewish by birth but disengaged from this aspect of her background. As the narrative unfolds, it becomes apparent that Danny's father, Simon, has developed an identity crisis about his own Jewishness. This is complicated by the fact that his own mother (Jack's wife) was not in fact Jewish. So, he occupies a strange position within the matrilineal tradition of Jewish designation: although both his father and his son are Jewish, Simon is not. I shall return to broader issues relating to contemporary explorations of half-Jewish or Jew-ish identities in Chapter 8, but here I want to retain a focus on how these questions of partial identification impact on the representation of Jewish masculinity.

As Simon has recently begun to explore his (not) Jewishness, so his son who has hitherto been brought up with little familial awareness of Jewishness, is left with a rather confused understanding of his own identification. When Danny and Jack go out for a pizza, an inter-generational tension about some of these complex variations of Jewishness erupts. Danny tells Jack that he does not want ham on his pizza. Simon has told him about kosher and non-kosher foods. Jack's angry response typifies an internal contradiction. As he vehemently rejects his grandson's interest in claiming a Jewish identity, so he expresses the rejection in stereotypically Jewish terms: '"Jewish? I should be Jewish?" ... "Who says we're Jewish?" ... "Oy yoy yoy yoy! I have failed. I wanted to be English and have an English grandson"' (206). Jewishness, for Jack, is both defining and indefinable. It is something that is 'said', suggesting, alongside a sense of accusation, a constructed, performative type of identity; but it is also something that in its essence is incompatible with Englishness, which is represented in many ways as a distinct and unattainable difference.

Here Sanger's narrative brings to mind the short story, 'My CV', by Clive Sinclair.[23] In this obliquely dystopian narrative a presumably Jewish man, based in Eastern England, takes his wife and young son on a trip to some sites of supposed historic interest. As the journey develops, through bleak fenland to the abandoned industrial sites of middle England, it becomes apparent that antisemitism permeates this forlorn topography. An awareness of this Jew-hating heritage swells within the increasingly fevered consciousness of the narrator. Although he has named his son 'Pippen', after the local English apple, Jewishness becomes an increasingly uncontainable and intrusive difference. As he tells his son about the grim ways in which Jewishness is embedded into English history, the following inter-generational exchange reveals a fatalistic sense of both connection and disconnection:

> 'Daddy', asks Pippen, 'how come you know so much about Jews?'
> 'I used to live among them', I reply.[24]

The story, which has a darkly timeless quality, ends with a knock at the door and the narrator's final cry: 'the antisemites are without. We must hide!' (118).

Although written in an entirely different register to Sinclair's mordantly ironic story, Sanger's narrative also places antisemitism, particularly in relation to violence, at the centre of his exploration of Jewish masculinity. In the somewhat unsettling terms of the novel, this is what brings a seemingly authentic Jewishness into focus. At a pivotal point in the narrative Jack stumbles upon a disturbing street scene in which an elderly Hasidic man is being assaulted by four young white men. When Jack rushes in to help, the attackers turn on him. The assault is described from Jack's perspective in a blow-by-blow account of vicious and sustained Jew-hating violence. The attackers are bluntly drawn thugs who, as they beat him, taunt the old man with shouts of 'Die, yid!'. In this way the trauma reconnects Jack to his earlier formative memories of antisemitic violence which are never far from the surface. The antisemites are then simultaneously 'without' and within. 'Unable to see clearly' Jack recalls, 'I seem to hear a chorus of Yid! Yid! Yid! Pounding in my ears, echoing through a lifetime that I'm afraid is about to end' (113).

In an unlikely turn of events the attack is later avenged by Yoav, a local Israeli mechanic, and his sidekick Ehud. Jack tracks down his attackers and in a sustained and brutal scene, his Israeli accomplices beat them up, using Krav Maga, an Israeli army form of contact fighting. The Israelis are, in contrast to Jack, embodiments of new 'muscle' Jews. Yoav and Ehud are young, strong and brimming over with a kind of deranged confidence and a vengeful masculine vitality. Jack, old, frail and unresolved about his identity is rendered emasculate. Jack is an intellectual. The Israelis are fighters. Yoav, it emerges, is the more psychotically violent of the two. Like the bogus Jewish partisan fantasized by Wallenstein, he threatens to circumcise the 'boys', to 'make you into proper Jews like us' (227). This section of the novel is an uncomfortable read for a number of reasons: the depiction of violence, and the concurrent representation of brutish working-class men, is reductive; the plot develops in implausible ways; and the section in which Jack debates the rights and wrongs of antisemitism with one of the attackers stretches credulity even further.

As the novel attempts to resolve various identity crises in Jewish masculinity it picks up anxieties about identity that are inflected in different ways through the three generations. Danny's bar mitzvah is perhaps inevitably the point at which tensions begin to dissolve in order to begin a process of healing. However, the resolutions that are reached at the end of the narrative remain somewhat incomplete. Jack finally accepts his Jewishness, but the suggestion is that his life has been damaged by his disavowal of identity and that this damage has been passed on to the next generation. Simon reaches a compromise and finds a way in which to be Jewish (although technically he is not), but his mental health is still fragile. Danny will experience a different and perhaps healthier sort of Jewish manhood to both his father and his grandfather. His Jewishness, it is suggested, will be partial but not incomplete.

The excesses produced by these resolutions are thought-provoking. Antisemitic violence is presented as a real and current threat to contemporary Jews in Britain. Jack's rejection of Jewishness and Simon's ensuing psychological breakdown suggest that not being connected to a distinct heritage, even within the diffuse conditions of contemporary Britain, can create surprisingly fragile subjectivities. Finally, the way that the narrative has presented British-Jewish masculinity as vulnerable to crisis from within and without leaves a disconcerting sense of irresolution.

Many of these themes are worked through in Mark Glanville's memoir: *The Goldberg Variations*. The subtitle, From *Football Hooligan to Opera Singer*, suggests some of the interlocking and contradictory aspects of identity that Glanville explores.[25] Here the non-fictional form, which combines aspects of memoir, meditation and confession, allows for a nuanced reflection on identity in process. Glanville charts four variations: the football hooligan, the Oxford classist, the opera singer and the Jew. Mark Glanville is the son of Brian Glanville, the football-writer and novelist. In his son's account of growing up, 'King Brian' was a womanizer, a charmer and a competitive father. Like Simon, in *The J-Word*, Glanville's story is marked by a sense of confusion about his Jewishness. Once again, in a family in which his mother was not technically Jewish, the father in many ways possesses the Jewish identity which then has to be claimed, in a somewhat oedipally inflected struggle, by the son. So, the memoir is about Jewishness, but it is equally about masculinity.

Football is seminal in the development of Glanville's sense of identification and connection. Matches are remembered in relation to the edgy masculinity that pervaded the terraces and a concomitant sense of coming home within such an environment. He recalls his first experience of the terraces, explaining how 'the atmosphere was charged with a sense of menace that left me shivering as I exited the ground, not with fear but elation … Feeling that I'd successfully completed a rite of passage, I experienced a warm tingle of acceptance' (27). Glanville's story is quite particular in the way that it relates to Jewishness but it can also be linked to more general aspects of British masculinity towards the end of the twentieth century. Some of his reminiscences, for example, can be read alongside Nick Hornby's *Fever Pitch* (1992) which, in its account of obsessive football fandom, also presents an exploration of masculine identity in crisis.[26] Like Glanville, Hornby is in many respects a middle-class outsider in the predominantly working-class culture of Arsenal supporters of the time. Like Glanville, Hornby describes a difficult relationship with his father and a profound sense of alienation. And, like Glanville, masculinity is placed at the centre of his fixation on the communal connection of football. He recalls how at his first match he was struck by 'the overwhelming *maleness* of it all' (11). Unlike Glanville, however, Hornby is not also attempting to work out what it means to be a Jewish man.

Issues of belonging and masculinity are clearly not related only to Jewishness. There are many ways in which to belong or to be excluded in contemporary Britain. And there are many ways in which to be troubled by the conflicts and confusions that inform identities. But Jewishness, as I have argued throughout this chapter, inflects these themes in certain respects. *The Goldberg Variations* brings together themes that have underpinned the chapter as a whole. Fissured Jewish identities, fraught father-son relationships, antisemitism, sexual insecurity, Englishness, sport and belonging; these themes all structure Glanville's account of becoming a Jewish man in contemporary Britain. But, the type of Jewish man he will become is presented as both an essential connection and as a performed identity. When he finds himself drawn to the unfamiliar setting of a synagogue he feels 'an almost physical sensation of belonging' (224), but he realizes that he must also learn how to behave within such a context. Such knowledge is not innate.

The last section of Glanville's memoir, which focuses on another key Jewish ritual of manhood, a marriage ceremony, is presented as an answer to the troubling stages that have come before. Glanville describes a sense of completion in his marriage to Julia, a Jewish woman, but he recognizes that identities are always, to a certain extent, in flux. On his wedding day he recalls that he felt himself to be somehow impersonating the role of a Jew, noting that 'as the day progressed, my gentile features began to show through the Jewish mask' (253). Throughout his account he has worn a number of masks and performed several roles. These are all variations on masculine identities. Jewishness is, in a sense, as inherent or as conditional as any of them.

At the end of the memoir, Glanville returns to a Jewish joke with which he had opened his story. The joke is based on a parody of Abey, a heavily accented, self-aggrandizing, 'ghetto Jew', who is duped into buying an ill-fitting suit. The point of the joke is manifold. But the key aspect, here, is the way in which Glanville's charismatic, anglicized, un-dupable, Jewish father, routinely performed this set piece, a performance which united the family in 'an unspoken sense of belonging engendered by the joke and its teller'(2). On his wedding day, Glanville's wife despairs over her new husband's badly fitted suit. 'Nu?', he responds, recognizing that his different identities might not be so tragic after all: 'like the stock hero in a thousand Jewish jokes.... I'd long since given up hope of finding a suit that actually fitted' (254). It is a moment of ironic awareness which suggests that there are many ways in which to be a Jewish man in contemporary Britain. Telling a joke that shows an understanding of the provisional but strangely compelling nature of identity is perhaps as good as any.

Notes

1. Daniel Boyarin, *Unheroic Conduct: The Rise of Heterosexuality and the Invention of the Jewish Man* (Berkeley: University of California Press, 1997), p.xiii.

2. Paul Weiland, dir., *Sixty-Six* (2006).

3. The 2003 film *Wondrous Oblivion* directed by Paul Morrison is also worth noting in this context. It is set in 1960s London and looks at issues of immigrant identities in another coming of age story for a Jewish boy. Here the exploration of identity, sport and Englishness is focused on cricket.

4. Tamar Garb, 'Modernity, Identity, Textuality', in Linda Nochlin and Tamar Garb, eds, *The Jew in the Text: Modernity and the Construction of Identity* (London: Thames and Hudson, 1995), pp.20–30, p.22.

5. Sander Gilman, *The Jew's Body* (London: Routledge, 1991), p.39.

6. James Shapiro, *Shakespeare and the Jews* (New York: Colombia University Press, 1996), p.38.

7. For a useful discussion of Weininger see Ritchie Robertson, 'Historicizing Weininger: the Nineteenth-Century German Image of the Feminized Jew', in Bryan Cheyette and Laura Marcus, eds, *Modernity, Culture and 'the Jew'* (London: Polity, 1998), pp.23–39.

8. As Todd Presner notes, like the 'muscular Christianity' movement in Victorian England, Nordau's idea 'can be understood as a call for corporeal and spiritual regeneration', *Muscular Judaism: The Jewish Body and the Politics of Regeneration* (London: Routledge, 2007), p.1.

9. Howard Cooper and Paul Morrison, *A Sense of Belonging: Dilemmas of British Jewish Identity* (London: Weidenfeld and Nicolson, 1991), p.95.

10. Presner, p.xvii.

11. Victor Jeleniewski Seidler, *Shadows of the Shoah: Jewish Identity and Belonging* (Oxford: Berg, 2000), p.50.

12. Harry Brod, ed., *A Mensch Among Men: Explorations in Jewish Masculinity* (California: Crossing Press, 1988). For a more recent consideration see Harry Brod and Rabbi Shaw Israel Zevit, eds, *Brother Keepers: New Perspectives on Jewish Masculinity* (Harriman, TN: Men's Studies Press, 2010).

13. See Daniel Boyarin, Daniel Itzkovitz and Ann Pellegrini, eds, *Queer Theory and the Jewish Question* (New York: Columbia University Press, 2003).

14. David Baddiel's recent novel, *The Death of Eli Gold* (London: Fourth Estate, 2011), presents an explicit engagement with the 'Great Man' literary tradition of Roth and Bellow. For a comment on this see Aida Edemariam, 'David Baddiel: from stand-up to Saul Bellow', *Guardian*, 24 July 2010.

15. See http://www.guardian.co.uk/books/audio/2010/sep/28/howard-jacobson-kalooki-nights. Accessed 20 June 2012.

16. Howard Jacobson, *Kalooki Nights* (London: Jonathan Cape, 2006), p.12.

17. For discussions about male menstruation see Shapiro, pp.37–38 and Boyarin, pp.208–216.

18. See *Peeping Tom* (London, Vintage, 1999).

19. Giles Coren, *Winkler* (London: Vintage, 2006), p.3.

20. Winkler's father is, in fact, alive but is revealed to have been a wayward husband who had run off many years before with a non-Jewish woman.

21. Omer Bartov, *Mirrors of Destruction* (2000), quoted from Jon Stratton, *Jewish Identity in Western Pop Culture: The Holocaust and Trauma through Modernity* (Basingstoke: Palgrave, 2008), p.162. Stratton's discussion of the complex issues relating to pornography and the Holocaust is useful. See, pp.158–164.

22. Andrew Sanger, *The J-Word* (London: Snowbooks, 2009), p.10. See also Natasha Solomons, *Mr Rosenblum's List* (London: Sceptre, 2010) which I have discussed in previous chapters.

23. Sinclair is an interesting and important voice in post-war British-Jewish writing. I have not, in this study, been able to include an exploration of Sinclair's writing. Some of his most significant work, such as *Hearts of Gold* (1979), *Bedbugs* (1982) and his memoir, *Diaspora Blues: A View of Israel* (1987), predate the post-1990 period on which *Writing Jewish* focuses. For readings of Sinclair's work see Bryan Cheyette, *Contemporary Jewish Writing in Britain and Ireland: An Anthology* (London: Peter Halban, 1998), pp.liii–lvi; David Brauner, *Post-War Jewish Fiction: Ambivalence, Self-Explanation and Transatlantic Connections* (Basingstoke: Palgrave, 2001), pp.170–184; and Michael Woolf, 'Negotiating the Self; Jewish Fiction in Britain since 1945', in A. Robert Lee, ed., *Other Britain, Other British: Contemporary Multicultural Fiction* (London: Pluto Press, 1995), pp.124–141.

24. Clive Sinclair, 'My CV', in *The Lady with the Laptop* (London: Picador, 1997), pp.107–118 (p.111).

25. Mark Glanville, *The Goldberg Variation: From Football Hooligan to Opera Singer* (London: Flamingo, 2004).

26. Nick Hornby, *Fever Pitch* (London: Penguin, 2010).

7

'A Vortex of Contradictory Forces': British-Jewish Women

As I have discussed throughout *Writing Jewish*, contemporary representations of British-Jewishness draw from a number of powerful, yet often contradictory, stereotypes. The previous chapter considered this in relation to Jewish masculinity and argued that some familiar ideas about gender and difference are both reiterated and reconfigured in recent writing by British Jews. The following discussion, which focuses on the representation of Jewish women, demonstrates that stereotypes relating to Jewish women are as charged and as contradictory as those relating to Jewish men, and perhaps even more so.

The chapter will outline some of these stereotypes and present an overview of recurring issues in contemporary British-Jewish writing by women, but I want to begin by looking at Lana Citron's short story, 'Mordecai's First Brush with Love'.[1] The story, as it narrates how Mordecai, a 14-year-old 'slow-developer', embarks on a romantic adventure, presents a witty take on Jewish gender relations and introduces some of the themes that will become the focus of the chapter as a whole. When Mordecai returns from his first date, his mother, who is described as being 'of a nervous disposition, in a constant state of worry, obsessed with food' (35), is waiting for him. Poised by the 'stacked to capacity' fridge, Marlene sets about interrogating her son. Later, as she watches him eat, Mordecai understands the damaging dynamic that lies at the heart of their relationship. He realizes at that moment 'exactly why he hated his mother: she was the one he cleaved to and always would' (39) and he is compelled to disclose the horrible revelation that had ruined his evening. Under the bright lights of a

KFC takeaway, Mordecai had noticed that Rachel Reuben, the girl of his dreams, had a moustache.

Marlene responds with the voice of experience. She 'looked at her son, thinking: A nice Jewish girl: what did he expect? She placed her hand upon his and said, "Don't worry – you'll get yours soon"' (39). But what, the reader might wonder, of Rachel Reuben? The narrator tells us:

> Though beautiful, intelligent and destined to be the controller of the BBC, three miles down the road, in floods of tears, choking on snot, with her mother's Jolen burning her upper lip, was the young Rachel. Throughout her life this humiliation would always plague her, and she would wax, pluck, Immac, and have electrolysis until, aged thirty, finally, she could afford laser treatment. (39)

It is a comic tale of woe, which, balancing naivety against neurosis, nascent masculinity against fraught femininity, signals the profound dysfunction that has so often characterized the representation of Jewish gender relations. The story invokes concisely a range of stereotypical figures, each of whom contributes to this problematic scenario: the overbearing mother, the dominated son and the high-achieving girl, forever damaged by this moment in which her femininity is compromised by a hairy upper lip. The story thus presents, in Mordecai, an already emasculated, moustacheless, form of Jewish masculinity, and in Marlene, a fatefully dominant form of femininity. Rachel, the teenage girl, in some ways mediates these two extremes and is excluded from the intensity of the mother-son dyad; but we might reflect on how she will eventually come to understand herself as an adult Jewish woman, beyond the challenges of depilation. This thought informs the discussion to come. As the young Rachel is yet to discover, the Jewish woman in contemporary Britain can absorb or refuse the stereotypes that inform ideas of Jewish gender relations, but she must first of all identify the ways in which such stereotypes are constructed.

The chapter begins by outlining some familiar stereotypes, looking at historical constructions of 'the Jewess' and moving on to more recent figurations of Jewish women, particularly that of the Jewish mother. The discussion then looks more closely at how Jewish women in Britain represent themselves in contemporary writing and asks why, within a context in which British Jews are in many ways more confident than ever, are anxieties about belonging and alienation still repeatedly expressed within such writing? The final part of the chapter addresses this issue more fully in its readings of two high-profile recent novels by British-Jewish women: Naomi Alderman's *Disobedience* and Charlotte Mendelson's *When We Were Bad*. These novels, whilst distinct in their own terms, both raise interconnected questions about what it means to be a Jewish woman in Britain today.

'The Devil that Haunts': stereotypes of the Jewish woman

The Jewish woman has been both celebrated and vilified. In this respect, one might note, that way she is no different from women in Western culture in general. It is obvious that images of Jewish women are variations on more widespread stereotypes of women. So, in the discussion that follows, I am of course drawing implicitly from general issues relating to women in the past and in the present. However, as the previous chapter set out to explore the particularity of British-Jewish masculinity in contemporary representation, here I am interested in looking at the ways in which depictions of Jewish femininity are inflected by some rather specific concerns. From the matriarchs, temptresses and warrior women of the Old Testament to the suffocating Jewish mothers and spoiled Jewish princesses of contemporary representation, Jewish women have been constructed in a variety of compelling yet contrary ways.

The term 'Jewess' has always been a charged and equivocal designation. It could connote the *belle juive*, the innocent and beautiful Jewess of so many nineteenth-century novels, a figure who, as Nadia Valman has demonstrated, was idealized within a culture of ostensible philosemitism but was also coded in some problematic ways.[2] Most often the Jewish woman was seen as an eroticized figure of excess. As Tamar Garb puts it, looking at the ways in which such representations circulated within nineteenth-century culture, 'in the Christian imagination, the sexuality of the Jewess is both dangerous and desirable'.[3] She goes on to explain that 'the Jewess can stand for warmth, love, and sensuality, a constellation of characteristics that always threatens to spill over into excess' (27). The 'Jewess' thus combines and compounds already complex ideas relating to both women and to Jews.

Nathan Abrams has observed that even within a contemporary context the idea of the 'Jewess' is highly charged. For him, the term 'rankles', bringing to mind 'heavy locks of black hair, long skirts, clinking bracelets, a musky odour'. A 'Jewess', he explains, 'sounds juicy and slightly dirty'.[4] Howard Jacobson's *The Finkler Question* presents a knowing image of the sexualized 'Jewess' in these terms.

Here Jacobson describes how Julian Treslove, the gentile who is intrigued by Jewishness, falls for Hephzibah Weizenbaum, a distinctly Jewish woman. In the sensual headiness of their first encounter (at a Passover dinner) Treslove is dazzled by her exotic otherness. In contrast to the brittle Anglo-Saxon women, to whom he has previously been subjected, Hephzibah is fleshy and bejewelled. Her eyes are 'more purple than black'; her mouth is 'vivacious'; she is dressed in layers of such voluptuous extravagance that she appears 'tented and suggested the Middle East'.[5] As Treslove struggles repeatedly to pronounce her name, she wonders if she is 'too much of a mouthful' (133). As a Jewish man, Jacobson ventriloquizes Treslove's gentile perception of Jewish femininity with comic precision. In a novel that plays with the fascinating unpronouncibility of Jewishness in general, the Jewish woman brings another deliciously unutterable layer of difference into the narrative.

Historically, and perhaps even currently, the 'Jewess' embodies a series of contradictory signifiers and these cannot be easily contained. She is a figure of virtue and seduction, vulnerability and power, extreme femininity and dangerous womanliness. She bears the cultural load of women in Western culture in general and this sense of otherness is intensified in terms of her Jewishness. I want now to look at some of the ways in which stereotypes figure in the self-representation of Jewish women in contemporary Britain. Drawing from first-person reflection, short stories, poetry, and novels, the discussion sets out to explore the ways in which British-Jewish women are rewriting such stereotypes and to reflect on some of the preoccupations and tensions that surface throughout this writing

'Mother Chicken Soup': stereotypes and self-representation

One of the most notable stereotypes associated with the Jewish woman is of course, that of the Jewish mother. As Cooper and Morrison make explicit, 'you don't have to be Jewish to be a "Jewish mother". To manipulate, and provoke guilt in others, through self-abnegation or over-protective control is not a Jewish (or female) monopoly'.[6] This is undoubtedly the case. Yet, the image of the Jewish mother has a particular resonance within post-war culture. As Nadia Valman argues, the Jewish mother 'is consistently made to stand for Jewishness itself, and all the romantic, raging or ambivalent feelings that it arouses'.[7] So the Jewish mother comes to represent an intensified version of Jewishness and, moreover, taps into a myriad of complex cultural ideas relating to femininity and the maternal. Jew, woman, mother. These are all highly charged terms.

However, although the Jewish mother is an enduring stereotype, the image has evolved over time and in different contexts. Whereas the 'yiddisher mama' was an idealized character, embodying the warmth and nurture of the old world, the Jewish mother is a more recent and troubling creation. The stereotype, as Abrams outlines in a discussion of the representation of the Jewess in contemporary film, shifted in the 1960s and 1970s.[8] Most notably, the publication of Philip Roth's *Portnoy's Complaint* in 1969 cemented an image of the anxious, overbearing Jewish mother which has circulated ever since.[9] In an article titled 'Hearts and Bowels', published in 2005, the British-Jewish writer Michele Hanson presents a wry examination of what it means to be labelled as a Jewish mother. 'Sometimes', she admits, 'I pretend I am not a Jewish mother'. She goes on to explain that 'if I own up...people will nail me to the dreaded stereotype'.[10] Reflecting on her own mother's anxiety, her loudness and her extreme interest in her daughter's bodily functions, Hansen recalls that this had seemed 'entirely normal' until she had read *Portnoy's Complaint*. 'Portnoy's mother', Hansen realized, 'was rather similar to mine, lurking outside the lavatory, worried to death about what's going on in there, and it is this awful physicality that I think of as Jewish mothering: food, bowels, lavatories' (131). Although Hansen resituates the stereotype within a British context, it is through reading Roth, that she found a way in which to frame her own experience. The 'awful physicality' associated with her mother becomes explicable, if still horrifying, when understood within the structure of the stereotype.

Hansen is part of the immediate post-war generation.[11] For this, and subsequent generations of British Jews, the American stereotype of the Jewish mother continued to exert a powerful hold on the popular imagination. It was developed in the UK domestic context through two key home-grown representations: Jack Rosenthal's television play *Bar Mitzvah Boy* (broadcast in 1976) and the popular British Telecom adverts featuring the character Beattie Bellman (played by Rosenthal's wife, Maureen Lipman), which ran from the late 1980s and throughout the 1990s.[12] The Jewish mothers depicted here are stereotypically anxious, over-invested in their offspring and endlessly reproachful. But these are generally affectionate portrayals in which Jewish neuroses function as a kind of cultural tic rather than a pathological character flaw. The Jewish mother in this form is irritating, maybe even infuriating, but she is not necessarily the root cause of acute psychological damage.

More recent television depictions of Jewish families in the British sitcoms *Grandma's House* and *Friday Night Dinner* present Jewish mothers that are updated for the twenty-first century. Such programmes arguably signal the confidence of Jews in contemporary Britain. The families they portray may house a degree of eccentricity but, it is suggested, they are not so different from any other family today. It is questionable whether many young Jewish men of a secular persuasion would really gather at their mother's and grandmother's tables with the regularity that these sitcoms suggest, but this is not the point. Instead these programmes present Jewish families as both particular and general in terms of contemporary British life. There is an interesting double consciousness at play here. Gender and Jewishness intersect in ways which are clearly identifiable to a Jewish audience, but may or may not be picked up by a non-Jewish viewer. Jewish mothers are at the heart of such coding.

Alongside these sharp and self-aware sitcoms, which have been created from a Jewish perspective, there is currently a more generalized wave of popular media interest in representing Jewishness. Here, Jewishness functions as a largely unthreatening form of ethnic vibrancy within contemporary Britain and the Jewish woman seems, ostensibly, to exemplify reassuring family values.[13] So, in this vein, we can note, Channel 4's announcement in March 2012 that they were launching a televised competition to find the 'Jewish Mum of the Year'. The publicity stated that:

> The competition will seek out the traditional, the overbearing, the cheek-pinching and the charming. The winner is out there somewhere in the land of the Jewish Princess and the over-pampered Bar Mitzvah boys, and no strudel will be left unturned in his quest to find the perfect Jewish mum.[14]

This suggests a cheerfully ironic yet also rather nostalgic impulse. The Jewish mother in this mode embodies ideas about Jewish warmth, family and cultural durability. It is a compelling image that keys into ideas that are fundamental to Jewish self-representation as well as the stereotypes that are perpetuated about Jewishness by non-Jews. Yet, in a culture in which Jewish women are increasingly less likely to conform to this stereotype, does this popular reiteration of the Jewish mother motif perhaps also reveal current insecurities about femininity, maternal identities and Jewishness from within as well as beyond Jewish culture?

In fact, when the Jewish Mum of the Year programme was broadcast in the Autumn of 2012, not only did it evoke some highly negative responses from British Jews, but it also demonstrated a significant sense of strain as it struggled to find its own register.[15] The women in this programme, who were rarely seen with their own families, were then oddly disassociated from their purported identities as Jewish mothers. In this way they became somewhat evacuated ciphers. As A.A. Gill put it: 'This was all stereotypes and racial profiling. A group of mad Jewish mothers compete to be the next agony aunt for a newspaper. They ticked every single cartoon prejudice and racial truism'.[16] However, the effect of the programme was not just to evoke irritation or even offence. Perhaps more unexpectedly, even in relation to other TV reality shows, it was a remarkably dull viewing experience. As it somehow managed to convey a sense of exhaustion, rather than vivacity, the programme ended up suggesting that the stereotype on which it was premised was at best a rather brittle construction and may have even run its course.

Whereas, some contemporary representations, such as Tanya in *Grandma's House* and Marlene in 'Mordecai's First Brush with Love', manage to convey the deranged and innately disturbing quality of the classic Jewish mother with considerable self-awareness, the concept can become caricatured to such an extent that it functions only in terms of empty clichés. In this way the Jewish mother becomes, potentially, no more than a byword for an anxious nature and an exaggerated preoccupation with food. In terms of popular literature, Olivia Lichtenstein's, *Mrs Zhivago of Queen's Park* (2007), illustrates this tendency.[17] This post-chicklit novel about a forty-something Jewish woman in crisis, in keeping with its genre, deploys some familiar tropes relating to contemporary gender relationships and adds Jewishness into the mix. For Chloe Zhivago, Jewishness manifests itself principally through a connection to cooking. As we have seen in the discussion of cultural memory in Chapter 3, food can play an important role in the construction of Jewish identity, but in Lichtenstein's novel it becomes a formulaic signifier of Jewish femininity. Chloe announces, perhaps a little defensively, that 'my compulsion to feed people was the most Jewish thing about me' (64) and in this spirit each chapter of the book is prefaced with a symbolically-laden recipe. In these terms, Chapter Five, 'Chloe Zhivago's Jewish Penicillin', 'proven to cure guilt, remorse and all major illnesses' (51), is a key chapter. As it narrates a 'Chicken Soup Tournament' between Chloe and her gentile husband, Greg, so ideas about the transmission of women's knowledge come to the fore. Discussing the essential properties of matzo balls, Chloe explains that 'it's the sort of thing you have to learn at a grandmother's knee, as I did at mine' (58). She recalls that:

When I turned thirteen, the age when Jewish boys become men, she took me by the hand, saying 'it's time'. We marked my important rite of passage into womanhood in her kitchen, where she taught me the art of chicken soup with *kneidlach* while telling me stories of her life 'back home'. (59)

It is a schmaltz-infused passage in which Jewish womanhood is seen through the nostalgic glow of the past rather than the more refracted light of the present.

The novel does what it sets out to do in terms of its own genre. But what interests me about the use of Jewishness as a trope here is in the insecurity that it invokes. Chloe, repeatedly comments on her sense of disconnection from Jewishness, comparing herself to her friend Ruthie, 'a better Jew than me' (10), and admitting early on in the narrative that, 'in spite of the fact that I'm a psychotherapist, make fantastic chicken soup and do all that soul food business, I'm fundamentally ignorant about Judaism' (10). This ignorance becomes an anxious presence in the text. However casual this representation of Jewish women in contemporary London appears to be, it also suggests the more serious struggles about fractured Jewish identities, which we saw articulated in the previous chapter in texts by Andrew Sanger and Mark Glanville. As Lichtenstein's narrative repeatedly circles around issues of identification, self-consciously peppering the text with Yiddish words and clichéd Jewish motifs, the effect, in the end, is one of confusion. Jewishness here is not just a narrative accessory within a popular generic mode. It is, instead, a surprisingly unresolved aspect of the novel.

Lichtenstein's novel deploys a revealing but vague use of the Jewish mother motif in her novel. In contrast, the poet, Joanne Limburg, presents a far spikier reworking of the stereotype. Limburg has written astutely about Jewish identity in contemporary Britain and her poem 'Mother Chicken Soup', published in 2000, presents a mordant spin on the traditional image of the self-sacrificing Jewish mother. 'God forbid', it begins:

her family should starve,
So mother is boiling herself down
for soup,[18]

The poem has a fable-like quality as the Jewish mother, taking the stereotype to its logical conclusion, offers herself cannibalistically to her offspring. In a grotesque realization of the invasive qualities associated with the Jewish mother, no boundaries between mother and children are allowed to remain. 'The oven clock pings', it continues,

time to dissolve her life into theirs,
dive into the broth.

The mother leaves a note behind telling her children that she does not 'expect gratitude', and advising them on how they should heat up this maternally infused broth. In this way the stereotype of the Jewish mother is presented with such macabre excess that the poem effectively deconstructs any complacency that might have built up around this myth. This is chicken soup without the schmaltz.

'Am I – ?': British-Jewish women's writing and identity

In subjecting the stereotype of the Jewish mother to the pressure of intense overstatement Limburg both exposes its pervasiveness and explodes its power. She has explored the potency of such stereotypes and the impact that they have on identification elsewhere. Her poem 'The Nose on My Face' considers the ways in which ideas of otherness are internalized. It begins with the narrator fielding a question about her identity: 'Someone hopes I don't mind/them asking, but am I –?'.[19] The hesitant enquiry opens a series of associated thoughts that scrape at the edges of what might seem to be a thoroughly assimilated identity as a Jewish woman in twenty-first century Britain. The narrator recalls her 16-year-old self, poised in front of a mirror, scrutinizing the ways in which her nose reveals her Jewishness:

What was it about my nose? Did it
have a pushy way of forcing
itself into a room, a vulgar
nose-come-lately, embarrassing
and overdressed? Did it mark its owner as a fleshy, suburban
princess condemned to a life of shopping
and eating and smothering sons? Was it
transparently over-emotional? Was it
lubricious, dishonest or dirty?

Limburg here reads her nose as a metonymic signifier of Jewish excess. 'It' becomes the defining mark of difference in a face that is otherwise characterized by 'inoffensive adequacy'. For the young Jewish woman, images of suburban princesses and smothering Jewish mothers form part of an inventory of undesirable Jewish associations. The poem, as it invokes a rush of antisemitic stereotypes, can be read as ironic (surely no single nose could carry such cultural freight); but it is astute in its understanding of the ways in which antisemitic discourse can be internalized. The word 'Jew' is not once spoken. As the nose stands in for a series of cultural stereotypes, it does not need to be. 'Yes' the speaker says at the end of this meditation on the Jewish nose, 'that would tell the world': 'I am'. In a moment of bathos, following this angst-ridden self-scrutiny, 'someone says/that's funny, they'd never have guessed'.

The poem presents an interesting double manoeuvre. On the one hand it seems to articulate a perhaps surprising sense of insecurity; an anxiety about Jewishness that does not seem entirely relevant to a contemporary British-Jewish woman such as Limburg, who was born in 1970. And yet, in the way that it insists on speaking the unspeakable, in cataloguing the internalized stereotypes of antisemitic discourse, it also moves beyond them. This doubleness is, I would argue, a strategy that characterizes other contemporary writing by British-Jewish women. In 2004, Laura Phillips and Marion Baraitser, the editors of a collection of short stories by Jewish women, claimed that there was currently a 'Jewish cultural renaissance' taking place in Britain. The aim of the collection was, therefore, 'to announce a new confidence and ability among disparate authors bound by a common culture, gender, history and, sometimes, faith'.[20] Phillips and Baraitser register the improved conditions for Jewish women in contemporary Britain, noting that 'we are better educated and more culturally confident, which allows a new pluralism and diversity of self-expression and openness in Jewish women writers' (8). But, even within this positive context of self-asser-tion, there remains a sense of hesitant identification and irresolution. Phillips and Baraitser thus sound a note of caution, explaining: 'We still do not seem to have escaped the old dilemma of the split-personality of the Jew', adding, 'although we no longer feel oppressed, we are coming to terms with our sense of being outsiders within another culture' (8).

A sense of disjunction, between confidence in what it means to be a British-Jewish woman, and a lingering sense of in-betweenness, runs through much of the writing in the collection. The self-representation of the writers in their biographies is revealing in this respect. So, for example, Rachel Castell Farhi, a 'matrilineal Jew' who has written 'about dual identity' presents an emotive sense of what it means to be doubled and divided. In a complex expression of identification, Farhi explains that:

> I love being a Jew but I am proud of being British. Judaism tugs at my heart like a guilty child wanting attention; Englishness is my father in his military uniform, standing on a Remembrance parade in silent dignity. Both need nurturing. (22)

As British and Jewish identities are separated, so Judaism is femi-nized, associated with love, and cast not as a mother but as a needy child. 'Englishness', in contrast, is masculinized, linked to a sense of pride and presented as patriarchal, stoical and silent.

Farhi's story, 'The Mezuzah Gatherer', explores an ontological uncertainty that underlies much contemporary British-Jewish writing. As it begins, the narrator, Susie, opens the door to a Lubavitch woman whose mission is to prepare lapsed Jews for the arrival of the Messiah: 'She asks me if I am Jewish and I hesitate. "No, yes – I mean, not really, any more."'[21] From Rachel Lichtenstein's *Rodinsky's Room* to Andrew Sanger's *The J-Word* and the subtle interlocution of Limburg's poem, this is the question that runs through many texts and attempts to answer it, however hesitant, fraught and even confused, provide the creative impetus for a considerable amount of British-Jewish writing today.

The story, as it develops, explores the relationship between familial history, cultural memory, religious belief and contemporary Jewish identity. Different versions of Jewish women are presented, ranging from the messianic Lubavitch woman, to Susie's mother, a child of East End immigrants, who refuses to romanticize the past. The other female figure that shapes the story is, Anna, Susie's father's daughter from his first marriage. Anna had been gassed in a domestic accident during the war and comes, in the imagination of her disconnected half-sister, to stand in for the horrors of the Holocaust. As she haunts the edges of this narrative she is figured as 'the past's ungathered recollec-tion' (32). Anna is not the only ghostly presence in the text, however. The more intense loss is the Jewish tradition that has passed. In a diffuse act of substitution, Susie collects mezuzahs from the doors of the East End houses which are no longer inhabited by Jews. 'I gather mezuzahs', she says, 'like so many un-recollected thoughts' (33).

In this way, the story is reminiscent of Rachel Lichtenstein's nostal-gized yearning for a site of Jewish authenticity in *Rodinsky's Room*, a non-fictional self-reflexive text that I discussed in relation to loca-tion in Chapter 4. As Lichtenstein's narrative meditates on identity, place, collection, recollection and un-recollection, so Farhi's story raises similar issues. At one stage of her tale Lichtenstein focused on Bertha Rodinsky, the shadowy, superimposed and uncannily haunting photographic image which signalled an absent female presence in the mystery of Rodinsky's life. Similarly, in Farhi's story, Anna comes to represent that which is repressed and its return. Lichtenstein charted an obsession with retrieving and cataloguing archival material relating to Rodinsky, a figure who is deployed as a metonymic signifier of the lost Jewish East End. Similarly, for Susie, the collection of mezuzahs becomes a fetishized remnant of Jewishness.

The question that runs through many of these texts, in the frothy chicklit of Chloe Zhivago as well as in the traumatized world of 'The Mezuzah Gatherer' is what, in the end, remains? As Jewishness becomes increasingly more dissipated, is a recipe for chicken soup and a drawer full of reclaimed mezuzahs all that are left? When identities are increasingly disjointed how can a sense of cultural connection be meaningfully sustained? These questions preoccupy much recent writing but they also provide a sense of creative potential. As Tamar Yellin puts it:

> Woman, Briton, Jew – all these are identities that have been imposed upon me. 'Writer' is the identity I have chosen for myself. To be a Jew, a Briton and a woman means to live in a vortex of contradictory forces: loss, longing, pride, guilt. Exile and alienation. Only by writing is it possible to harness these forces and make my contradictions whole.[22]

To be a British-Jewish woman is, in these terms, to embody a fraught set of identifiers and to inhabit 'a vortex of contradictory forces'. Like Farhi, Yellin expresses a sense of existential incongruity but choosing the identity of a writer creates the potential for resolution.

The poet and fiction writer, Michelene Wandor, presents a less troubled summation of a composite identity. She explains that 'my writing draws in different ways on my main cultural sources of Britishness, Jewishness and being a woman....I hope I am more than the sum of these parts, as well as the sum of these parts'.[23] For Wandor, multiple influences lead to literary riches. Her writing, which draws from biblical tradition, Jewish myth and English history, bears out this point. Alongside Wandor, writers such as the playwrights Diane Samuels and Julia Pascal, the poets Ruth Fainlight and Elaine Feinstein, and novelists such as Linda Grant and Jenny Diski, have contributed significantly to recent developments in British-Jewish women's writing. As these women rewrite traditional stories, engage with history, and reflect on what it means to be a British Jew, so British-Jewish women's writing is becoming an increasingly notable aspect of the contemporary literary field.

Subjectivity and subversion: Naomi Alderman's *Disobedience* and Charlotte Mendelson's *When We Were Bad*

Popular awareness of British-Jewish women writers in recent years has been augmented by the work of Naomi Alderman and Charlotte Mendelson. Alderman's 2006 Orange-prize winning novel

Disobedience focuses on orthodox Jewish life in suburban Hendon, North-West London.[24] Mendelson's *When We Were Bad*, which is set in the Belsize Park area of North-West London, also depicts contemporary British-Jewish life, but from a less orthodox perspective. Both novels were highly publicized and both have contributed to a sense of growing visibility in the representation of British-Jewish women. So, despite Mendelson's understandable irritation about being 'routinely lumped together with Alderman', I am going to discuss these two texts alongside each other.[25] Both novels share an acute sense of location; both raise issues about the constraints of Jewish family life; both focus on key Jewish occasions (a death, a wedding, a Passover dinner); both explore the power of secrets; both, as their titles signal, work through a sense of transgression, and both raise issues of sexual desire as providing the focus of such transgression.[26]

Both novels also feature rabbis. But it is at this point that similarities become differences. Mendelson's Claudia Rubin, a luminous, progressive, media-focused rabbi, is situated at the epicentre of her family and of the narrative. Rav Krushka, the rabbi in Alderman's story is, in contrast, a traditional male patriarch who dies in the first chapter, leaving a vacuum that the remaining characters in the narrative will strain to fill. Whilst interrogating the constraints that the Jewish orthodox tradition places on women, *Disobedience* also presents the religious aspects of Judaism in a nuanced way. Alderman's own orthodox background is apparent in the understanding of Jewish liturgy that she brings to the novel. Each chapter is prefaced with an extract of a text used in Jewish service and the religious motifs that run through the narrative are not incidental. They provide a serious and powerful structure in which ideas of faith as well as community, family and personal desire are treated with equal respect. So, whilst hypocrisy, repression and compromise are undoubtedly key themes in the novel, so too are matters of belief, forgiveness and acceptance.[27]

Alderman has discussed, in frank terms, the way in which the novel is in some respects a working through of her own background. In a blog for *Granta* she reflects on her experience of growing up within the orthodox community in Hendon, recalling how at primary school boys in daily prayers would thank God for not making them women. 'I was vaguely aware by the time I reached nine or ten that something disturbed me about these lines', she notes, 'but didn't realize how grotesquely offensive they were until I included them in the novel I was writing, *Disobedience*'.[28] Elsewhere, she comments on the disparities between Jewish orthodoxy and feminist principles, describing her experience as a Jewish feminist as being 'like holding two glass vessels in my head. Here is feminism and equal rights, and here is Judaism – and it took me a long time to kind of bash them together'.[29] The danger implied by such an image is that bashing together two glass vessels will inevitably lead to a shattering of both and *Disobedience* might well have become a jarring act of destruction in this way. However, the novel does not simply reject Jewish orthodox tradition or abandon feminist principles. Instead, it captures the profound ambivalence that an attempt to reconcile these two aspects of committed belief can evoke.

It is a structural dilemma. As Alderman puts it, 'there's some really good stuff in the way I was brought up. There's some really rubbish stuff as well'. However, as she also recognizes, the nature of orthodoxy is that it is essentially un-malleable. It resists reinterpretation. 'The trouble is', she explains, 'the point at which you start sifting and saying this is great and this is rubbish, that's no longer an orthodox way of thinking... I suppose the idea about all orthodox religion is that it's a kind of submission, obedience'.[30] So, for the women in the novel, and perhaps for Alderman herself, the challenge is to reposition themselves in relation to this fixed pole of orthodoxy, rather than attempting to remould the tradition it embodies. And it is here that some quite complex ideas relating to obedience and disobedience are worked out.

The dilemma is enacted through the two main female characters in the novel, Ronit and Esti, who, initially at least, appear to epitomize opposite positions in relation to orthodoxy and feminism. Ronit's character demonstrates a superficially violent rejection of the orthodox world, a conspicuous refusal to submit and a statement of blunt disobedience. Some of this is focused on what she sees as a particularly British form of repression. She decries the cramped and self-effacing tendencies of Anglo-Jewry, contrasting this to the vitality and confidence of New York Jews. 'It's as though', she says:

> Jews in this country have made an *investment* in silence. There's a vicious circle here, in which the Jewish fear of being noticed and the natural British reticence interact. They feed off each other so that British Jews cannot speak. Cannot be seen, value invisibility above all other virtues. (55)

However, although she seems to embody the progressive possibilities of voice and visibility, Ronit is unsettled and abrasive. She has escaped the restraints of orthodox Hendon and lives instead a kind of *Sex in the City* secular, sexually-liberated, but emotionally unresolved, existence in New York. When her father dies, Ronit returns to England and is jolted into a confrontation with her past, in terms of the religious as well as social bonds that she has so forcefully disavowed.

Reflecting on the restrictions and exclusions that orthodoxy places on women she notes that:

> These are subtle things. We don't condone wife-beating here, or genital mutilation, or honour killings. We don't demand head-to-toe coverings, or cast-down eyes, or that a modern woman must not go out in public unaccompanied. We are modern. We live modern lives. All that we demand is that women keep to their allotted areas; a woman is private, while a man is public. The correct mode for a man is speech, while the correct mode for a woman is silence. (242)

But Ronit has been formed by this tradition. She knows it and it knows her. Like the piece of bark that had lodged itself in her elbow when, many years before, she had tripped on a tree root, it is part of her. The fall, when she was 13, marked a charged moment in the story of the triangular relationship that was to develop between her, Esti and Dovid (the Rav's shy, unprepossessing nephew and heir apparent). The wound, which 'healed unevenly', leaves a scar (183). Throughout the course of the novel, Ronit comes to realize that her past has left its mark on her in a number of ways and the narrative ends with a cautious sense of resolution. Her mother's candlesticks, artefacts of the Shabbat ritual particularly associated with women, are returned to her and she reconciles herself to a relocated understanding of her British-Jewish subjectivity.

In contrast to Ronit's ostensible reinvention of self, Esti, her teenage love, lives a seemingly thwarted and alienated life. She has remained within the confines of the orthodox community in Hendon, has married Dovid, and has struggled to repress her lesbian desires. Ronit's return brings this chronic longing to the surface, creating a more acute sense of crisis within her relationships and her community. However, by the end of the narrative, Esti embodies a more subtle and complex reconfiguration of belief, tradition and identity. Dovid's role in this reconfiguration is central. He is neither oppressive patriarch nor modern silencer, but presents instead a different model of masculinity. Dovid is in many ways a version of Boyarin's 'sissy' Jew, a figure that, as I discussed in the previous chapter, embodies a subtle masculinity, and provokes a reconsideration of cultural assumptions about sex and gender. At the denouement of the novel, the synagogue community waits expectantly for Dovid. He is supposed to speak about the deceased Rav and thereby claim his place within the patriarchal chain. But Dovid cannot be found. It turns out that he is ensconced in the women's section of the segregated synagogue. When he is revealed, the effect is disruptive and radically disconcerting:

> Heads twisted and craned. Women nudged their neighbours. There was a sort of laughing gasp as the people saw that Dovid was standing in the *ladies' gallery*. Some of the congregation wondered privately if it might not be forbidden for him to be there. The thing seemed a terrible, forbidden mingling. (243)

Esti, at this stage of the narrative, is the subject of much gossip and condemnation. Dovid gives her something that is denied women in the orthodox tradition, a voice; and with that voice comes an opportunity for some kind of resolution. This sense of 'forbidden mingling', of all sorts, invokes the interrogation of (dis)obedience that lies at the heart of the novel; but Dovid's transgression, this temporary mixing up of gender divisions, also provides a moment of restorative potential for both individual characters and the community as a whole.

Esti makes a bold declaration about her sexual identity and the moment seems to be one of transformative dramatic potential. Ronit, who significantly has only been able to attend the occasion in disguise (by passing as an orthodox Jewish woman) observes the scene with detachment. Noting the absolute difference between US and British Jews, she thinks how, in New York, such a moment would have been a 'show-stopper'. But, 'because this is Britain' the response to Esti's revelation is characterized by a slight pause, a few whispers, and some eye-rolling and then the event continues as if nothing shocking had happened. 'The next-half an hour was proof', Ronit thinks, 'if proof were needed, that':

> What we say about ourselves is not true. There is a myth – many of us believe it – that we are wanderers, unaffected by the place in which we live ... It's a lie. These British Jews were British – they shuffled awkwardly, looked at their feet and drank tea. (247)

So, the myth of Jewish unrootedness is called into question. In the terms of this novel it would seem that Jews are formed by their cultural environments in the same way that Ronit is fundamentally marked by the Hendon tree root that has become part of her.

Charlotte Mendelson shares a similar interest in teasing out the particularity of British-Jewish identity and a shared sense of frustration about the lingering timidity within Anglo-Jewry. Of course, it could be argued that both Alderman and Mendelson's novels, whilst depicting some aspects of this culture of apology, have in fact also contributed to what many regard as a new wave of confidence within British-Jewish life. Mendelson has said that in writing *When We Were Bad* she set out to explore:

> What it's like to be Jewish in England – how weird it is, and how different to being Jewish in America or being not-Jewish in England. It's a particularly odd experience. Whatever kind of Jew you are – Orthodox, liberal, practising, non-practising – you are never quite fully English, even in multicultural, cosmopolitan 21st-century London. England is the least Jewish country in the world.[31]

To address this weirdness, this innate sense of difference, Mendelson presents a conspicuously and self-consciously Jewish book. In interview, she recalls meeting Howard Jacobson at a party and telling him, excitedly, 'Howard. Howard. I'm writing this really *Jewy* book'.[32] Ignoring his advice not to do it, she writes a story that centres on a North-West London Jewish family that is both held together and held back by its matriarch, Rabbi Claudia Rubin. Claudia is bold, ambitious and highly visible. Like Ronit she despises 'those who insist all English Jews must keep their heads down, in that crouching self-loathing way she cannot stand' (47).

The characterizations of Claudia, her dysfunctional family and her extended community, are drawn from a particular kind of North London Jewish life. The Rubins inhabit a progressive, cosmopolitan and media-orientated world, but one that harbours a multitude of its own repressions and restraints. Claudia seems to be, as her daughter Frances describes it, 'so openly welcoming to every racial and sexual and liturgical permutation, so vigorously liberal' (101). But, as the narrative unfolds, it is clear that Claudia exercises a powerful and constrictive control over her family. The crises that come to the surface in Mendelson's novel, like Alderman's, are focused in part on the potentially disruptive effects to social order brought about by sexual desire but, although geographically very close to the Hendon of *Disobedience*, this is a different world. The kinds of badness that the title suggests are not the manifest disobediences of Alderman's text, in which religious orthodoxy provided a focus for transgression. The taboos here are more nebulous, but no less pervasive.

Although the novel features a rabbi as a central character, includes many Yiddish and Hebrew words, and depicts key moments of Jewish ceremony and celebration, it is a relatively secular work. Jewishness here is articulated through family, ritual and culture rather than religion.

Whereas Alderman drew directly from her own orthodox background, Mendelson describes a less secure relationship to Jewishness and her account of her experience of being Jewish in Britain is revealing at a number of levels. In an interview with Laura Phillips for *Jewish Quarterly*, Mendelson confesses that it felt 'scary coming out as a Jew':

> Because although I'm very proud and very open about being Jewish, I don't know how to put this ... I am not all that confident about being Jewish in some ways. I am not a member of a shul, I don't have safety in numbers and I work in a company where I am the only Jew out of about 80 people. If you are a pretty secular Jew in Britain today, it is hard to feel entirely confident or safe perhaps, so it did feel a real head-above-the parapet thing. I also worried about what Jews would think. Would it be 'Shush, keep your voice down, don't draw attention to us' or 'She doesn't know what she's talking about'.[33]

This contains an interesting and, I would argue, very current, dual anxiety about belonging in relation to both Britishness and Jewishness. As a minority within the mainstream of British life, Mendelson perceives the novel to be a 'coming out' in terms of identifying publicly as Jewish. It is perhaps surprising that in the publishing world of twenty-first century London, Mendelson still feels isolated and a little vulnerable about being Jewish in Britain. But, as we saw in relation to texts as diverse as Rachel Lichtenstein's *Rodinsky's Room* to Olivia Lichtenstein's *Mrs Zhivago of Queen's Park*, the more fraught, and indeed more contemporary, issue seems to be a lack of confidence in connection to Jewishness itself. The fear expressed by Mendelson is that the novel might expose her as an ignorant and ultimately unconvincing Jew; not to non-Jews, but to a Jewish community in Britain of which she is not really a part.

Although generally well-received, some of Mendelson's apprehensions were realized in a few reviews in the Anglo-Jewish press. Rabbi Sybil Sheridan in the *Jewish Chronicle* picks up on some 'inaccuracies' in Mendelson's depiction of Jewish life which makes the novel, in her view, less than 'convincing'.[34] Deborah Smith, reviewing in *Jewish Renaissance*, admires many features of the narrative but also notes some 'jarring aspects of the religious elements of the book' that 'make it appear as if it were written by an outsider'.[35] The critique is based on such seemingly unthinkable errors as 'a Rabbi of any denomination serving chicken and camembert together' on a Shabbat dinner (44), blunders which result in the novel being seen as 'not completely authentic' from a Jewish perspective.[36] But, the question of authenticity here is complex. Perhaps what is most authentic to contemporary experience for Jews in Britain is, in fact, a somewhat fractured relationship to Jewishness, characterized by insecurity, displaying pockets of ignorance, but demonstrating curiosity and a sense of engagement with what it might mean to be a contemporary Jew.

Reading the two novels alongside each other suggests the variety of Jewish life in contemporary Britain. The women in these texts, like their authors, represent different ways of being Jewish women in today's Britain and show how these possibilities are changing. Perhaps unsurprisingly, issues of family, tradition and identity are especially prominent within such works. But, in refusing to subdue an understanding of British-Jewishness as a set of identifications that are in process, as well as a culture which is embedded in tradition, they contribute to a dialogue about contemporary British-Jewish life.

So, returning to Rachel Reuben, the voiceless girl in 'Mordecai's First Brush With Love', we might imagine her today, as controller of the BBC, having resolved her problem with facial hair, and commissioning a programme on the diverse lives of Jewish women in contemporary Britain. The documentary might well include stereotypes: Jewish mothers and chicken soup, cruise ships and kalooki, rituals and rebellions. But it might also include a discussion of the ways in which these women are working out how to connect to their Jewishness in the increasingly disparate conditions of twenty-first century Britain. In the end, the stereotypes about Jewish women might form a basis for identity but they do not contain it.

The next chapter looks at these issues of doubled, divided and disconnected identifications more fully, bringing *Writing Jewish* to a conclusion by asking questions about what becomes of Jewishness in a context in which identities are increasingly composite and shifting constructions. For many Jews in Britain today perhaps the most troubling focus of anxiety is not so much about *being* different but about *losing* difference.

Notes

1. Lana Citron, 'Mordecai's First Brush with Love' in Laura Phillips and Marion Baraitser, eds, *Mordecai's First Brush with Love: New Stories by Jewish Women in Britain* (London: Loki Books, 2004), pp.35–39.
2. Nadia Valman, 'La Belle Juive', *Jewish Quarterly*, 205 (2007), 52–56.
3. Tamar Garb, 'Modernity, Identity, Textuality', in Linda Nochlin and Tamar Garb, eds, *The Jew in the Text: Modernity and the Construction of Identity* (London: Thames and Hudson, 1995), pp.20–30, p.27.

4. Nathan Abrams, *The New Jew in Film: Exploring Jewishness and Judaism in Contemporary Cinema* (London: I.B. Tauris, 2012), p.45.

5. Howard, Jacobson, *The Finkler Question* (London: Bloomsbury, 2010), p.130, 131.

6. Howard Cooper and Paul Morrison, *A Sense of Belonging: Dilemmas of British Jewish Identity* (London: Weidenfeld and Nicolson, 1991), p.43.

7. Nadia Valman, '"the Most Unforgettable Character I've Ever Met": Literary Representations of the Jewish Mother', in Mandy Ross and Ronne Randall, eds, *For Generations: Jewish Motherhood* (Nottingham: Five Leaves Press, 2005), pp.58–66, p.66.

8. Abrams, pp.47–48. For a comprehensive history of the Jewish Mother stereotype in American popular culture see Joyce Antler, *You Never Call! You Never Write: A History of the Jewish Mother* (Oxford: Oxford University Press, 2007).

9. However, as David Brauner has observed, although 'Philip Roth has often been vilified for his portrait of the suffocating, infantilizing, emasculating oedipal Jewish mother ... [Bernice] Rubens was there first.' David Brauner, 'Bellow at Your Elbow, Roth Breathing Down Your Neck: Gender and Ethnicity in Novels by Bernice Rubens and Linda Grant', in Claire Tylee, ed., *'In the Open': Jewish Women Writers and British Culture* (Delaware, NJ: Associated University Presses, 2006), pp.96–109, p.98.

10. Michele Hansen, 'Hearts and Bowels', in *For Generations: Jewish Motherhood*, pp.128–31, p.128.

11. Hansen's recent memoir nicely evokes the particularity of the post-war British-Jewish suburban setting. See Michele Hansen, *What the Grown-Ups Were Doing* (London: Simon and Schuster, 2012).

12. The Jewish mother stereotype was also seen in the TV series *Agony* (1979–1981) in which Maria Charles played Maureen Lipman's over-bearing mother. Charles had, of course, also played the mother in Rosenthal's *Bar Mitzvah Boy* in 1976. For a nuanced discussion of the representation of British-Jewishness in Rosenthal's TV drama see Sue Vice, *Jack Rosenthal* (Manchester: Manchester University Press, 2012), chapter 8.

13. See, for example, the two BBC2 *Wonderland* documentaries, *A Hasidic Guide to Love, Marriage and Finding a Bride* (broadcast, May 2011) and *Two Jews on a Cruise* (broadcast, February, 2012); and ITV's pro-grammes about the Jewish community in Manchester, *Strictly Kosher* (broadcast, July 2011, June 2012).

14. http://www.channel4.com/info/press/news/channel-4-crowns-jewish-mum-of-the-year. Accessed 03 June 2012.

15. Maureen Lipman was particularly vocal in her response to the pro-gramme. She noted that 'people will say, "Oh, well you did Beattie" in the BT adverts, but that was affectionate. This isn't.' Tim Walker, 'Channel 4's Jewish Mum of the Year Show is "Disgusting" Says Maureen Lipman',

The Telegraph, 18 October 2012. See also, Josh Glancy, 'These Jewish Mother Clichés Aren't Kosher', *The Sunday Times*, 21 October 2012.

16. A.A. Gill, 'Who Exactly is the Enemy Within?', *The Sunday Times*, 14 October 2012.

17. Olivia Lichtenstein, *Mrs Zhivago of Queen's Park* (London: Orion, 2007).

18. Joanne Limburg, 'Mother Chicken Soup', *Femenismo* (Tarset, Northumberland: Bloodaxe Books, 2000), p.45.

19. Joanne Limburg, 'The Nose on My Face', *Femenismo*, p.22.

20. Laura Phillips and Marion Baraitser, 'Introduction', *Mordecai's First Brush with Love*, pp.6–9, p.6.

21. Rachel Castell Farhi, 'The Mezuzah Gatherer', *Mordecai's First Brush with Love*, pp.23–39, p.23.

22. Tamar Yellin, *Mordecai's First Brush with Love*, p.57.

23. Michelene Wandor, *Mordecai's First Brush with Love*, p. 187.

24. Naomi Alderman, *Disobedience* (London: Viking, 2006); Charlotte Mendelson, *When We Were Bad* (London: Picador, 2007). Alderman's profile has increased further since the publication of *Disobedience*. As well as her journalistic work and broadcast media appearances, she has written short stories and published a second novel, *The Lessons* (London: Viking, 2010); and, most recently, *The Liar's Gospel* (London: Viking, 2012).

25. Interview with Natasha Lehrer, *Tablet*, 26 September 2007.

26. Francesca Segal's, *The Innocents* (London: Chatto and Windus, 2012), which is set in the Jewish community of Hampstead Garden Suburb, continues this trend. *The Innocents* has come a little late for close attention in *Writing Jewish* but is interesting in the way that it develops themes of contemporary British-Jewish identity in relation to family, community and location. I shall be incorporating a sustained reading of the novel into future work.

27. Reva Mann's controversial memoir, *The Rabbi's Daughter: A True Story of Sex, Drugs and Orthodoxy* (London: Hodder, 2007), also raises issues about the relationship between tradition, belief and transgression.

28. Alderman, 'According to Your Will', Granta Blog, 20 May 2011. See http://www.granta.com/New-Writing/According-to-Your-Will. Accessed 04 June 2012.

29. Alderman in interview with Aida Edemariam, *The Guardian*, 20 February 2006.

30. Interview with Aida Edemariam.

31. Interview with Natasha Lehrer.

32. Interview with Natasha Lehrer.

33. 'Bagels and Pork Sausages', Interview with Laura Phillips, *Jewish Quarterly*, 206 (2007), 39–42 (39).

34. *Jewish Chronicle*, 27 April 2007, p.51.

35. Deborah Smith, 'Chicken and Camembert for Shabbat', *Jewish Renaissance*, 6.4 (2007), 45.
36. The *Jewish Quarterly* article on Mendelson signals what is described as her 'appetite for antithesis' in a far more positive sense, indicating the playfully subversive juxtaposition of bagels and pork sausage which were served together at the book's launch.

8

Jewish, Half-Jewish, Jew-ish: Contemporary Identities

Writing Jewish has explored the ways in which British-Jewish culture has increased in confidence and visibility in recent years. However, it is also apparent that this current wave of self-assurance has emerged from an earlier backdrop of insecurity. So, in my survey of contemporary British-Jewish writing in Chapter 1, it was necessary to contextualize this insecurity in order to understand how certain anxieties have permeated even recent Anglo-Jewish writing. The following chapters on the importance of memory within Jewish culture, and the effects of postmemory in relation to the Holocaust, articulated some of the profound uncertainties that have characterized the experience and self-perception of British Jews. These chapters also considered the importance of memory and postmemory in constructing and perpetuating a sense of Jewish identity for an increasingly disconnected generation of British Jews.

An exploration of the relationship between place and displacement in Chapters 4 and 5 developed these themes. We saw here how issues of diaspora and belonging have created a complex series of identifications for British Jews. Chapters 6 and 7 moved on to the more intimate terrain of the body. These chapters focused on the ways in which Jewishness impacts on constructions of gendered and sexual identities and explored some of the ways in which stereotypes are deployed, internalized and resisted in contemporary British-Jewish writing.

I set out to consider the ways in which contemporary British-Jewish writing reflects on what it might mean to be a Jew in Britain today. My focus in *Writing Jewish* has been on the mainstream of British-Jewish culture and this has encompassed a variety of identifications. I have looked at the work of some writers who are engaged with the religious aspects of Judaism and others who identify as Jewish in a cultural, and perhaps entirely secular, sense. Some of these identifications are relatively secure; but many are ambiguous. And others are really quite confused. In researching this book I have noted what seems to be a subtle, yet significant, process of transition in the self-representation of British Jews. Many of the memoirs and novels from which I have drawn have been written by writers of the immediate post-war generation, the so-called 'baby boomers', born in the late 1940s and 1950s. Jewishness for these writers was sometimes troubling, perhaps even burdensome, but it was generally known. Throughout this study I have also been looking at the work of British Jews born in the 1960s, 70s and 80s, generations for whom connections to their Jewish identities have become, in many cases, increasingly diluted. Overall, there has been a shift: where once British Jews articulated anxieties about how they belonged in relation to their Britishness, now they are equally or more likely to express uncertainty about how they belong in relation to Jewishness.

In Chapter 4 I focused on *Rodinsky's Room* (1999), written by Rachel Lichtenstein (with Iain Sinclair), a text that explores such a tension.[1] Writers of the immediate post-war generation, such as Linda Grant and Howard Jacobson question the complexities inherent in categorizing British-Jewish identity but seem, nevertheless, to have a workable notion of what Jewishness is and how to place themselves within this identification. Lichtenstein, however, perhaps more typically of her generation (she was born in the late 1960s), articulates a relatively solid connection to Britishness but a far less confident sense of her own Jewishness. Lichtenstein's text illustrates a wider tendency of this generation in ruing the loss of an imagined Jewish past. As I discussed in Chapter 4, it emerges almost half way through the book that Lichtenstein's mother is not in fact Jewish, and so, according to orthodox law, neither is Lichtenstein. The text seeks to reconcile this repressed aspect of her identity, rejecting the blandness of a thoroughly assimilated English existence (summed up by the flatness of the Essex landscape) in order to appropriate a rather more textured identity based on nostalgic ideas of an authentic Jewish East End. But, as I argued, in my discussion of this text, Lichtenstein's narrative works through some of this tension and, in the end, proposes a more progressive sense of what it means to be a Jew in the diverse conditions of Britain at the dawn of the new millennium.

Rodinsky's Room in many ways provided the impetus for *Writing Jewish*. Reading it, some years ago, during a sleepy Christmas break in Dorset (a long way from both the East End of London and the suburbs of Essex), instigated the process of thinking that I have developed throughout this project.[2] Lichtenstein's reflections on identity undoubtedly speak to a shared experience for many British Jews who feel displaced from their collective past and lament the loss of ethnic and cultural distinctiveness that Jewishness seems to bestow. In this respect, *Rodinsky's Room* seems, ostensibly, to articulate insecurity; but it is a deceptively confident story. It narrates a tension in Jewish identity and recognizes, implicitly, that there is perhaps an exhilaration, or at least kind of pleasure, to be found in the friction that is generated by uncertain identifications. It is this creative tension that, I would argue, characterizes so much contemporary British-Jewish writing.

So, in this final chapter, it is fitting that a return to *Rodinsky's Room* inaugurates a discussion about, not what it means to be Jewish and perhaps not quite British; but what it means to be British and perhaps not quite Jewish.

Half-Jewish

In a 2005 *Jewish Quarterly* article titled 'On Not Being Jewish Enough' the artist Jonathan Leaman articulated a hesitant identification with Jewishness.[3] His mother was Jewish (she was born into a long established line of English Jews) and his father was non-Jewish. He begins his reflection on how Jewishness has informed his artistic practice with the somewhat mischievous claim, 'I am not Jewish, and this is a line or two on the kind of Jew I am not' (49). Leaman avoids the nostalgic tone that infused Lichtenstein's search for identity but, like Lichtenstein, Jewishness is for him also located in the past not the present. 'Jews were archival notes', he says 'and nothing seemed further from myself'. He explains that his mother's Jewishness was 'an enlightened, liberal and watered-down Judaism, the more so for not sharing the motifs of exile, transit and extinction', the very motifs that Lichtenstein pursues in searching for her own Jewish identity (50). Leaman recognizes that the effect that this rather mild form of Jewishness had on him was of a nebulous and diffuse nature:

> Jewish boys were let off assembly – I wasn't Jewish enough for that. We ate matzos and hot-cross buns, cold fried fish and sausages – Jewishness was a distant echo of smoked cod's roe, winks and disembodied shadows happening through other people's half-open doors. (51)

It is an evocative description. The Jewish writer today often inherits such a legacy, whilst not necessarily having any really immediate connection to what seem to be authentic Jewish experiences. In many ways Leaman's 'not-Jewishness' is the cooler flip-side to Lichtenstein's more emotionally charged journey of self-discovery. Both accounts underscore the point that the Jewish past, for third, fourth and fifth generation British Jews, is often made up of echoes, winks and shadows. Like the lingering smell of yesterday's chicken soup, it pervades in subtle ways.

This is not say that all Jews today feel entirely connected to their Britishness or entirely disconnected from their Jewishness. Clearly this is not the case. What I am suggesting is that whilst some sense of exclusion might still exist, it is increasingly likely to be developed in response to and alongside a range of other differences. In Chapter 4, when I was focusing on issues of location, I looked at the way in which Tamar Yellin, who was born in Britain but has parental roots in Poland and Jerusalem, situated herself as an eternal outsider. Yellin explores these themes in her story 'Kafka in Brontëland', a tale in which a Jewish woman living alone in a Yorkshire village becomes fascinated by an enigmatic stranger of uncertain origins whom the locals call Kafka. 'Kafka the outcast, Kafka the Jew' the narrator comments.[4] By the end of the story she has found a way to belong. From the Irish backgrounds of some village families, to the half-Jewish shop owner and the south-east Asians who live down the valley, this is, Yellin suggests a landscape populated by Kafkas.

Towards the end of the *Jewish Quarterly* article in which she reflected on these issues of belonging and identification, Yellin notes that her sense of her own Jewishness had been further complicated by the recent discovery that her great-grandmother was in fact an Irish Catholic.[5] So, what we see here is not just that the Yorkshire community is ethnically and culturally mixed but that plurality exists within the genealogy of most identities, including Jewishness. Many Jews in contemporary Britain have mixed backgrounds and increasingly they will create more diverse new families. Chapter 3 explored some of these issues in relation to memory and identity and suggested that whilst such connections remain significant, contemporary forms of identification are becoming inevitably more diffuse. How Jewishness evolves within such a context is yet to be seen. But for some writers Jewishness is connected to identity and creativity in ways that are figurative as well as literal and embodied. Jewishness is in this way a trope, signifying a collective history that has been marked by dispossession, but also a more current sense of identities that are provisional, partial and performative.

In the same 2007 issue of the *Jewish Quarterly* to which Yellin had contributed, Adam Thirlwell wrote a piece titled, 'On Writing Half-Jewishly'.[6] In this, Thirlwell takes up the idea of Jewishness as a trope. He reflects on Jewishness 'as a motif for placelessness', and argues, in what is really a modernist gesture, that exile is the root of literary writing. Thirlwell goes on to explain on a more personal level why this is particularly meaningful to him: 'Perhaps', he acknowledges, 'this is a belief of mine which is intimately related to the fact that, although my mother is Jewish, I still feel half-Jewish. I can be sensitive, there-fore, to overly stringent demarcations' (4). One can detect here some defensiveness about identification. However, unlike Lichtenstein's often painful journey into the Jewish past, or Leaman who seems to rather enjoy exploring 'not being Jewish enough', or even Yellin's realization that cultures are not fixed in windswept moments from nineteenth-century novels, Thirlwell resolves his own sensitivities by pronouncing that, 'like me, the Jewish is always half-Jewish' (4).

This idea that 'Jewish is always half-Jewish' is provocative. Whilst themes of not belonging are clearly central to much Jewish writing, Thirlwell's claim effectively dismisses the idea that there could ever be a wholly Jewish identity. To the extent that all identities are, argu-ably, provisional, constructed and contingent this might be the case; and I have certainly suggested throughout this study that partial iden-tifications with Jewishness characterize much contemporary British-Jewish writing. However, there is a danger that Thirlwell's contention threatens to dispose of any meaningful sense of what it is to be Jewish and this proposition is not entirely playful. The implications of such a manoeuvre are explored in Andrew Sanger's *The J-Word*, which reflects on the problematic potential of inchoate identities. In Chapter 6 I looked at Sanger's novel, as well as Mark Glanville's memoir, *The Goldberg Variations*, focusing specifically on the ways in which they explore the construction of Jewish masculinity in contem-porary Britain. I want now to revisit these texts in order to focus in more detail on the ways in which being half-Jewish can be read as the preoccupying theme.

In the *J-Word* we see Simon, a middle-aged man in the throes of an identity crisis. He is the son of a Jewish father and non-Jewish mother (and, therefore, according to Jewish tradition not Jewish himself). By marrying a Jewish woman, Simon has fathered a Jewish son, but he comes to question where exactly he belongs in this Jewish family. The question pivots on how Jewishness itself is conceptualized. As Jack, Simon's father puts it, encountering a woman who seems to epitomize all the qualities of the gentile world but who it turns out is 'a bit' Jewish on her mother's side: 'All Jews are equally Jewish. There are no half Jews. There are no proportions or fractions or half-measures in Judaism'.[7] However, for Simon, who is on the wrong side of this certainty principle, identity is far less clearly defined. His crisis is predicated on a sense of ontological incompleteness that becomes progressively more critical after watching a documentary about Auschwitz. 'If I had been murdered in the Holocaust', he thinks, 'I would be Jewish. But alive, I am not Jewish' (152). Sanger's novel suggests that it is this knowledge of a simultaneously doubled and divided identity that comes to rupture Simon's sense of self. He sees himself as an outsider, a potential victim of the Nazis (whatever his status within Jewish law); but he also feels excluded from the Jewishness that, for him, is the quintessence of all other excluded identities. Describing his increasingly fractured sense of subjectivity and his ensuing psychological collapse, he explains: 'It was like being two people who are both angry – with each other. Or two half people, a half-Jew and a half-non-Jew. The whole being less than the sum of the parts. Because I consist only of fragments' (246). The work of the novel is to present the possibility of repair to this shattered self.

Danny, Simon's son, will find a new way in which to be Jewish. Drawing from the mathematical motif that runs through the novel, and echoing his grandfather's belief in whole identities, he reflects that Jewishness is ultimately based on indivisibility:

> Jewish people are sort of like a country, which, even if you take the country away and try to smash it up and throw its people all over the world and kill millions of them, nothing changes, they still stay the same, and can't be broken up. So Jews are like a prime number. And a prime letter. And a prime word. (328)

Both grandson and grandfather understand Jewishness as fundamentally unbreakable and, as the narrative progresses, so Simon also finds a way in which to reconcile his split sense of self. Although suspicious about religious faith, he nevertheless achieves a resolution through connecting to collective Jewish ritual. Attending his first synagogue service, 'he shivered with recognition':

> It seemed to him that each congregation of Jews at their Sabbath services around the globe on that day, listening to the unchanging proclamation

in untranslated words of prehistory, were joined in some larger congrega-
tion, Jews of every time and place, all of that most hated and despised and
enduring tribe....he could almost feel the sand beneath his feet, and the
desert sun. (319)

It is a curious moment that suggests an ineffable quality to Jewishness.
This is not the first or the last example of this that we see in contemporary British-Jewish literature. From Bernice Rubens' *I Dreyfus*, in
which Alfred Dreyfus displays an innate knowledge of Judaism; to the
far more ironic self-interrogation of, for example, Howard Jacobson
in *Roots Schmoots*; or, Chloe Zhivago's instinctive, chicken-soup
connection to Jewish tradition in Olivia Lichtenstein's frothy novel,
Jewishness is repeatedly presented as an intrinsic and enduring tribal
condition. All Jews, such a formulation suggests, however disconnected, disenchanted or lost they might be, can somehow return to an
essential condition of Jewishness.

In this way, Sanger's novel which suggests that half-Jewishness, even
in today's Britain, might be bad for the psyche, presents a moment of
healing. So it is that Simon, an atheistic, intellectual, Londoner, experiences the comfort of connection and even feels the distant warmth
of an autochthonous beginning in the Middle-Eastern 'desert sun'. He
also, through making this connection to Jewishness, finds a way in
which to be English. As he explains: 'I used to feel that I was half
Jewish and half English. Two halves that didn't add up to a whole
anything. Now I feel both fully Jewish and fully English' (337). The
resolution offered here is both strained and strange. It suggests an
idealistic conclusion, in which belonging can be achieved, but it also
presents an oddly restrictive and somewhat disheartening view of
identity within contemporary British culture.

Mark Glanville's memoir tackles some related issues through auto-
biographical exploration. It opens with the line, 'happy the man who
can celebrate his diversity'.[8] He continues, using strikingly similar
terms to Sanger's fictional character Simon, by presenting himself as
embodying a condition of violent internal division: 'For a large part of
my own life', he explains, 'the contradictory elements of my identity
have been at war, and have fragmented rather than fused me' (1).
Like Simon, Glanville's father is Jewish but his mother, born of a
German-Jewish father and a gentile mother, is not then technically
Jewish. Thus, according to the oft-cited orthodox principle, Mark
Glanville is not Jewish. His clever, charming and dominant father
teases Glanville about this identity glitch throughout his formative

years. So, for example, he tells the young Glanville that at least he will not have to contend with antisemitism. The exchange that follows, signals a complex set of identifications: 'What do you mean?' he asks his father:

> 'Well you don't look Jewish'.
> 'Of course I do'.
> 'Darling, you don't'. Mum's sweet tone heightened the provocation.
> 'You should be grateful for that', Dad continued.
> 'For what? I'm not going to hide. They can all know I'm Jewish as far as I'm concerned'.
> 'But, my dear, you're not Jewish'.
> 'What do you mean? Of course I am'.
> 'By Jewish law you're not...'
> 'Seventy-five per cent of my blood is Jewish. It's what I am'.
> 'The wrong seventy-five per cent, schmendrick!' (37)

His father's final word, which both draws from and claims a Yiddish lexicon, plays Jewishness as a trump card in this generational power struggle.

Much of the narrative circles around this snag in identification. As it charts Glanville's youthful attachment to football hooliganism, his unsatisfactory relationships with women, his time at Oxford and his developing career as an opera singer, the memoir demonstrates a profound sense of disconnection and a concurrently strong desire to belong to something, even if that is a violent gang of Manchester United supporters. When, later in life, the confused Glanville discusses his identity with a mixed heritage girlfriend, she asks him, 'What do you feel you are yourself?' He replies, 'Jewish. One hundred per cent' (142). So, the 'seventy-five percent' that he had claimed in arguing with his father has been adjusted to the full one hundred. Again, a mathematical imperative surfaces as a way in which to think about degrees of belonging. But, then admitting that this is not technically the case, Glanville adds 'it makes me feel very rootless' (142); and this rootlessness is presented as a dangerously ungrounded condition.

As Jacobson reflected, in a quote from *Roots Schmoots* that I cited in Chapter 4, but which seems apposite to cite again here, for the immediate post-war generation, 'the problem of how it felt not to feel Jewish' was not the cause of pain that it would later become. The priority for his generation was to become English. 'Roots we didn't think about,' he notes, 'tendrils we needed. You don't look down when you're climbing'.[9] For subsequent generations of British

Jews the predominant imagery is perhaps not so much of climbing, o looking upwards, but rather a perception of skimming, without any secure foundations, across the surface of a series of possible selves So, for someone such as Glanville, who has been brought up with a confused awareness of simultaneously being and not being Jewish, the desire to belong becomes acute.

He begins a process of reconciliation when he attends a synagogue memorial service for his first singing teacher, Mark Raphael. Again like Simon, in Sanger's novel, he describes a powerful sense of reinte gration as he enters the synagogue:

> Despite Dad's, daily reminders of our provenance, albeit accompanied with caveats that we weren't thoroughbreds, I'd never actually been inside a synagogue before ... So I went with very mixed feelings, excited at the prospect of entering a shul for the first time ... I certainly nurtured no expectation of returning to the fold. (223)

The experience is, in fact, transformative: 'As I walked into the temple itself', he recalls, 'I experienced a wonderful inner tranquility'; adding 'I felt an almost physical sensation of belonging' (224). This sense of belonging is completed when he falls in love with a Jewish woman, who he recognizes as his 'perfect woman' (234), and he begins to attend a Reform synagogue. As he sings in the synagogue he experiences a hitherto unknown sense of fulfilment. When the synagogue warden the shammas, compliments him, Glanville is overwhelmed, recalling that: 'Tears came into my eyes on finally receiving the acceptance I'd so longed for without, until now, ever really knowing from whom it was I'd sought it' (246). To complete this circle of belonging it turns out that the shammas, who is the same age as Glanville, and shares a number of physical characteristics, is also a keen football fan. For Glanville, the connection is healing. Earlier in the memoir he had quoted some lines from the poetry of Celan whose idea of *pneuma* he finds profoundly moving. 'The breath of Celan's Jewishness', he explains, is 'an essence like music, that couldn't be caught, and codified in law or defined by race'. And, in a powerful statement on identity he announces, 'I wasn't a racial or a religious Jew. I was a pneumatic Jew' (247).

In some respects, it is as good a definition as any. Jewishness, as we have seen throughout *Writing Jewish*, is a slippery and perhaps indefinable term. Glanville's somewhat mystical redefinition is open to question but it makes sense for him, and *of* him. His story, as I discussed in Chapter 6, ends with a note of humorous self-awareness but the drive towards reconciliation in both Sanger and Glanville's texts is strong. For both Simon in fiction and Glanville in memoir the idea of half-Jewish does not work. They both instead seek ways in which to become differently whole, rather than fatally incomplete, Jews. Returning now to the heated debate that followed Thirlwell's declaration of half-Jewishness in the *Jewish Quarterly*, I want to explore what else might be in play in such a formulation.

'Multicultural Heaven'? Jews and other others

Cynthia Ozick responded to Thirlwell's article in the *Jewish Quarterly* with outrage.[10] Interestingly, Ozick attacked Thirlwell for what she perceived as particularly *British* brand of Jewish self-consciousness which resulted in what she termed, the 'ahistorical lukewarmness' of his essay. 'The ... hallmark of Jewishness', she argues, 'lies precisely in its distinction-making: the knowledge, the bold assertion ... , that one thing is not another thing ... that people are born wholes, not halves. And that the purpose of seeing distinction is to make choices'.[11] Partly this is a clash between a US and British perspective, a matter again of confidence in asserting the existence of what could be termed a 'Jewish sensibility', or as Ozick puts it elsewhere, a '*substratum* that is recognizably Jewish'.[12] So an American writer such as Nessa Rapoport can talk about 'the possibility of a literature whose spine and sinews would not be simply Jewish experience, but Jewish materials and Jewish dreams', and another American writer, Robert Lasson, can define himself as 'a gastrointestinal Jew'.[13] These are explicit, definite and gutsy identifications against which Thirlwell's 'half-Jewishness' might well look irresponsibly timid and even Glanville's pneumatic Jewish essentialism might seem altogether less robust.

This conflict perhaps also signifies a generational shift in perception. Put simply, Ozick, born in New York to immigrant parents in 1928, and Thirlwell, who was born in North London in 1978 in comfortable and privileged circumstances, have distinctly different experiences of Jewishness. Thirlwell's approach to identity is formed by a postmodern sense of subjectivity in flux. One could argue that perhaps Thirlwell's generation is generally far more comfortable with not quite belonging to any identity in particular. Whereas some writers in their forties and fifties such as Sanger and Glanville might have a more fraught sense of wanting to belong, other, younger writers are possibly less attached to a singular or even dual sense of defining identity. Increasingly, British-Jewishness is being understood as an evolving series of identifications. For younger writers, there is undoubtedly still an interest in understanding oneself in relation to a collective Jewish history, but, as the twenty-first century unfolds, British-Jewishness is increasingly figured as a matrix of connections that form ever more imbricated ways of belonging. The final part of this discussion focuses on the ways in which some recent British Jewish writers explore these possibilities.

Thirlwell's character Moshe, in *Politics* (2003), typifies a loose and uncommitted form of Jewishness. 'This was partly', the narrator explains, 'because only his father was Jewish. It was also because his father was not a very Jewish Jew'.[14] So here we have a self-consciously tepid Jewishness, that having been passed down the paternal, rather than maternal, line amounts to an inflection, rather than a summation of identity. Despite bearing a name that connotes a pronounced connection to Jewishness, Moshe is not 'a serious Jewish boy' (75): he cannot locate Israel on a map, he is not circumcised, and although he owns a 1996 Union of Jewish Students Haggadah (which includes an essay by the Chief Rabbi, 'Why Be Jewish?'), he is not concerned about the future of the Jewish people. Moshe thus provides an insight into the parameters of the contemporary condition. 'Occasionally', the narrator tells us:

> Moshe enjoyed being overtly Jewish. Sometimes he felt loyal. But he was not inclined to worry about his nation. He did not worry about his Jewishness...Sometimes he felt loyal. But, more often, he did not. He did not understand allegiance. (76)

Jewishness, for this disconnected generation, is one root among many. So, although in crisis Moshe finds himself feeling fondly towards the Hasidim in Hatton Garden, and drawn to the *Kosher Knosherie*, he is not so much a pneumatic Jew, as a rather breezy one. He allows Jewishness to pass over him in small, mostly unruffling, moments.

Politics, which treats Jewishness not as an essence but as a constituent element within a range of identities, also places Jewishness within a wider context of multiculturalism. Thirlwell situates Moshe in the north-west London suburb of Edgware, a place that has a markedly Jewish population evidenced, amongst other ways, by the 'ten-foot high menorah for Chanukah' that is erected each year outside the tube station. But this is not all there to celebrate about 'the odd variety of happiness' that Edgware invokes. The narrator explains that:

> On Saturday nights, when Shabbat is over, a collection of Jewish boys and girls congregate with black and Asian boys and girls outside McDonald's. They sell each other drugs. Sometimes, to pass the time, they get on the

tube to Golders Green and stand outside Golders Green station. Then
they come back to Edgware station.

Edgware is multicultural heaven (250–251)

Here the youth of Edgware are united in shared aimlessness as
different ethnic and racial groups exist easily alongside each other.
The Jewish boys and girls, like the black and Asian boys and girls,
are, it is suggested, all engaged in the same meaningless looping journeys, travelling but going nowhere. It is a mordantly postmodern kind
of equality located within an archetypally 'dismal, quiet, lovable and
kitsch' (251) suburban environment.

Sander Gilman has argued that 'the figure of the Jew, defined
within the world of fiction, is a key to the understanding of the
very nature of the multicultural society represented in it'.[15] In this
context, Gilman reads Hanif Kureishi's 1997 short story 'We're
Not Jews' as an example of the way in which the Jew functions as
a 'litmus test to define a particularly multicultural world' (147).
The story, which is set in the 1960s, focuses on an encounter
between an English woman, who has married a Pakistani man,
her son and their teddy boy neighbours. As mother and son are
verbally abused the mother responds with the statement, 'We're
not Jews'.[16] It is a strange and seemingly disconnected response.
However, as the story explores the complexities of exclusion, and
the strategies of displacement and disavowal that they invoke, it
makes more sense. Kureishi paints a bleak picture of race and class
in 1960s Britain. This retrospective context is important to note.
Whilst it is evident that racial and religious tensions clearly exist
still in contemporary Britain, more recent representations, set in
the present, have tended to approach the relationship between
Jews and other minority groups by presenting unlikely hybridiza-
tions, reversals and renegotiations of identity. Such explorations
often form the basis for comic encounters. So, to take a mainstream
example, the British film *The Infidel* (2010), uses the stock narrative convention of swapped identities to explore the intersecting
identities of British Jews and British Muslims. The film, which
presents some astute moments of observation, arrives at a rather
unchallenging but upbeat conclusion. It suggests that beneath all
the obvious dissimilarities and deep-rooted animosities, Jews and
Muslims are not essentially so different after all.[17] Thus the pain
underlying Kureishi's story becomes reconfigured, in a mainstream
comic mode, as a thing of the past.

There is then, in some recent representations, a cheery embrace
of diverse and hybridized forms of Jewishness. In these figurations,
the angst described by Sanger and Glanville comes to seem unnec-
essarily morose. As issues of divisibility and indivisibility become
re-envisioned as a celebration of multiplicity, we see some playful
explorations of the ways in which Jewishness becomes deployed as a
component of fused rather than *con*fused identities. So, for example,
Olivia Lichtenstein, in *Mrs Zhivago of Queens Park*, introduces the
character of Abraham 'Abe' Green, a six-foot Rastafarian Jewish deli
owner, who is studying to be a rabbi, and whose speech is littered with
'Oy Veys' and 'ai yai yais'. His ancestry, it is explained, is derived from
the Portuguese-Spanish colonizers of sixteenth-century Jamaica. As
he rolls a joint, he discusses the impact of this hybridized identity in
enthusiastic terms:

> Genes, shmenes, they're complementary, two halves that make a per-
> fect whole: Rasta grass to give you an appetite, Jewish food to feed
> your munchies. Yin and Yang, you should pardon the expression. The
> Rastafarian Jew is the most highly evolved human being on the planet.[18]

So, in this formulation, a character such as Sanger's divided Simon,
who has felt himself to be 'two halves that didn't add up to a whole
anything', is reconfigured to be 'a perfect whole'. Perhaps beyond the
obvious stylistic and tonal differences in these novels, the difference
in terms of their representation of identity is that the gentile half of
Simon is figured as a rather blank, English, non-self, whereas Abe,
the Rastafarian Jew, merges two equally, if stereotypically, vibrant
parts. Abe is an incidental character in a light-hearted novel, but, as
I argued in Chapter 7, Lichtenstein's text exposes a seam of anxiety
about Chloe Zhivago's lack of connection to her Jewishness and this
Rastafarian Jew in some ways answers such unease. He is more than
the sum of his parts.

Olivia Lichtenstein's characterization of hybridity is then brief and
celebratory. Jake Wallis Simons', *The Exiled Times of a Tibetan Jew*
(2005) in the style of Salman Rushdie, presents a more experimental
literary text that tackles both the seriousness and the absurdity that
underpins identification.[19] In particular he draws out the comic pathos
of bizarre and mismatched combinations through the character of
Rabbi Chod, a Tibetan Jew who presents himself as a reincarnation of
Moses and gathers followers to his lost tribe of Israel. Chod, who runs
his synagogue from a pet shop in Golders Green, feels unfairly marginalized by the more conventional Tibetan immigrant community, the

Anglo-Jewish population and the British authorities. In essence, he wants to belong. Trying to find a suitable site for sky-burial in London, he focuses on Hampstead Heath, reasoning that 'this prominent location will make a bold statement that Tibetan Jews are truly part of the fabric of British life' (12).

Identities here are not so much hybridized as thrown into collision and the character is created with considerable comic brio. Chod's pet shop/office/synagogue is a muddled hotchpotch of religious and cultural signification and contains the detritus of many years and many cultures. It jumbles together rosaries, Bibles, pictures of the Dalai Lama, a Torah scroll, posters of Tibet and Jerusalem, Israeli flags and a Tibetan canopy. As the narrator explains: 'The entire room had an uncanny, discordant atmosphere. Everywhere I looked, Jewish symbols had been self-consciously positioned within an otherwise Tibetan environment, with a hint of Englishness of course' (32). The effect of such juxtaposition is comical but also disconcerting. It is a desperate and overdetermined attempt to merge cultural identities, but it ends up marking the gaps between them.

The ludicrous implausibility of Chod's endeavour is apparent, but this drive towards conjunction, with Jewishness functioning as a factor within ever more complex and compounded identities, is, as we have seen, a serious and recurring theme in other recent writing. These texts, in strikingly different ways, suggest that there is an interactive loop in which Jewishness alters the conditions around it and is itself altered by a range of other differences. Some of these figurations are idealistic, or somewhat simplistic, but they signal an openness to reconfiguration, however absurd or awkward that might be. Certainly, some leading contemporary British-Jewish writers are approaching such issues from a nuanced perspective. So, we see, for example, in Naomi Alderman's astutely observed short story 'Other People's Gods', an impulse to engage with difference from the Jewish perspective. Reuben Bloom, the thoroughly Jewish optician who is the protagonist of the story, has led a 'blameless life' in Hendon.[20] However, when he sees a statue of the Hindu god Ganesha on a market stall, he buys it, brings it home and is changed by it. Alderman presents here another fable about disobedience, in this case the worshipping of idols, which suggest that Jewishness cannot remain impervious to the influences around it within the diverse conditions of contemporary Britain.

In *White Teeth* (2000), Zadie Smith famously articulated what has come to be seen as the millennial zeitgeist of British multiculturalism. In exploring variations on themes of hybridized identities she introduces the Chalfens, an upper-middle class, liberal, half-Jewish family. A passage extracted from Joyce Chalfen's book on cross-fertilization explains that:

> Where once gardeners swore by the reliability of the self-pollinating plant in which pollen is transferred from the stamen to the stigma of the same flower (autogamy), now we are more adventurous, positively singing the praises of cross-pollination.[21]

For many British Jews today, this pseudo-horticultural paean to cross-fertilization might be the reality of the situation as Jews increasingly marry out and parent children who are Jewish in different ways to previous generations of British Jews.

In an article for the *Guardian*, Jake Wallis Simons has discussed his own British-Jewish identification in such terms. He was born to a Jewish mother and non-Jewish father and his early childhood was broadly secular in nature. When his parents divorced, and his mother became more orthodox, so Simons became more fully identified with Jewishness but less secure in terms of Britishness. He describes how as orthodox young Jews, even in the 1980s, he and his brother 'felt profoundly alienated from the Britain that surrounded us'.[22] Yet, through a process of shifting identification, he has in adult life become detached from orthodox Judaism and, like many other contemporary British Jews, he has gone on to create a different type of family. 'I have three children now', he explains,

> and my partner is not Jewish – or at least, her father is Jewish but not her mother, which is unacceptable from the orthodox perspective. What is missing for people such as me, who have found the dominant cultures of their birth untenable, is a coherent group mythology, shared traditions and a sense of belonging... As a parent it is my duty to acknowledge that the strands that weave the tapestry of our identities are not singular, but multiple.

Simons' acknowledgment of loss in relation to a coherent 'sense of belonging' is important. For many Jews in contemporary Britain feelings of disconnection can be complex and troubling and this is undoubtedly a theme that has informed much recent British-Jewish writing. But, as Simons also notes, for the next generation, multiplicity is a progressively more defining aspect of identification. How Jewishness endures as a meaningful and distinctive identity in this context is the focus of anxiety for some, but not all, elements of the Anglo-Jewish population in Britain today. As Jews increasingly marry out and parent children who experience Jewishness in diverse ways, the answer to the Chief Rabbi's question of 1994, 'will we have Jewish grandchildren?' is difficult to answer.[23] Perhaps such a question can only really be addressed, in a stereotypically Jewish manner, by reframing it as another question; asking, instead, what does 'Jewish' mean?

Jew-ish, Jew-ish-ish ...

Some years ago the British-Jewish atheist, Jonathan Miller, described himself as 'Jew-ish'.[24] He has been asked to explain this ever since. In an interview with Mark Lawson at Jewish Book Week in 2009, Miller articulated a cheerfully disconnected sense of Jewishness, describing his father as a 'Jewish amphibian' and himself as only really 'a Jew for antisemites'.[25] Jewishness for him is neither something to be denied, nor an identity to be claimed. In this sense all identities are equally meaningful and meaningless. They are not, for Miller, a matter for angst or overly stringent definition and he adds that as well as Jew-ish, he might also say that he is 'Brit-ish'. Neither identification is comprehensive or defining.

In 'Not Jewish but Jew-ish', a 2009 *Guardian* article, Jonathan Margolis develops the theme:

> We are those cop-out, fair-weather Jews that 'real' Jews despise more than they do antisemites: the secular, cultural Jews, the amoral majority, the ones who want to have their bagel and eat it. The ones who, with their marrying out, their going to the pub on Yom Kippur and to the football on Saturdays, and – God forbid – with their ambivalent view of the Middle East, are doing Hitler's work for him and conspiring in the erosion of the already disappearing UK Jewish community – currently about 250,000 and counting, downwards.[26]

In admitting to this apparently compromised Jewish identity, Margolis effectively claims the contemporary ground. He continues by acknowledging that his form of 'fair-weather' Jewishness has undoubtedly impacted on the Jewishness of his offspring and, by implication, the declining Anglo-Jewish population.

> So has being merely Jew-ish rather than a proper Jew, marrying a woman who was half-Jewish, half-Methodist, and eating non-kosher food these five decades thwarted my children's option to be Jews, and by doing so played its part in the slow decline of Britain's Jewish population? In an odd way, it hasn't entirely.

He goes on to outline the ways in which each of his three children is finding new ways to connect to Jewishness: through relationships, work and political engagement, and he ends with the thought that 'all this activity by our Jew-ish-ish children seems to suggest our particular Jew-ish line might limp on for a while yet, rather than collapse in an apathetic heap'. His grandchildren, might not be Jewish but they will, he thinks, be Jew-ish-ish. Or perhaps that should be Jew-ish-ish-ish?

So, in the end, neither anxieties about diminishing identities nor blasé celebrations of cultural plurality quite describe the contemporary situation for British Jews. Jewishness still exists; it has a distinct history and particular flavour in British life. But, increasingly, it exists alongside a range of other differences in the form of Jew-ishness. However, in focusing on the ways in which identities are increasingly connected and overlapping, we might also need to attend to the interstices that exist between Jewishness and other identities. Throughout *Writing Jewish* I have looked at the tensions between Jewish and British identities and the tensions within Jewish identities. We have seen a shift from insecurity about being not quite British, to insecurity about being not quite Jewish, and finally a playfulness, or at least a willingness, to explore gaps in identity. However, such a trajectory is never entirely clear and questions about what it really means to be a Jew in Britain today continue to disturb, engage and energize contemporary writers.

Recent reflections on Jewish identity circle round these questions of distinctiveness and definition. Perhaps it is apt to end with a non-Jewish writer who demonstrates an acute understanding of precisely these issues. In her 2002 novel, *The Autograph Man,* Zadie Smith's hero is Alex-Li Tandem, a Chinese-Jewish hero born and bred in North London. Following Lenny Bruce's example, Tandem compiles a potentially endless compendium that sets out to divide the world into that which is deemed to be Jewish and that which is (in these terms) 'Goyish'. So for example, in the category of office items: the stapler is clearly Jewish whilst the paper-clip and mouse-mat are Goyish.[27] Tandem is of course, as his name suggests, the embodiment of hybridized, multiple, postmodern subjectivity, and his list points to the ludicrous and futile nature of trying to fix and itemize identities. And yet, however risible the project is, it is also somehow compelling. Whilst in many ways the contemporary mode celebrates the dissolution of certainties we also seem to crave distinction. Peculiarity is appealing. As readers we might be left wondering, despite our better judgement, if there is, after all, something more Jewish about a stapler than a paper-clip?

In twenty-first century Britain, Jewishness is one difference among many. Contemporary British-Jewish writers highlight the desire to identify the particularity of their difference, whilst acknowledging that that difference is neither fixed nor final, but always open to change, re-signification and re-interpretation. The question is, not if Britishness and Jewishness are attached, but perhaps instead *how* they are attached? Is it a staple or paper-clip that holds such identities together?

Notes

1. Rachel Lichtenstein and Iain Sinclair, *Rodinsky's Room* (London: Granta, 1999).
2. I am grateful to Rachel Lichtenstein for her generous comments on an early article I published on *Rodinsky's Room*.
3. Jonathan Leaman, 'On Not Being Jewish Enough', *Jewish Quarterly*, 196 (2004/2005), 49–51.
4. Tamar Yellin, 'Kafka in Brontëland', *Kafka in Brontëland and Other Stories* (London: The Toby Press, 2006), 11–22, 14.
5. Tamar Yellin, 'A Jew in Brontëland', *Jewish Quarterly*, 208 (2007), 68–69.
6. Adam Thirlwell, 'On Writing Half-Jewishly', *Jewish Quarterly*, 208 (2007), 4–5.
7. Andrew Sanger, *The J-Word* (London: Snowbooks, 2009), p.173.
8. Mark Glanville, *The Goldberg Variations: From Football Hooligan to Opera Singer* (London: Flamingo, 2004), p.1.
9. Howard Jacobson, *Roots Schmoots: Journeys Among Jews* (London: Penguin, 1993), p.2.
10. The debate was developed further by Gabriel Josipovici who framed it in terms of a contest between realism and postmodernity. Gabriel Josipovici, 'Boxing Clever', *Jewish Quarterly*, 210 (2008), 70–72. These issues were also the focus of a Jewish Book Week discussion, 'A Beginner's Guide to Jews on the Edge', between Thirlwell and Will Self (28 February 2010). See: http://www.jewishbookweek.com/2010/beginners-guide-jews-on-the-edge.php. Accessed 08 June 2012.
11. Cynthia Ozick, 'Responsa', *Jewish Quarterly*, 209 (2008), 5.
12. Ozick, cited in 'Forward', in Sonja Lyndon and Sylvia Paskin, eds, *The Slow Mirror and Other Stories: New Fiction by Jewish Writers* (Nottingham: Five Leaves, 1996), p.3.
13. Nessa Rapoport and Robert Lasson, cited in 'Forward', *The Slow Mirror and Other Stories: New Fiction by Jewish Writers,* eds, Sonja Lyndon and Sylvia Paskin (Nottingham: Five Leaves, 1996), p.2.
14. Adam Thirlwell, *Politics* (London: Vintage, 2006), p.75.

15. Sander Gilman, *Multiculturalism and the Jews* (London: Routledge, 2006), p.146. See also Efraim Sicher and Linda Weinhouse, *Under Postcolonial Eyes: Figuring the 'Jew' in Contemporary British Writing* (Nebraska: University of Nebraska Press, 2013). Sicher and Weinhouse's book, in its emphasis on issues of multiculturalism and globalization, appears to be an interesting and useful contribution to the field of British-Jewish studies. Unfortunately its publication has come too late for consideration in *Writing Jewish*.

16. Hanif Kureishi, 'We're Not Jews', *Love in a Blue Time* (London: Faber and Faber, 1997), pp.41–51 (p.45).

17. Josh Appignanesi, Josh, dir., *The Infidel* (2010). David Baddiel wrote the screenplay for the film. He has noted that 'the idea for the film came, in part, out of my own ethnic ambiguity. At school, a lot of people thought I was from Pakistan; I was bullied by racists both for being Pakistani and for being Jewish.' David Baddiel, 'I'm not worried about a backlash', *Guardian*, 8 April 2010. Sarfraz Manzoor charted an interesting response to the proposition of Muslim-Jewish interchangeability in 'My month of being Jewish', *Guardian*, 8 April 2010.

18. Olivia Lichtenstein, *Mrs Zhivago of Queen's Park* (London: Orion, 2007), p.221.

19. Jake Wallis Simons, *The Exiled Times of a Tibetan Jew* (London: Polygon, 2005).

20. Naomi Alderman 'Other People's Gods', BBC National Short Story Award (2009), http://fileserver.booktrust.org.uk/usr/library/documents/bbc-nssa-2009/other_peoples_gods.pdf. 15-31. Accessed 05 June 2012.

21. Zadie Smith, *White Teeth* (London: Penguin, 2001), p.309.

22. Jake Wallis Simons, 'I broke out of my orthodox cocoon', *Guardian*, 13 March 2010.

23. Jonathan Sacks, *Will We Have Jewish Grandchildren: Jewish Continuity and How to Achieve it* (London: Vallentine Mitchell, 1994).

24. See http://www.thejc.com/arts/arts-interviews/jonathan-miller-yes-im-a-jew-and-a-chimpanzee. Accessed 09 June 2012.

25. http://www.jewishbookweek.com/2009/220209r.php. Accessed 09 June 2012.

26. Jonathan Margolis, 'Not Jewish but Jew-ish', *Guardian*, 30 November 2009.

27. Zadie Smith, *The Autograph Man* (London: Penguin, 2003), p.90.

Afterword: Reality Gaps

In 2009 Naomi Alderman published a short story, titled 'United'.[1] The story responds explicitly to *Connection, Continuity and Community*, a recently published report which reflected on findings from a survey of Jewish women in contemporary Britain. The question underlying the project, and the continuity and renewal agenda in general, is what will become of Anglo-Jewry?[2] In an ever more disconnected and discontinuous culture, will it eventually become extinct? The report begins by noting that:

> There appears to be something of a reality gap between the ways in which Jews today live (and will increasingly live) their diverse lives and the ways in which the leaders of institutional Judaism would ideally wish they might live their lives. (6)

The anxiety here is that this 'reality gap' will widen. If the Anglo-Jewish leadership is neither willing nor able to adapt to the changing conditions of the twenty-first century, so British-Jewishness might become a thing of the past.

Alderman's story presents a future Britain in which Jewishness has, in effect, died out. It is, instead, reproduced in a mediated form at the annual 'Festival of Judaism'. The story is narrated from the perspective of Ellie Markowitz, a single woman in her thirties, who reflects somewhat wistfully on what has been lost in this heritage park version of Jewishness. When Ellie asks her grandmother what her experience of 'real' Jewish life had been like, the old woman does not romanticize the past:

> She rolled her eyes to the ceiling with the effort of recollection, 'well, it had been dying for a long time you know. People didn't feel comfortable anymore in those synagogues. Everyone thought that Real Judaism was meant for someone else. Not the average person. It's better now: everyone can enjoy the Festival'.

The festival has become a hyper-real version of Jewishness. It is in this way, far more inclusive than the 'real' Jewishness had ever been. Ellie's struggle to understand her identity as a Jew in this dislocated contemporary milieu illustrates a tendency that I have traced

163

throughout *Writing Jewish*. For her generation a perceived disconnection from Jewishness can lead to a rather nostalgic yearning
for a more congruent Jewish identity. Alderman's story, however,
neither romanticizes nor disavows such yearning. Instead it explores
some of the tensions that are evoked in re-visiting a simulacrum of
Jewishness.

The story is set in the year of a new development for the festival.
The innovative young expo team have organized a display in
which a 'real, authentic Jewish family' (3), the Blattsteins, live
their traditional Jewish lives in public view. In the same issue of
Jewish Quarterly in which Alderman's story was published, Ruth
Ellen Gruber reflects on 'virtual Jewishness', the trend that she
had identified in mid-1990s post-communist Europe.[3] Gruber
observed that Jewish culture festivals were taking place in locations across Poland, for example, where few if any Jews remained.
Since Gruber's book, *Virtually Jewish*, was first published in 2002,
internet communications have accelerated the possibilities to
engage with 'virtual Jewry' in a variety of ways. She cites, by way
of example, the 'Virtual Diaspora' of Second Life and the 'Virtual
Shtetl' which is under construction in Warsaw. The festivals and
interactive sites on which Gruber focuses, allow otherwise dislocated Jews to explore their 'culture, heritage and identity' (25);
and non-Jews to experience some of the flavour of Jewishness
within these simulated and sanitized environments. Alderman's
story functions in a similarly virtual vein. The 'Festival of Judaism'
allows visitors to experience a replicated sensation of connection
to an imagined past; but it also offers the security of detachment,
positioning the viewer as a tourist who can pass safely through this
landscape of faded identifications.

Ellie visits the exhibition with her friends, Adam and Steve, a gay
couple who are bringing up a child together in a new kind of family.
They ponder the lives of the Blattsteins and the ways in which the
narrow and exclusionary nature of traditional Jewish life in Britain
had led to its demise: 'Just like pandas', Steve notes, 'if they'd really
had any kind of survival instinct they'd have moved with the times'
(4). But Ellie's response is ambivalent. As she contemplates the
Jewish past, she is neither simply nostalgic nor condemnatory. She
realizes that this was a culture in which neither she nor her friends
would have a place and reflects on a complicated set of connections and disconnections: 'not everything that is lost is good', she

acknowledges, 'but it has still been lost and perhaps it is right to mourn for it' (5).

Late at night, when she is the only visitor left in the exhibition, Ellie shares a brief moment of affinity with the Blattstein daughter who, it will emerge, has fallen in love with a non-Jewish man (in fact, one of the expo organizers), and will soon walk out on the installation. When, as midnight approaches, the attendant finds that Ellie is still on the premises, his words could perhaps serve as a warning for a generation of British Jews who do not know quite how to remember their Jewish pasts, but do not know, either, quite how to forget: 'Time now please', he says, 'time to leave now' (5).

In the end Ellie struggles to resolve what it means to be a Jewish woman in this virtually Jewish world. Her final exchange with Steve encapsulates the tension between the imagined Jewish past and the increasingly diffuse Jew-ish present. 'Maybe', Ellie suggests:

> 'When the last one's gone, the last person who felt like they had a right to call themselves a Real Jew, Jewish can just be something you...'
> 'Something you can choose to be?' said Steve, 'something you can call yourself? Something where you are the one who gets to decide what it means...'
> 'I don't know', said Ellie. 'When you say it like that, it sounds a bit improbable'. (5)

I started *Writing Jewish* by reflecting on Judah Passow's photographs of Jews in contemporary Britain. I want to end now by suggesting that Passow's images, which in many respects show the resilience of British-Jewish life, and Alderman's story, which explores the fictional possibilities of its extinction, lead us to a similar conclusion. British-Jewish identities are continuously evolving and always under construction. Steve, in Alderman's story, could have the right idea, however 'improbable' it might sound. *Writing Jewish* has suggested that history, memory, geography, stereotypes, bodies, dispossession and desire all play important roles in constructing a sense of British-Jewish identity; but, in the provisional, shifting and multiple conditions of twenty-first century Britain, a 'Real Jew' might also signify, 'something you can choose to be'.

Notes

1. Naomi Alderman, 'United', *Jewish Quarterly*, 214 (2009), 3–5.

2. Women's Review Taskforce, *Connection, Continuity and Community*, 2009. http://www.boardofdeputies.org.uk/file/ ConnectionContinuityCommunity.pdf. Accessed 30 June 2012. For an outline of the continuity and renewal agenda see Keith Kahn-Harris and Ben Gidley, *Turbulent Times: The British Jewish Community Today* (London: Continuum, 2010).
3. Ruth Gruber, 'Virtual Judaism', *Jewish Quarterly*, 214 (2009), 22–25.

Bibliography

Abrams, Nathan, *The New Jew in Film: Exploring Jewishness and Judaism in Contemporary Cinema* (London: I.B. Tauris, 2012).

Alderman, Naomi, *Disobedience* (London: Viking, 2006).

Alderman, Naomi, 'United', *Jewish Quarterly*, 214 (2009), 3–5.

Alderman, Naomi, 'Other People's Gods', BBC National Short Story Award (2009). http://fileserver.booktrust.org.uk/usr/library/documents/bbc-nssa-2009/other_peoples_gods.pdf. 15-31. Accessed 05 June 2012.

Alderman, Naomi, 'According to Your Will', Granta Blog, 20 May 2011. http://www.granta.com/New-Writing/According-to-Your-Will.

Alderman, Naomi, 'Anne Frank and So On', *Jewish Quarterly*, 221 (2012), 27–30.

Anderson, Benedict, *Imagined Communities* (London: Verso, 1991).

Antler, Joyce, *You Never Call! You Never Write: A History of the Jewish Mother* (Oxford: Oxford University Press, 2007).

Appignanesi, Josh, dir., *The Infidel* (2010).

Appignanesi, Lisa, *Losing the Dead* (London: Vintage, 1999).

Appignanesi, Lisa, *The Memory Man* (London: Arcadia, 2004).

Assmann, Jan, 'Collective Memory and Cultural Identity', trans. by John Czaplicka, *New German Critique*, 65 (1995), 125–33.

Aviv, Caryn and David Shneer, *New Jews: The End of the Jewish Diaspora* (New York: New York University Press, 2005).

Baddiel, David, *The Secret Purposes* (London: Abacus, 2004).

Baddiel, David, 'I'm not worried about a backlash', *Guardian*, 8 April 2010.

Baddiel, David, *The Death of Eli Gold* (London: Fourth Estate, 2011).

Bhabha, Homi, *The Location of Culture* (London: Routledge, 1994).

Boyarin, Daniel, *Unheroic Conduct: The Rise of Heterosexuality and the Invention of the Jewish Man* (Berkeley: University of California Press, 1997).

Boyarin, Daniel, Daniel Itzkovitz and Ann Pellegrini, eds, *Queer Theory and the Jewish Question* (New York: Columbia University Press, 2003).

Boyarin, Jonathan, *Storm from Paradise: The Politics of Jewish Memory* (Minneapolis: University of Minnesota Press, 1992).

Boyarin, Daniel and Jonathan Boyarin, 'Diaspora: Generation and the Ground of Jewish Diaspora', in Jana Evans Braziel and Anita Mannur, eds, *Theorizing Diaspora* (Oxford: Blackwell, 2003), pp.85–118.

Brauner, David, *Post-War Jewish Fiction: Ambivalence, Self-Explanation and Transatlantic Connections* (Basingstoke: Palgrave, 2001).

Brod, Harry, ed., *A Mensch Among Men: Explorations in Jewish Masculinity* (California: Crossing Press, 1988).

Casey, Edward S, *Remembering: A Phenomenological Study* (Bloomington, Indiana UP, 1987).

Cesarani, David, *The Making of Modern Anglo-Jewry* (Oxford: Basil Blackwell, 1990).

Cesarani, David, *The Jewish Chronicle and Anglo-Jewry* (Cambridge: Cambridge University Press, 1994).

Cesarani, David, 'A Funny Thing Happened on the Way to the Suburbs: Social Change in Anglo-Jewry Between the Wars, 1914–1945', *Jewish Culture and History*, 1 (1998), 5–26.

Cesarani, David, 'How Post-War Britain Reflected on the Nazi Persecution and Mass Murder of Europe's Jews: A Reassessment of Early Responses', in Hannah Ewence and Tony Kushner, eds, 'Whatever Happened to British Jewish Studies?', special issue of *Jewish Culture and History*, 12.1–2 (2010), 95–130.

Cesarani, David, Tony Kushner and Milton Shain, *Place and Displacement in Jewish History and Memory* (London: Vallentine Mitchell, 2009).

Cheyette, Bryan, 'Ineffable and Usable': Towards a Diasporic British-Jewish Writing', *Textual Practice*, 10.2 (1996), 295–313.

Cheyette, Bryan, 'Englishness and Extraterritoriality: British-Jewish Writing and Diaspora Culture', *Literary Strategies: Studies in Contemporary Jewry*, 12 (1996), 21–39.

Cheyette, Bryan, *Contemporary Jewish Writing in Britain and Ireland: an Anthology* (London: Peter Halban, 1998).

Cheyette, Bryan, 'British-Jewish Literature', in Sorrel Kerbel, ed., *Jewish Writers of the Twentieth Century* (New York: Fitzroy Dearbon, 2003), pp.7–10.

Cheyette, Bryan, 'Diasporas of the Mind: British-Jewish Writing beyond Multiculturalism', in Fludernick, ed., *Diaspora and Multiculturalism* (New York: Rodopi, 2003), pp.45–82.

Cheyette, Bryan and Laura Marcus, eds, *Modernity, Culture and 'the Jew'* (London: Polity, 1998).

Cohen, Robin, *Global Diasporas: An Introduction* (London, Routledge, 2010).

Cohen, Steven M. and Keith Kahn-Harris, *Beyond Belonging: The Jewish Identities of Moderately Engaged British Jews* (London, UIJA/Profile Books, 2004).

Connerton, Paul, *How Societies Remember* (Cambridge: Cambridge University Press, 1989).

Cooper, Howard and Paul Morrison, *A Sense of Belonging: Dilemmas of British Jewish Identity* (London: Weidenfeld and Nicolson, 1991).

Coren, Giles, *Winkler* (London: Vintage, 2006).

'Debating the Debate', *Jewish Quarterly*, 213 (2009), 50–54.

Eaglestone, Robert, *The Holocaust and the Postmodern* (Oxford: Oxford, University Press, 2004).

Edemariam, Aida, Interview with Naomi Alderman, *Guardian*, 20 February 2006.

Edemariam, Aida, Interview with David Baddiel, *Guardian*, 24 July 2010.

Endelman, Todd, *The Jews of Britain 1656–2000* (Berkeley: University of California Press, 2002).

Ewence, Hannah and Tony Kushner, eds, 'Whatever Happened to British Jewish Studies?' special issue of *Jewish Culture and History*, 12.1–2 (2010).

Figes, Eva, *Tales of Innocence and Experience* (London: Bloomsbury, 2004).

Finkielkraut, Alain, *The Imaginary Jew,* trans. by Kevin O'Neill and David Suchoff (Lincoln: University of Nebraska Press, 1994).

Finlay, Joseph, 'There's No Place Like Home', *Jewish Quarterly,* 213 (2009), 2–3.

Fludernick, Monika, ed., *Diaspora and Multiculturalism: Common Traditions and New Developments* (New York: Rodopi, 2003).

Foer, Jonathan Safran, *Everything is Illuminated* (London: Penguin, 2002).

Freedland, Jonathan, *Jacob's Gift* (London: Penguin, 2006).

Freedland, Jonathan 'Minority Report' in *No Place Like Home: Photographs by Judah Passow* (London: Jewish Museum, 2012), pp.5–6.

France, Louise, Interview with Deborah Wearing, *Observer*, 23 January 2005.

Gavron, Jeremy, *The Book of Israel* (London: Scribner, 2003).

Gavron, Jeremy, *An Acre of Barren Ground* (London: Scribner, 2006).

Gilbert, Ruth, 'Ever After: Postmemory, Fairy Tales and the Body in Second-Generation Memoirs by Jewish Women', *Holocaust Studies*, 12.3 (2006), 23–39.

Gilbert, Ruth, 'The Golem in the Attic: Jewish Memory and Identity in Rachel Lichtenstein and Iain Sinclair's *Rodinsky's Room*', *Jewish Culture and History*, 9.1 (2007), 51–70.

Gilbert, Ruth, 'Displaced, Dysfunctional & Divided: Contemporary British Jewish Writing', in *Whatever Happened to British-Jewish Studies?* special issue of *Jewish Culture and History*, ed. by Tony Kushner & Hannah Ewence, 12. 1–2 (2010), 267–280.

Gill, A.A., 'Who Exactly is the Enemy Within?' *The Sunday Times*, 14 October 2012.

Gilman, Sander, *The Jew's Body* (London: Routledge, 1991).

Gilman, Sander, *Multiculturalism and the Jews* (London: Routledge, 2006).

Glanville, Mark, *The Goldberg Variations: From Football Hooligan to Opera Singer* (London: Flamingo, 2004).

Graham, David and Jonathan Boyd, *Committed, Concerned and Conciliatory: The Attitudes of Jews in Britain Towards Israel* (Institute for Jewish Policy Research, 2010).

Graham, David, Marlena Schmool and Stanley Waterman, *Jews in Britain: A Snapshot from the 2001 Census* (Institute for Jewish Policy Research, 2007).

Grant, Linda, *Remind Me Who I am Again* (London: Granta, 1998).

Grant, Linda, *The Cast Iron Shore* (London: Granta, 1998).

Grant, Linda, *When I Lived in Modern Times* (London: Granta, 2000).

Grant, Linda, 'It's Kosher', *Guardian*, 20 September 2005.

Grant, Linda, *The People on the Street: A Writer's View of Israel* (London: Virago, 2006).

Grosz, Elizabeth, 'Judaism and Exile: The Ethics of Otherness', in Erica Carter, James Donald and Judith Squires, eds, *Space and Place: Theories of Identity and Location* (London: Lawrence and Wishart, 1993), pp.57–71.

Gruber, Ruth, 'Virtual Judaism', *Jewish Quarterly*, 214 (2009), 22–5.

Halbwachs, Maurice, *On Collective Memory*, ed. and trans. by Lewis A. Coser (Chicago: University of Chicago Press, 1992).

Hansen, Michele, *What the Grown-Ups Were Doing* (London: Simon and Schuster, 2012).

Herman, David, 'Where Are the Novelists?' *Jewish Chronicle*, 20 October 2006, p.43.

Hirsch, Marianne, *Family Frames: Photographs, Narrative and Postmemory* (Cambridge MA: Harvard University Press, 1997).

Hoffman, Eva, *Lost in Translation* (London: Vintage, 1998)

Hoffman, Eva, *After Such Knowledge* (London: Vintage, 2005).

Jacobson, Howard, *Roots Schmoots: Journeys Among Jews* (London: Penguin, 1993).

Jacobson, Howard, *Peeping Tom* (London: Vintage, 1999).

Jacobson, Howard, *The Mighty Walzer* (London: Vintage, 2000).

Jacobson, Howard, 'Dinner in the Diaspora', *Jewish Quarterly*, 193 (2004), 87–88.

Jacobson, 'Now We are 350', *Jewish Quarterly*, 20 (2006), 41–46.

Jacobson, Howard, *Kalooki Nights* (London: Jonathan Cape, 2006).

Jacobson, Howard, *The Finkler Question* (London: Bloomsbury, 2010).

Jacobson, Howard, 'Anti-Zionism – facts (and fictions)', *Jewish Chronicle*, 30 July 2010, p.22.

Jagendorf, Zvi, *Wolfy and the Strudelbakers* (Stockport: Dewi Lewis, 2001).

Josipovici, Gabriel, 'Boxing Clever', *Jewish Quarterly*, 210 (2008), 70–2.

Julius, Anthony, *Trials of the Diaspora: A History of Anti-Semitism in England* (Oxford: Oxford University Press, 2010).

Kahn-Harris, Keith and Ben Gidley, *Turbulent Times: The British Jewish Community Today* (London: Continuum, 2010).

Karpf, Anne, *The War After* (London: Minerva, 1996).

Kenny, Michael G., 'A Place for Memory: The Interface between Individual and Collective History', *Comparative Studies in Society and History*, 41 (1999), 420–437.

Kerbel, Sorrel, ed., *Jewish Writers of the Twentieth Century* (New York: Fitzroy Dearbon, 2003).

King, Nicola, *Memory, Narrative and Identity: Remembering the Self* (Edinburgh: Edinburgh University Press, 2000).

Kugelmass, Jack, 'Jewish Icons: Envisioning the Self in Images of the Other', in Jonathan Boyarin and Daniel Boyarin, eds, *Jews and Other Differences: The New Jewish Cultural Studies* (Minneapolis: University of Minnesota Press, 1997), pp.30–53.

Kureishi, Hanif, 'We're Not Jews', *Love in a Blue Time* (London: Faber and Faber, 1997), pp.41–45.

Kushner, Tony, *The Jewish Heritage in British History: Englishness and Jewishness* (London: Frank Cass, 1992).

Kushner, Tony, *The Holocaust and the Liberal Imagination* (Oxford: Blackwell, 1994).

Kushner, Tony, 'Wandering Lonely Jews in the English Countryside', in Hannah Ewence and Tony Kushner, eds, 'Whatever Happened to British Jewish Studies?' special issue of *Jewish Culture and History*, 12.1–2 (2010), 223–250.

Lassner, Phyllis, *Anglo-Jewish Women Writing the Holocaust: Displaced Witnesses* (Basingstoke: Palgrave, 2008).

Lawson, Mark, Interview with Jonathan Miller, Jewish Book Week 2009. http://www.jewishbookweek.com/2009/220209r.php. Accessed 09 June 2012.

Lawson, Peter, ed., *Passionate Renewal: Jewish Poetry in Britain since 1945* (Nottingham: Five Leaves, 2001).

Lawson, Peter, 'Otherness and Affiliation in Anglo-Jewish Poetry', in Axel Stähler, ed., *Anglophone Jewish Literature* (London: Routledge, 2007), pp.123–32.

Leaman, Jonathan, 'On Not Being Jewish Enough', *Jewish Quarterly*, 196 (2004/2005), 49–51.

Lehrer, Natasha, ed., *The Golden Chain: Fifty Years of the Jewish Quarterly* (London: Vallentine Mitchell, 2002).

Lehrer, Natasha, Interview with Charlotte Mendelson, *Tablet*, 26 September 2007.

Leigh, Mike, *Two Thousand Years* (London: Faber and Faber, 2006).

Lezard, Nicholas, 'Is Howard Jacobson the only person writing British Jewish novels?' *Guardian*, 15 October 2010.

Lichtenstein, Olivia, *Mrs Zhivago of Queen's Park* (London: Orion, 2007).

Lichtenstein, Rachel and Iain Sinclair, *Rodinsky's Room* (London: Granta, 1999).

Lichtenstein, Rachel, *On Brick Lane* (London: Hamish Hamilton, 2007).

Limburg, Joanne, *Femenismo* (Tarset, Northumberland: Bloodaxe Books, 2000).

Lyndon, Sonja and Sylvia Paskin, eds, *The Dybbuk of Delight: An Anthology of Jewish Women's Poetry* (Nottingham: Five Leaves, 1995).

Lyndon, Sonja and Sylvia Paskin, eds, *The Slow Mirror and Other Stories: New Fiction by Jewish Writers* (Nottingham: Five Leaves, 1996).

Mann, Reva, *The Rabbi's Daughter: A True Story of Sex, Drugs and Orthodoxy* (London: Hodder, 2007).

Manzoor, Sarfraz, 'My Month of Being Jewish', *Guardian,* 8 April 2010.

Margolis, Jonathan, 'Not Jewish but Jew-ish', *Guardian*, 30 November 2009.

Mendelson, Charlotte, *When We Were Bad* (London: Picador, 2007).

Mullen, John, Interview with Howard Jacobson, Guardian Book Club, 29 September 2010. http://www.guardian.co.uk/books/audio/2010/sep/28/howard-jacobson-kalooki-nights. Accessed 20 June 2012.

Nochlin, Linda and Tamar Garb, eds, *The Jew in the Text: Modernity and the Construction of Identity* (London: Thames and Hudson, 1995).

Neuberger, Julia, *On Being Jewish* (London: Heinemann, 1995).

New Statesman, special issue 'Who Speaks for British Jews?' 28 May 2012.

Ozick, Cynthia, 'Responsa', *Jewish Quarterly*, 209 (2008), 5.

Phillips, Laura and Marion Baraitser, eds, *Mordecai's First Brush with Love: New Stories by Jewish Women in Britain* (London: Loki Books, 2004).

Phillips, Laura, 'Bagels and Pork Sausages', Interview with Charlotte Mendelson, *Jewish Quarterly,* 206 (2007), 39–42.

Presner, Todd, *Muscular Judaism: The Jewish Body and the Politics of Regeneration* (London: Routledge, 2007).

Raczymow, Henri and Alan Astro, 'Memory Shot Through With Holes', *Yale French Studies*, 85 (1994), 98–105.

Roden, Claudia, *The Book of Jewish Food: An Odyssey from Samarkand and Vilna to the Present Day* (London: Penguin, 1996).

Romain, Gemma, *Connecting Histories: A Comparative Exploration of African- Caribbean and Jewish History and memory in Modern Britain* (London: Kegan Paul, 2006).

Rose, Steven, *The Making of Memory: from Molecules to Mind* (London: Vintage, 2003).

Roskies, David G, *The Jewish Search for a Usable Past* (Indiana University Press, 1999).

Ross, Mandy and Ronne Randall, eds, *For Generations: Jewish Motherhood* (Nottingham: Five Leaves, 2005).

Rossington, Michael and Anne Whitehead, eds, *Theories of Memory: A Reader* (Edinburgh: Edinburgh University Press, 2008).

Rubens, Bernice, *When I Grow Up* (London: Abacus, 2006).

Rubens, Bernice, *I Dreyfus* (London: Abacus, 2000).

Sacks, Jonathan, *Will We Have Jewish Grandchildren? Jewish Continuity and How to Achieve It* (London: Vallentine Mitchell, 1994).

Sacks, Jonathan, *The Home We Build Together: Recreating Society* (London: Continuum, 2007).

Samuels, Diane, *Kindertransport* (London: Nick Hern Books, 1995; revised ed., 2004).

Sanger, Andrew, *The J-Word* (London: Snowbooks, 2009).

Segal, Francesca, *The Innocents* (London: Chatto and Windus, 2012).

Seidler, Victor Jeleniewski, *Shadows of the Shoah: Jewish Identity and Belonging* (Oxford: Berg, 2000).

Shapiro, James, *Shakespeare and the Jews* (New York: Colombia University Press, 1996).

Sicher, Efraim, *Beyond Marginality: Anglo-Jewish Literature After the Holocaust* (New York: SUNY, 1985).

Sinclair, Clive, *The Lady with the Laptop* (London: Picador, 1997).

Silverstone, Ben, Interview with Jonathan Miller, *Jewish Chronicle*, 24 August 2006.

Simons, Jake Wallis, *The Exiled Times of a Tibetan Jew* (London: Polygon, 2005).

Simons, Jake Wallis, *The English German Girl* (London: Polygon, 2011).

Simons, Jake Wallis, 'I broke out of my orthodox cocoon', *Guardian*, 13 March 2010.

Smith, Deborah, 'Chicken and Camembert for Shabbat', *Jewish Renaissance*, 6 (2007), 45.

Smith. Golda Zafer, 'Mike Leigh Comes Out', *Jewish Renaissance*, 4 (2005), 6–8.

Smith, Zadie, *White Teeth* (London: Penguin, 2001).

Smith, Zadie, *The Autograph Man* (London: Penguin, 2003).

Solomons, Natasha, *Mr Rosenblum's List* (London: Sceptre, 2010).

Solomons, Natasha, *The Novel in the Viola* (London: Sceptre, 2011).

Stähler, Axel, ed., *Anglophone Jewish Literature* (London: Routledge, 2007).

Stähler, Axel, 'Metonymies of Jewish Postcoloniality: the British Mandate for Palestine and Israel in Contemporary British Jewish Fiction', *Journal for the Study of British Cultures,* 16.1 (2009), 27–40.

Stebbing, David and Evelyn Kent, *Jewish Memories of the Twentieth Century* (London: Evelyn Kent Associates, 2003).

Stratton, Jon, *Coming Out Jewish: Constructing Ambivalent Identities* (London: Routledge, 2000).

Stratton, Jon, *Jewish Identity in Western Pop Culture: The Holocaust and Trauma through Modernity* (Basingstoke: Palgrave, 2008).

Sutton, David Evan, *Remembrance of Repasts: An Anthropology of Food and Memory* (Oxford: Berg, 2001).

Theobald, Stephanie, 'We're All Kosher Now', *Sunday Times*, 4 November 2012.

Thirlwell, Adam, *Politics* (London: Vintage, 2006).

Thirlwell, Adam, 'On Writing Half-Jewishly', *Jewish Quarterly*, 208 (2007), 4–5.

Tucker, Eva, *Becoming English* (London: Starhaven, 2009).

Tylee, Claire, ed., *'In the Open': Jewish Women Writers and British Culture* (Delaware NJ: Associated University Presses, 2006).

Valman, Nadia, 'La Belle Juive', *Jewish Quarterly*, 205 (2007), 52–56.

Vice, Sue, *Holocaust Fiction* (London: Routledge, 2000).

Vice, Sue, *Jack Rosenthal* (Manchester: Manchester University Press, 2012).

Wade, Stephen, *Jewish American Literature Since 1945: An Introduction* (Edinburgh: Edinburgh University Press, 1999).

Walker, Tim, 'Channel 4's Jewish Mum of the Year Show is "Disgusting" Says Maureen Lipman', *The Telegraph*, 18 October 2012.

Wandor, Michelene, *Gardens of Eden Revisited* (Nottingham: Five Leaves, 1999).

Weber, Donald, 'Anglo-Jewish Literature Raises Its Voice', *JBooks*, 12 July 2007.
http://www.jbooks.com/interviews/index/IP_Weber_English.htm.

Weiland, Paul, dir., *Sixty-Six* (2006).

Whitehead, Anne, *Memory* (London: Routledge, 2009).

Wides, Cara, 'Howard Jacobson Talking', interview with Howard Jacobson, 21 January 2006, http://www.somethingjewish.co.uk/articles/1730_howard_jacobson_talk.htm.

Wilson, Jonathan, *A Palestine Affair* (Nottingham: Five Leaves, 2007).

Woolf, Michael, 'Negotiating the Self; Jewish Fiction in Britain since 1945', in A. Robert Lee, ed., *Other Britain, Other British: Contemporary Multicultural Fiction* (London: Pluto Press, 1995), pp.124–141.

Women's Review Taskforce, *Connection, Continuity and Community*, 2009.
http://www.boardofdeputies.org.uk/file/ConnectionContinuityCommunity.pdf. Accessed 30 June 12.

Yellin, Tamar, *Kafka in Brontëland and Other Stories* (London: The Toby Press, 2006).

Yellin, Tamar, 'A Jew in Brontëland', *Jewish Quarterly*, 208 (2007), 68–69.

Yerushalmi, Yosef Hayim, *Zakhor: Jewish History and Jewish Memory* (Seattle and London: University of Washington Press, 1982; 1996).

Index